It is Forgiven

Surviving abuse and betrayal

E M P

iUniverse, Inc.
Bloomington

It is Forgiven
Surviving abuse and betrayal

iUniverse books may be ordered through booksellers or by contacting:

iUniverse
1663 Liberty Drive
Bloomington, IN 47403
www.iuniverse.com
1-800-Authors (1-800-288-4677)

ISBN: 978-1-4620-8591-0 (sc)
ISBN: 978-1-4620-8592-7 (hc)
ISBN: 978-1-4620-8593-4 (e)

Printed in the United States of America

iUniverse rev. date: 1/18/2012

In memory of the woman who took me under her wing,
To the man for whom I can thank my life,
To the other woman, who made it possible for me to survive, and
To my children who were my light in the darkness.

God bless you all.

Author's Note/Introduction

English is my second language. My "course" began in 1998 and my first words were: *police, abuse, court, refugee and custody.* In the first five years of living in Canada and learning English, I was lost; very self-conscious about not knowing the language, I avoided conversations, and people in general. I was reading and writing, though—at least, I was trying to. Even after thirteen years, I'm still learning, but I did write this book, to share my story with you.

Although my book has been thoroughly edited and proofread, you'll probably encounter an awkward sentence here and there, or some expressions that strike you as a little odd. That's my voice filtering through the editorial work.

So many of us take good relationships for granted, yet every happy moment, every kind word is extremely precious, and having someone in your life who loves you for who you are is truly a treasure. In early 1998, when I was facing a situation that I didn't know how to handle, I felt an overwhelming urge to write. I didn't stop until I had handwritten eighteen pages on graph paper, filling up every line with my outpourings of pain and frustration. Those eighteen pages are the foundation of this book.

This particular journey was incredibly long and agonizing. I've experienced a life that I didn't even know could exist; thus, it feels like a miracle that I am actually here today. It took me more than ten years to complete this book. Why? Because I was learning the English language along the way and the more I learned, the more corrections I made. I was also struggling with ill health, hardship, and had doubt about the book itself, so several times I simply stopped working on it. Then my inner urge asserted itself too strongly to be ignored, and I returned to writing.

So who am I, or who *was* I, and why did I write this book? I *was* a bullied child; I *was* a rape victim; I *was* a battered woman; I *was* a betrayed daughter and goddaughter. And because of all this, I *was* a refugee. Also, I was and am a single mother of two beautiful children, and I am now a landed immigrant in Canada. Above all, I *am* a survivor and more blessed than I can imagine.

Abuse doesn't discriminate and I know I'm not alone in what I have experienced. That is why this book exists: to bring light to the many others who have faced, are living through, or might be confronted with similar situations.

I'm quite sure that many women suffer in silence for a variety of reasons. No doubt, it takes extreme courage to step away, to go against everything and everybody, to take that leap of faith in order to save yourself and your children. After all, *you* are living your life, and not everybody else. So listen to yourself and remember: you are worthy of every good thing in life!

Even though I cannot know the nature of your life—you are the judge of that—I know that no one deserves to be mistreated, no matter who you are or what your age. Every one of us deserves a better life than being tortured and torn down by the men in our lives. It is much better to be alone than in a harmful and destructive relationship.

For me, it is still quite shocking to realize that such people exist— people who believe they have the right to selfishly and possessively extinguish the life of their partner. They forget that we women have our own minds and feelings, and our free will, with which not even God interferes. Yet some people do just that. These individuals try desperately to break us down, perhaps because we are unique and captivating individuals of whom they envy beyond their own recognition.

I start my story with some significant events of my childhood and teens. Then I recount my experience of domestic violence, of abuse and betrayal year after year. It's quite amazing to see how one event led to another, and how the abuse escalated in frequency and violence. Certain events also repeated themselves and insidiously became patterns in my life. My experience clearly shows that if you don't have enough self-confidence and self-worth, you may become very easy prey, a ready target for manipulation and abuse.

So please, let me share my story with you. Hopefully, it will bring you to the realization that your situation is better than you might have thought. But if my story reminds you of yours, do not think twice about taking the necessary steps to save yourself and your children, if you have any. Do something before it's too late!

I honestly hope that I can give your soul a much needed lift, a tiny spark of strength that will encourage you not to give up, no matter what your age or situation is. Each of us is much stronger than we think or feel. After all, God resides within us, and the sun never stops shining above the clouds.

Unfortunately, any kind of issue can be enough cause to surrender hope and life, but for whom and why? We may turn to drugs and alcohol, might even try to commit suicide. Those choices, though, won't bring us the solutions we crave so deeply.

But whatever you do, please don't beat yourself up. Know that "we are God's masterpiece, His finishing touch. We are God's glory, the Crown of Creation," as Stasi and John Eldredge have said in their book, *Captivating*. I am still getting used to this idea, because I was scarcely ever treated as someone special.

I'm no longer ashamed of my past, although it still causes me discomfort. It made me who I am today and also gave me the opportunity and the knowledge to offer help where it may be needed. So do not feel sorry for me. But you have every reason and right to feel sorry for yourself if you are in or heading toward a situation like the one I describe in the following pages. It is an experience that I don't want you to go through or even have a taste of, as it can devastate your whole existence. Rather than having to face such a nightmare, read about it, educate yourself, if I may suggest, so you can be aware and avoid becoming stuck in a similar, almost annihilating series of events.

Because of this story's nature and the involvement of certain people, some individuals may be worried about their reputations—although they weren't at the time. Accordingly, names have been changed to protect those people's dignity and privacy. Some events may also have occurred in a slightly different order; nevertheless, they all happened.

Also, I want to emphasize that this is not written as punishment or revenge for what has been done to me and my children. And since every story has two sides, let's give my family members and my abuser the benefit of the doubt. He would tell you that none of what I say is true, that he was only good to me and I am just an ungrateful, stupid, intolerable creature. Let's add to that my parents' vote as well. I'm quite sure that is what they would say.

But this is what happened…

PROLOGUE
My foundation for life

CHAPTER 1

I HAVE ONLY A FEW memories of my life before age six. I remember being in preschool, playing in the pool there with my girlfriend, who became my best friend for life. On some other occasions of school, I was paired up with the tallest boy because I was the tallest girl.

When I was four or five years old, we had a family gathering, which is also quite memorable. As we were getting ready for a family photo, I asked my paternal grandmother for her beer, to sip off the foam. But instead, by the time the camera clicked, I had finished the whole glass. My grandma was utterly horrified, while I was grinning from ear to ear and couldn't deny what I had done; I was caught in black and white by the camera. That was my first and only glass of beer in my life to date.

I still vividly remember how afraid I was every time we walked by a pub on our way to visit my maternal grandfather. The patrons were drunk, loud and quarrelsome. Even when I got older, I remained fearful of such places, and I still avoid them. That fear was probably planted in me because my parents were always moderate drinkers.

However, I have no recollection of being born with a dislocated hip and living my first months in straps. I also have no memories of my paternal grandfather, who according to my mother loved and adored me deeply. She said that I was his favourite granddaughter, which caused jealousy within the family. He allowed me to do everything I wanted, even mess up his hair, which was a huge thing since he was a very orderly man. As I later learned, there was a reason for his love and favouritism: my grandfather appreciated clean people very much and I was always kept clean and neat and beautifully dressed...

This bond was broken very early, though, as I was only three years old when he died. Still, I never liked to "visit" him, because the moment I stepped through the gate of the cemetery, the air turned so cold that I shivered. Yet when we left and I walked out of the gate the air became balmy and warm again. I never understood why we had to go there. After all, *he* wasn't there.

I often missed him. Somehow I felt that he would have understood me no matter what. Sometimes I was quite angry and disappointed with him for passing on before I could even know or remember him. I missed that love and adoration he had apparently given me.

However, I do remember asking my parents for a baby and having a naming contest with them. And when I was six years old my wish came true—my brother was born. But instead of joy and happiness in our house, I mostly remember stress and frustration. He was a very demanding, fussy little boy and cried endlessly, which exhausted our mother. Most of the time she would begin crying in desperation, and yelling to release her frustration. When she had no strength left to deal with him, it was my duty to rock and push his pram until he fell asleep. Although I was always eager to help her with my baby brother, it wasn't particularly exciting to be with him when he wailed endlessly.

On one particular occasion my brother wouldn't fall asleep. My mother went through everything she knew, but it was no use. He was screaming in his pram, which I was again assigned to push forth and back, while our mother was screaming and crying in the kitchen. At age six it seemed to me that they went on screaming simultaneously for hours. Thankfully, after awhile our father came to my aid and the burden was lifted off my shoulders.

Regardless of his difficult infancy, and the fact that we fought and had arguments, as do nearly all other siblings growing up together, we got along very well.

I remember that each time our grandfather gave us chocolate bars, my brother ate his at once, while I had some and hid the rest, just in case. When I got home from school and wanted another piece of my chocolate, it was gone. Who had taken it? My brother of course denied everything, wearing an innocent "I don't know anything" expression. But this happened many, many times. My hidden chocolate was always gone. Finally, I had to do something about it, because I liked my sweets as well. Since I couldn't save my chocolates from him, I instead threw his favourite toy into the garden or onto the roof of the terrace: "Mickey is flying!"

As a child, I was really close to my mother's mom and sister, my godmother, and although we didn't have too much time together, we had a great relationship. I especially loved being with my grandma. She was so cool. She didn't even freak out when she learned that the son of her neighbour was interested in me, although we were barely ten years old at the time. He was the first boy who actually liked me and gave me my first little kiss, which quite honestly made me uncomfortable and ended that story.

My godmother, as a greatly talented violinist, was part of a symphony orchestra and lived in a big city. It was quite an adventure whenever I had the chance to be with her for a couple of weeks, which happened two or three times over the course of a decade.

I was also very close to my uncle (my mom's half-brother), who was a faithful friend or rather like a big brother to me. Whenever he came to visit us, I never left his side. He took me for short rides on his bike, taught me to play badminton, and was very patient when I repeatedly hit the air instead of the bird. But when I had finally mastered that activity, my father and I had many hours of fun.

I was really in my element when I could be with my uncle. He was one of the most important people in my life, even as I got older. I loved him so much, and was constantly trying to be helpful. Since he smoked, as his favourite little niece I took the privilege of protecting his health by breaking his cigarettes, one by one, into tiny pieces, or simply peeled off the wrappers right down to the filters. Who knows why, he never appreciated my help.

Altogether, I would on first consideration say that my childhood was pretty normal. On second thought, though, maybe it wasn't as normal as I would have liked it to be. I had great difficulties fitting in at school and at my swimming class. I was taller and skinnier than the other girls, and had shorter hair than most boys. Being a swimmer made it essential to have short hair, but not as short as mine. My mother cut our hair, and she was no hairdresser. Invariably, she always got one side shorter than the other, so again and again she had to readjust the length. When finally she was finished, not much hair was left on my head. And that earned me a nickname which haunted me for years, while my own name was forgotten…

I lived in the midst of mockery and bitter sarcasm every day, and if that wasn't enough, at age eleven I had to wear glasses, starting with minus two lenses. That was the crowning touch to my humorous assets.

The other children were brutal to me. I was a constant target of ugly jokes and cruel remarks. My classmates laughed in my face and made fun of me daily. They even made me nervous about my laughter. It was ridiculous to them, although I didn't know why; I didn't think that I was laughing much differently from the rest. Nonetheless, I started to observe how they laughed and tried to adjust mine to match, since theirs was accepted and "normal". But it didn't matter, and after a while I was even afraid to laugh.

I didn't understand what was wrong with me, why I wasn't likeable, why I wasn't good enough for other children to befriend me. After all, I was just a young girl who wished to have nice hair and perfect vision. I simply wanted to have some friends like the other kids did, and also to be accepted, but for some reason things were not going my way.

Every time I went to the ophthalmologist she made me read the tiniest letters on the board. If I wasn't able to, she adjusted and readjusted the dioptres until *she* was satisfied, then prescribed the strongest glasses, which nearly knocked me out. I just had to get used to them, right?

So then I was able to see every speck of dust. But my hawk-eyed vision didn't last long. Less than two years later I was destined to wear minus five lenses, and at age fourteen I ended up wearing minus seven. When they fogged up and I had to take them off, the whole world became blurry. I had to grope around to even be able to manage the stairs. I thought that my eyesight would never stop failing and in the end I would go blind. And that wasn't funny to me at all.

Chapter 2

The other children's constant bullying and the condition of my eyes made feel like a total loser, destroying my already fragile self-esteem. I became very self-conscious and withdrawn. But thankfully the bullies never hurt my one and only friend from preschool, so I clung to her in the hope of safety. With her friendship it was a bit easier to ignore all the malice directed against me.

But of course, she wasn't able to shield me from my tormentors, and after a short period of time I was literally afraid to go to school and to swimming. I was physically sick from the agony; my stomach twisted every time I had to face those mean kids. But they were my classmates and there was no way I could avoid them.

Each and every cruel word was a punch that made me feel utterly worthless. In an attempt to help myself, I tried different methods to deal with them. Instead of showing my true emotions, I forced myself to play along when they made jokes about me. Unfortunately, I wasn't able to keep that up, because they never stopped targeting me, never got tired of their games. I also made every effort to stay out of the bullies' ways and just be invisible. Ironically, though, when I tried to avoid or ignore them, they accosted me even more.

Plus, from time to time they tried to turn my one and only friend against me. They stirred up arguments between us, telling various lies, and sometimes they succeeded in convincing her to take their side. When my friend had been sucked into being with the bullies, I was entirely alone. After a while, though, she always came back to me. God bless her for her faithful soul.

For years I tried to deal with the pressure by myself, but it became too much to bear. I cried a lot and was often sad. Of course, my parents noticed the difference in me. Unfortunately, though, their affection didn't come easily. I don't remember being kissed or hugged, or hearing

"I love you". I was fed, dressed, schooled, grew up in a modest but nice home; yet there was no expression of love, unless I initiated it. They were never interested in how I felt or what my fears were. They never asked me about *me*. But because of the situation I was trapped in at school, I needed a few warm, encouraging words or just a hug from my parents. I longed for the love and understanding of my mother, and for my father's support.

Even though they never asked, I told them what was going on in my life, that I didn't know what to do or how to protect myself from the constant bullying. I cried out for help. My mother listened while half-absorbed in her cooking, then she told me to bully them back. I wasn't convinced, but the advice came from my mother so I figured I ought to give it a try.

I didn't even know where to start and the results of my efforts were pitiful. The children laughed at me even harder than before. I sank into a deep depression and everything was written on my face, which annoyed my parents. My father often snapped at me: "Don't make yourself out to be such a martyr!" Or "Why do you look so sorry for yourself?" Or they just described me as miserable, mawkish and oversensitive.

Yes, I'd always been sensitive but I wasn't a spoiled, hysterical little brat. My feelings were important to me, just as they are now. Nonetheless, I received none of the warm words I yearned for, no encouragement, and no hugs. The disappointment was physically painful. I was alone and scared, and not even taken seriously by my own parents. Clearly, I wasn't important enough to be helped.

Do they love me? I wondered. *If they really loved me, would they reject and ignore me in a serious situation like this? Is there something wrong with me?*

I have very vivid memories of being ignored and belittled every time I reached out to them. I always had to behave in a certain way to please the people around me, no matter how I felt or what my needs were. So that meant not to whine, not to complain, and not to be annoying, sad, angry or sour. If I showed my negative feelings, I wasn't even considered sane. But if I didn't get on anybody's nerves and acted pleasantly, everything was fine.

Maybe I was so easy to ignore because I always tried to be a good girl and never cause any trouble. And although my schedule was pretty tight, I always looked after my duties independently and diligently. Nobody had to nag me about them. I went to swimming every morning from 5:30 or 6:00 a.m. until 7:00 or 7:15, then went to school, and by 3:00 p.m. I was at swimming again. I went home after 5:00 and studied for the next day.

Even though I wasn't an excellent student, my homework was always done. I never started smoking or drinking, never used drugs; I didn't even have a boyfriend. I never stayed out at night either. So my early teenage years went by without major incident. For some reason I skipped the teenage wildness or it skipped me. I did become a bit more vocal though; when I perceived an injustice, I gave voice to my feelings.

Then when I was fourteen, in the eighth grade, many of us, including from other schools, attended dancing classes, which were very popular. My mother was delighted by the opportunity: "You never know where and when you're going to need some dancing skills," she said. "If a boy asks you to dance, at least you won't step on his foot." I realized that she was right and although there wasn't a single boy on the horizon for me, I went to each and every dancing lesson. Unfortunately, all of them ended miserably and I couldn't wait to escape.

First, I was only uncomfortable. But soon the constant whispering and giggling behind my back got to me. And I had nobody to hide behind because for some reason my best friend was not there. The boys almost fought *not* to be paired with me. Everyone made it clear that I was simply too ugly and disliked, that I surely would mess up the steps.

One time we were dancing the czardas. At the end of the dance one of my classmates asked my dancing partner if I had made any mistakes. "No," the boy said, "she did every step well." Thank you. At least I received that much recognition, although neither of them acknowledged my presence otherwise.

All I wanted was to fit in, so I worked hard on each and every step. No way could I afford to embarrass myself. But again, despite all my efforts I ended up the laughing stock of the dancing class as well, which was more than enough reason for me not to show up at the final performance.

CHAPTER 3

AT THE END OF OUR street lived a girl with whom I spent some friendly hours. One time we went out in our neighbourhood to meet with other children. They already knew one another, so I was the new kid. The boys were playing soccer, kicking the ball all over the place, while we just watched them. Then I had to take off my glasses to clean them, and in that instant the leather soccer ball smashed into my right eye. The impact was so powerful it nearly knocked me off my feet. Half of my face was on fire. The others found the incident rather funny, and I wondered whether the ball had been kicked at me intentionally. I went home holding my face and thinking about what might have happened if I'd still had my glasses on.

I began to learn that Nature worked shamelessly, regardless of what was going on in my life or what difficulties surrounded me. I became interested in boys, wanting to know everything related to them, what made them tick. Although the interest wasn't mutual, I wanted to be in their company if possible, and to experience the thrilling excitement of being liked and successful among them.

It was a new chapter in my life and since I had no one else to turn to but my mother, I confided in her. She'd always had a good sense of humour and an easygoing attitude when it came to the other gender, so I was confident she would level with me. I asked her openly about everything I wanted to know and was shocked to see how uncomfortable she became, as she tried to avoid answering my questions. The fact was we had never ever discussed anything like that; these subjects were and remained taboo. Even when we were joking around, when we were just being silly, we never crossed that invisible line. But I did learn that the monthly periods were our curse. (She suffered a great deal each time.) I was also told: "If you're smart, you will never have a family. Once you have children your life is over. I've regretted many times having a family, since I had to abandon my dreams." I heard this repeatedly throughout my childhood and hoped that it was only her desperation talking. I knew she had numerous broken dreams…but the more she said such things, the more unwanted I felt. As I got older, though, I tried to understand her perspective.

Maybe that was why my emotions were important to me: there was no one else who cared. For my parents, emotional problems did not exist. They totally shut me out where my feelings were concerned. My priorities were different. *I* was different. They often told me: "You can't make a living from emotions." I never wanted that, of course. I only wanted to be listened to and understood. I wanted some affection and encouragement from them when I needed it, some acceptance. That was all.

I also wanted to enjoy my life, enjoy who I was, to feel happy, but my soul was empty and my heart was sore. I reached out to them again and again, and was coldly pushed away just as many times. In their opinion, I couldn't have any problems because I was only a child. And when I cried my eyes out and shared the pain I was carrying, I was considered an idiot and my problems were dismissed as stupidities. "When you grow up, you are going to have real and serious problems in life," they said.

Finally, I simply stopped confiding in my parents. What was the point? They taught me not to count on them and I eventually grasped the lesson. I stopped reaching out to them and spent most of my time alone within my family. I was labelled a weirdo who was oversensitive and annoyingly emotional, and was treated accordingly.

Yet through the years I learned that some people were rather envious of our seemingly idyllic family. My mother was the perfect homemaker, very talented and artistic. But what happened behind our private walls stayed there. If nothing else, my parents were still together—although my mother would eat my father alive—while many of my classmates' parents were divorced, including my one and only friend's.

Of course, we had our good times too. Often we went for long walks. My father and I went to the open market almost every Sunday. I loved being with him; he was great company. My mother and I had some special times as well. I loved to meet her after work, when we would either just return home or go for a walk in our little town. Everything was all right until I was in need of their help, or needed to be comforted and listened to; then I became the ultimate black sheep of the family.

My mother had an opinion on everything, and the whole family had to listen to her icy comments about others. She could go on for hours about why other people were so unacceptable or why I couldn't befriend certain children. She was right in her complaints about her sisters-in-law, though, as they took great advantage of her for years. But my mother's anger and loathing toward them poisoned our everyday life. Many times it was unbearable to be at home because her rages were often directed toward us as well.

One day, as I was working on my homework, my mother and brother were having a huge argument about something, angrily shouting at each other over my head. They went on and on until I thought my brain would explode. "Could you stop it?!" I finally snapped at them. "I can't concentrate." I had hardly finished my sentence before my mother was at my side like a shot and started to pound on my head with her fists, like an unstoppable machine, screaming at me frenziedly. I was too stunned to do anything but take it. My father was in the kitchen but when he realized what was happening, he rushed in and firmly held back my mother; otherwise I don't think she would have stopped until her or my last breath.

It was a one-off occurrence, and although it was rather painful both physically and emotionally, I was so caught off guard I didn't even cry. I didn't know why my mother had beaten me, other than that I had been stuck in the crossfire. I wasn't mad at her but I started to fantasize about running away just to have some peace. Actually, I wanted to leave the whole depressing little town behind me.

As I got closer to the end of my eighth grade year, which was the last year of elementary school, I tried to make a couple of new friends. I approached people who I had never befriended before, finding myself drawn toward those who came from broken families. My new friendships brought me the opportunity to go out one evening. I had never before felt that I belonged with a group of people; thus I was very excited about the promising time ahead of me.

The four of us, two girls and two boys, went out for a few hours to talk over Coca-Cola and we had a marvellous time. I enjoyed being with them so much that I forgot to check my watch. When I finally remembered, I was already late. Instead of being back by 10:00 p.m.,

I arrived home at 10:30. I was in good spirits, but I was also nervous about not getting back on time.

When I arrived, my parents were watching TV quietly, but I could feel the tension in the air. I greeted them and apologized for being late. They neither looked at me nor greeted me; they simply didn't acknowledge my apologies, or even my presence, but just kept staring at the TV in bitter silence. That was my punishment for being thirty minutes late.

All my joy was washed away, and that remained the first and last time that I went out with a group of friends. They weren't suitable for me anyway, right?

CHAPTER 4

HIGH SCHOOL TURNED OUT TO be a better place than elementary school had been, as most of the bullies went to other schools—unfortunately also my very best friend, who continued her studies in another town. But instead of giving in to sadness, I looked upon high school as a fresh start, which worked quite well. After eight years of victimization, I finally experienced some relief. Though I was still unpopular, at least I wasn't constantly bullied and ridiculed.

Compared with the other girls in my class, I was considerably different. All the painful experiences in my life had made me somewhat more mature. But when it came to boys, I was undeniably inexperienced. However, if any boys wanted to hang out with me, they didn't approach. I was still considered an embarrassment to be with: I already knew I wasn't pretty enough and I reasoned that not having a boyfriend was okay with me; after all, I didn't go to high school to chase boys. Still, I had to admit that when everyone had a boyfriend except me, I didn't feel too happy about myself.

To bolster my shaky self-esteem, I allowed my natural humour to surface. It made me feel good when I could make my class laugh, along with the teacher. I wasn't rude to anyone, I never disturbed anybody's work, and I always kept to myself, but when I was called on, I let myself be spontaneous. This gave me a safety net, making me a bit more acceptable among my classmates, although I still retained a fear of becoming the target of laughter again.

In the same way, I liked to clown around at home and make my family laugh. Their laughter always made me feel loved and accepted, so it became a mission of mine to make them laugh as much as possible.

Even though I struggled to keep the remains of my self-esteem afloat, I felt myself sinking. Years of problems and fears had piled up, and around age fifteen I hit rock bottom. I became emotionally handicapped.

My self-worth was dangerously low. I was paralysed with fear every time I had to go into a store and ask the clerk for something. My stomach felt upside down and my whole body trembled. Even when I walked to school my legs shook. I was afraid to go out by myself and I hadn't the courage to look people in the eye, because I thought that every one of them viewed me as the bullies did—just an ugly loser who nobody accepted or liked. I actually suffered just from being me.

I was old enough, though, to understand what had led me to that dreadful stage and I also realized yet again that I was alone; confiding in my parents would have made the situation even worse. In spite of this, I continuously longed for their love and attention, which they may have given me in their own way, but nothing that I could recognize. If they had any positive feelings and thoughts about me they kept them to themselves; but if they had negative ones I surely knew about them.

So the only person I could rely on was myself. I analysed my feelings and fears, and although they didn't make much sense to me, I had to find a solution, a way out of that deadly situation. I had always loved to read, but this time I was reading to save myself! Books became the friends, companions and support system that I couldn't find elsewhere. I became interested in psychology, self-help and meditation, discovering a new and wonderful world in which I could improve and grow.

I learned to speak to myself positively and encouragingly: "Every person is a human being, just like me. They aren't any different, neither less nor more than me. They are people, and I am one of them." Step by step, I lifted myself out of the pit. Although my belief in my worth remained rather shaky and frail, it was a real blessing when I finally started to feel somewhat "normal" again. I overcame my fear of people and was able to have healthy interactions with them. I also quit my swimming class without asking my parents' permission; it was something I had to do.

At age seventeen, I became seriously and unforgettably ill. High fever and an unbearable pain struck me. I had to go to a surgeon, who found nothing wrong with me so he sent me to a gynaecologist, to whose office I inexplicably went alone. The waiting room was empty and rather dark but I had to wait what seemed a very long time. With every passing second, I became more and more nervous. I so much wanted my mother to be there with me.

When the appointment finally began, the doctor didn't even try to crack a smile or ease my fear. She was cold and brutal. I cried all the way as I slowly dragged myself home. The good news was that she found nothing wrong with my female organs, so she sent me back to the surgeon. But after that painful, traumatic experience at the gynaecologist, I had no intention of yo-yoing between doctors. The abdominal pain subsided and eventually stopped, but the pain from the gynaecologist's examination lasted for a long time; I was unable to walk or sit properly for at least a week.

The challenges never let up. My glasses were still a big issue. I had worn them for five or six years, yet my sight was continuing to fail. But when hard contact lenses became available, my father took me to the capital to see a specialist and I received my first pair. With those I was able to put my glasses aside for a few hours a day.

At first, I had a very hard time adjusting to my face without the familiarity of my glasses. Although I had never liked them, they were a shield and there were times when I felt hopelessly unattractive without their protection. Plus, my contact lenses bothered me a lot. But they had some advantages. Finally, I was able to wear sunglasses, which I had always wanted to do. I also learned to apply a touch of makeup to emphasize my eyes. The biggest advantage was that the lenses didn't fog up, so I was able to see when I entered a warm place in wintertime. And when I finally learned to accept my face without my glasses, my self-esteem noticeably perked up.

CHAPTER 5

In 1988, at the same time as my high school graduation, the problems at home intensified: my mother was hospitalized. Suddenly, I was the woman of the house, so besides studying for final exams, I had to take over the household duties and the care of my brother, with some help from my father, who was doing shift work. I wanted everything I did to turn out perfectly. I even surprised my mother with my first homemade cookies, which were actually edible.

After several stressful, tiring months I thought it was fair to have my last summer to myself before joining the workforce. But my summer plans were shattered by my ailing mother, who insisted that I immediately apply for a job at the local bookstore, which was hiring. I had absolutely no experience with job interviews, so I told the manager, "I'm a new graduate from the local high school and I love books, I love to read, so please hire me!" And I got the job.

So, my plans and dreams for the summer, as with so many other things in my life, remained unrealized. I actually wanted to engage in further education—I dreamed of becoming either a fashion designer, or a window dresser, or maybe an interior designer—but we couldn't afford it. I even had the passing thought of becoming a nun, because of the years of rejection I had experienced, but I quickly realized that their life wasn't for me.

The bookstore was a totally new world: I became a member of a team. I very much wanted to fit in and do a great job. The store itself was like a treasure chest, as I could find more help in the books there to stabilize my self-esteem. I knew I had to work hard to help myself, so I was constantly searching for useful books and I always found something.

In fact, I spent my entire salary on books, which didn't make my father very happy because he expected that about thirty percent of my earnings would go toward helping with the household expenses. I found this a fair request but also a challenging one, because my salary was only 1,500 forint, which was about $29CAD a month. Thankfully, over the next two years it slowly increased to 3,000, then to 3,500 forint, so about $55 to $65CAD.

Despite the low wages, I loved my job and would have done it for free. I loved the store, my colleagues and being surrounded by books. As my knowledge widened, I started to feel more confident and I also no longer had any difficulty talking with people.

We were always busy, cleaning the shop windows, decorating, packing and unpacking. We also supplied the local schools with textbooks. I worked ten hours on weekdays and six hours on every second Saturday. My days were colourful and exciting, and I began to love life.

What a change! I didn't know that life could be so wonderful. To my surprise, I started to have more and more male friends too. I received a lot of attention from them, in a respectful way; they were never impolite or pushy. I was walked or driven home almost every day. I enjoyed their company very much, and felt honoured by their consideration, and their showing me some affection and interest. It felt very good to be noticed and acknowledged. But none of my relationships went any further than holding hands.

I had reached age twenty and still had had no boyfriends whatsoever. I wasn't a child anymore but I was hardly an adult; I still lived with my parents because I couldn't manage a way out. Sixty dollars a month wasn't enough to fund my independence. I also had no plans for the future, only dreams. By this point I had worked at the bookshop for one and a half years, and was certain that I would be doing the same thing for the rest of my life. In our small town there were no opportunities, no chances to get ahead and succeed. My generation's future wasn't promising at all, given the limited circumstances.

Despite this, I was extremely proud that I had been able to build a healthy self after the years of destruction. Finally, I loved being me. I had never experienced such happiness and freedom in my life, as the burden of feeling miserable had lifted off my soul.

I expected nothing would interfere with my newly found happiness, so I was rather shocked when I had a confrontation with my favourite colleague. We had grown quite close and become good friends, but then one day an ugly argument erupted between us. We were like two vicious cats, but a single remark of hers abruptly ended the quarrel: "You were just an ugly little frog when you came here," she said. "Look at you now! You can thank me for who you are today!"

I only heard the first part of what she said, and it hit me so hard that I wasn't able to respond to her. I loved and trusted her, even admired her. Up to that point I had believed that we had a very nice friendship, and I absolutely wasn't expecting she would hurt me like this. I tried to hide the pain that her statement had caused and acted as confident as I could, but the damage was done. Although she apologized immediately, I could barely keep my tears at bay. Her words echoed in my head for a very long time and I had to fight the menacing depression that rose up in me. I fought it desperately because I was terrified of sinking into it again.

But despite whatever happened between that girl and me, or between my parents and me, or even with the school bullies, I didn't hold a grudge against any of them. Somehow, I was at peace with myself and the world, and the last six months had been the best of my life. I was happy and free, and that felt especially good. Then…the rich man came.

1990

My initiation; I was the chosen one

Chapter 6

In early 1990, Communism fell from power and my country began selling its state-owned companies. This was when a member of our extended family, Joseph, came back home to Hungary from Canada to start his own business line. He also visited some of his long forgotten relatives—my father's cousin, Uncle Mike, and his family. And by virtue of being relations, we became involved as well, although I had no idea who he was to us.

Joseph's arrival in our small town in September 1990 changed everything. He was the rich "American uncle" who everyone in my country wanted to have, and now he had come to rescue his relatives from themselves. He promised job opportunities and a bright future and ten times our current salaries. Every adult in the family believed that their salvation had just arrived.

For two weeks, the only thing I heard was how rich Joseph was, how beautiful his house was, how many stores he had over in Canada, and how much he wanted to help us. When his attention turned toward us, my parents acted as if we were the chosen ones. Everybody was so excited about the future Joseph had promised. Having such a chance in life was remarkable for ordinary people like us, so the adults did their best to please him.

My parents had always worked hard, diligently and honestly. Both of them were highly respected but not well paid. I'd never thought that they were dissatisfied, even though we had lived from paycheque to paycheque for as long as I could remember. We had a nice home which my mother kept beautifying, there was always enough food on the table, and we were always neatly dressed however, it emerged that they were actually quite unhappy with their lives, so much so that they were willing to throw the whole family into the unknown, risking our sense of security. At least, they risked mine.

Even though I still hadn't met Joseph, his indirect presence was already overwhelming me. At home, nothing else existed anymore but him and what he had and what he wanted. It was even said that besides his business plans, he was determined to find a woman who would give him a boy. He already had five daughters from his two marriages but had always wanted a boy. The fact that he was very much married didn't seem to make him hesitate to go after what he wanted.

One night, around 9:30 p.m., he came to visit us. I was already in bed but I heard him arrive. A short time later, my mother came to me saying that Joseph wanted to meet me. I told her that I wasn't interested in meeting him. She nagged me for a while and I had to be very firm to make her understand that I had no intention of going out there. Thankfully, she didn't start an argument, probably because she didn't want to give a bad impression. Besides, she was just too nervous and excited by being honoured with Joseph's presence in our home. Seeing her as fidgety as she was made me uncomfortable. I'd never seen my mother act like this, never.

I wasn't able to fall asleep because I was worried that Joseph himself would come in to meet me. While he was at our home, which was for one or two hours, I could hear my parents' nervous bustling around him. They just weren't themselves; they even spoke and laughed differently.

The next day they told me about the previous night, how exciting it had been, but I couldn't share their thrill, let alone their interest, and they didn't at all appreciate my lack of enthusiasm. They were so worked up that they seemed ready to do anything to please him, while Joseph seemed fully energized and ready to swallow up my whole country. The more I heard about him, the more my uneasiness grew. I wished I could share my discomfort with my parents but there was no room for my feelings. They were so agitated that I knew they would never listen to me. When did they ever, anyway? What frightened me most was that my parents knew virtually nothing about this man.

Joseph had fled to Canada in 1956, and as far as I knew this was the first time he had met us. My parents knew him only through my father's cousin, and the tall tales Joseph himself told them during his first visit. From my parents' behaviour, I could tell that he was a brilliant speaker who always knew what to say and which button to push to make an impression.

Uncle Mike—who wasn't renowned for his moral values—

idolized Joseph and praised him endlessly. His behaviour was even more disturbing than my parents' because his mind was always on breasts and sex. He was full of dirty jokes and disgusting remarks, repeatedly putting his hand under us women as we sat down, and he had humiliated his beautiful wife many times by making passes at his older son's girlfriends. As far as I was concerned, he was the most repulsive person I'd ever known in my childhood.

Now, he seemed to be Joseph's pawn whose mission was to fill my parents' heads with notions. He came over more often than usual to discuss the present situation and Joseph's intentions. It wasn't hard to get to my parents because they were under Joseph's spell already and believed everything they heard—that Joseph was there to make our dreams come true. And they wanted to realize those magical dreams so badly that they neglected to consider any possible consequences.

While this eloquent stranger was building up my parents' hopes, I tried to manage the bad feelings that were welling up in me. I avoided Joseph for as long as I could. My mysterious gut feelings wouldn't go away and were much too strong to ignore. If my parents wanted to be involved with him, that was their decision. I didn't want any of it, though. I just wanted to stay away from the increasing chaos. But the pressure was on. My parents and Uncle Mike didn't let me stay away from their hero for very long.

In mid-September Uncle Mike and Joseph came to our home. Joseph stayed in the car while my father's cousin rushed in and invited him to join them on a trip to Romania. Of course, my father jumped at the chance. But first Uncle Mike turned to me. "He wants to see you," he said. "You must meet him!"

"Maybe so," I said. "But I don't want to see him!" And with that I stepped back. But he didn't stop there. The more he pushed, the more reluctant I became. I thought my answer was clear enough: I didn't want to meet Joseph.

The nagging went on and finally my father stepped in to side with his *cousin*. When they saw there was no way to persuade me, Uncle Mike grabbed my arm and literally dragged me out into the street.

Joseph jumped out of the passenger seat of his black Mercedes. What struck me first was that he looked very impressive for his fifty-four years and I immediately felt the air of authority around him, although he was wearing just a pair of old Nike running shoes, jeans and a white T-shirt. His snow white hair sparkled in the sun. And since he was a photographer, he had a Nikon camera slung over his shoulder. He took my hand as we were introduced, then didn't let go. I was standing in the middle of the street bare-foot, wearing a miniskirt and a tank top and my inevitable glasses. He surveyed me from head to toe and back, shamelessly enjoying my six-foot youth. Not a word passed between us and I grew very uncomfortable under his gaze. Uncle Mike's content grin just increased my discomfort.

When Joseph finally let my hand go, I ran into the house, collapsing into the nearest chair and telling my mother how "hot" he looked. My statement shocked my mom to her core. Obviously, I wasn't supposed to say anything like this about him, because I guess it sounded disrespectful.

But the troubling feelings I'd had ever since he'd shown up didn't diminish just because of his good looks. I retained a strong gut feeling that something was out of line. And when I heard that my casual remark had been repeated to Joseph, I was utterly mortified.

CHAPTER 7

SHORTLY AFTER THAT FIRST MEETING, Uncle Mike and his family gave a dinner in honour of Joseph. I had never addressed him in any way, but when sitting at the same table with him I decided to call him "Uncle" Joseph, as an indication that he was an older man. (He was nine years older than my father.)

The honoured guest's attention was entirely on me, and everyone else's attention was on him. In one way his observing me was flattering but on the other hand I was totally unused to such focused interest. He made me quite nervous.

When he wanted to take some pictures of me, I shyly declined. Uncle Joseph didn't take my refusal seriously and took pictures of me anyway, while the others pressured me to follow his instructions for posing. I quickly reached a point of wanting to run out of the house, but the rising mood kept me in my chair—I knew that if I pulled that stunt everybody would get mad at me. After all, who was *I* to refuse *him*?

He was full of incredible tales, had pictures of his Canadian life, his daughters, his boat, this and that. He described such luxurious ways of living which were beyond our dreams. To me he sounded condescending and after some time I became annoyed by his constant bragging. But everyone else hung on his words. They looked so certain that their ship had come in at last. And my parents' naivety really shocked me. Why was I the only one not taken in by all those stories or by the speaker himself?

The whole evening was so exhausting that I was greatly relieved when it was time to go home. At the door as we said our good-byes, Uncle Joseph took my hand and slightly but noticeably squeezed it. I knew it was a private sign, but not yet whether it was a good or a bad one. When I mentioned it to my parents on our way home, they were certain that it was positive.

Then the following Sunday morning, when my father and I had walked to the open market, we met Uncle Mike driving Uncle Joseph's silver Ford van. He was so anxious that he was totally out of breath as he told us that he was just on his way to pick us up because Joseph wanted to see me immediately. "So hurry up!" he said. "Joseph is waiting!"

My first reaction was that I wouldn't go. I'd had enough of watching the people I knew so well jumping at Uncle Joseph's commands as if they had no minds of their own. Every time he opened his mouth his wish was granted instantly. Yet I'd always believed that my parents at least had some backbone and were too proud to bow down to a rich stranger. And when I refused to get into the van, Uncle Mike looked panicky. "Don't do this!" he pleaded. "Joseph is expecting you."

So how could I have gotten away? Even without Uncle Mike's pressure, my father wouldn't have allowed me to let Uncle Joseph down. But I needed some time before I faced him, so we just casually walked to the store, where he was waiting.

On our way in we saw his daughter, Monica, surrounded by boys. At the dinner I had seen her for a few seconds, but she never joined us at the table. Now, when I had more time to observe her, my first thought was that we couldn't be more different; she was everything I wasn't. At age nineteen, she was a breathtakingly beautiful young woman. She had long, curly auburn hair, wore perfect make-up on her angelic face, and was dressed expensively and uniquely. She looked exciting and mysterious, but also unreachable and cold. Or she could have been just bored by the bustling boys around her; my cousins and their friends were almost suffocating her with their attention.

Compared to her, I felt unspeakably plain, ugly and insignificant; I had never caused such excitement in my whole life. I was also nervous to meet her face to face because I didn't know how to behave in her company. I couldn't even imagine how we would get along.

It was said that she was her father's right hand in the business. They were coming and going between Budapest and my town opening up stores, looking for employees, training people. Within just a few weeks they had set up a small photo store whose future manager was going to be Uncle Mike's wife; it was where we were expected now.

When we arrived Uncle Joseph looked very pleased. Not wasting any time, he told me his idea of my going to Budapest and working for him there. "It would be very convenient if you were there because then I would be able to train you directly. And you wouldn't have to worry about accommodation either; you could live with us."

His words made my father grow a few inches but my inner alarm went off immediately. I wasn't happy with the idea. Uncle Joseph's demanding tone of voice was also rather unsettling. He expected me to accept his offer and leave everything behind me at once. When I quickly declined, his face clouded over. Clearly, he wasn't used to being rejected.

But accepting his offer meant giving up everything and everyone I knew and loved, including my cat and dog, and that I just couldn't do. Besides, spending two hours in his company didn't allow me to get to know him. In a way, he still was a total stranger. He had shown up out of the blue, fanning his money in front of our noses, and so I was supposed to jump at his offer without thinking?

I had just surfaced from a dreadful bout of depression and I wanted to enjoy the fruits of my hard work. I wasn't ready to take such an enormous step. Although I had always wanted to leave our sleepy little town, I wanted to do it when *I* felt ready.

I only had a brief break when Uncle Joseph's uncle, Joe, came into the store, bringing Monica along, having succeeded in rescuing her from the swarming boys. Uncle Joe was a lively, cheerful old gentleman and very friendly. Even though at first he had thought I was a boy, I loved him instantly. And now that Monica was there I had a chance to actually meet her.

She still kept her distance, and I couldn't help noticing how sad she looked. I hadn't seen her smile yet. Her father told her about his job offer to me and asked her to take me for a walk and make friends with me. My lack of enthusiasm for his plan was obvious; therefore it was now Monica's duty to convince me otherwise.

I was pleasantly surprised to find that Monica was a very warm-hearted girl, easy-going and friendly, with a good sense of humour. We spent a nice hour together. She told me that the job offer was worth a try. Only *I* didn't see it that way.

My parents, though, didn't think twice about it. They were extremely proud that Uncle Joseph had chosen me over the cousin's two lazy sons. And the reason for that—as my mother told me—was that I was a neat and honest girl, and it showed. Uncle Joseph knew who he could trust; that was why he was choosing me. "Never again will you have an opportunity like this," she said. "At least your future will be safe and secure. Don't throw it away. Joseph knows who deserves a chance and you are the lucky one!"

CHAPTER 8

BUT I STILL COULDN'T BRING myself to say yes. I told my parents that I needed some time to think the whole situation over. I thought that at age twenty I would be respected enough to be allowed to make my own decision about my own life. How wrong I was.

When I tried to express my concerns and the reasons for my reluctance, my mother didn't listen to me at all; instead she started to shout, "There is nothing to think over! This is a perfect opportunity for you, so you'd better take it! Besides, you always wanted to leave town. So, now you can." This was true. But I didn't want to be kicked out of it.

Finally, our disagreement ended with her threatening to hit me if I kept refusing to take the offer. My mother's reaction didn't surprise me. When I was nineteen, my father had given me a huge smack just because I dared to voice my disapproval. Well, actually I had called him stupid, so maybe I deserved that one. This situation, though, was entirely different.

All this time while my mother was raging my father remained quiet, his silence weighing heavily on me. I wasn't afraid of my mom—for one slap wouldn't have made much of a difference—but I felt humiliated and offended by her treatment. It really hurt me to be treated like an idiot incapable of making the right decision about anything.

The mood was so tense and my mom was so angry that it crossed my mind they might disown me if I didn't comply. It was frightening enough to see how my parents had allowed Uncle Joseph to take over our lives. *My* familiar life was quickly disappearing, along with the parents I knew.

And the decision was made for me, although I never agreed to it. Nobody asked my opinion; nobody was interested in what I wanted. Plus I was expected to behave with only humility and gratitude toward Uncle Joseph. Besides, I couldn't really afford to turn down a millionaire's job offer. Or so went the argument. The fact that we still didn't know him never even reached the surface.

In the end, my family forced me out of my current life. Sure, it wasn't a totally satisfying existence, but at least it was familiar. So I quit my job, to my boss's dismay, said my goodbyes, and packed my two modest suitcases. Whether my parents were excited, sad or terrified about my leaving, I never knew. To me they just looked relieved.

On November 15, 1990, my father and Uncle Mike drove me to Budapest in Uncle Joseph's silver Ford van, which had been left in Uncle Mike's care for the sole purpose of transporting me.

The trip was about three hours but to me seemed much longer. I didn't want to arrive, because this one-way trip felt like the end of the road for me. When we hit a cat just before we reached the capital, my doubts and fear reached their peak even though I had never been superstitious.

Swallowing my tears, I quietly asked my father to take me back home. He gave a short laugh, indicating that my request was nonsense. I was on the doorstep of a bright future and of course they wouldn't let me ruin it. "Your mother would be very disappointed if we turned back," he said. Yes, her feelings or Uncle Joseph's or the whole family tree's or who knows whose, those were important. But why weren't mine?

When we arrived, only Monica was there to welcome us because Uncle Joseph was back in Canada. And now that I was safely delivered to my destination point, my father and Uncle Mike immediately left for home. Their departure just intensified my fear and I felt more like I had been discarded than launched into my new life.

To me my situation was very depressing. I didn't know the city I was in and I didn't know the people I was compelled to depend on and trust. I was just a country girl in the nation's biggest city, against my will. I felt alone and lost. Although Monica's presence and kindness helped to ease the tension a little, it wasn't enough to make me feel safe or even comfortable. But since I was given no other option, I slowly acquiesced to my situation.

She showed me where to put my suitcases, which were to serve as my closets as well, since the apartment was nearly empty. There were only two queen size beds in the same room, and I was supposed to share a bed with her. A small table and three chairs stood in the kitchen, a TV on its box and a chair in the living room. Well, that wasn't the sign of a bright future.

Now that I had been thrown into the unknown, my choices were very limited: I either learned to manage my new life or simply drowned in it. I chose the first option and was determined to put all my efforts into it. After all, I was on the doorstep of my bright future, right?

The fact that my boss at the bookstore had been very pleased with my work gave me the much-needed encouragement. I wasn't afraid of working hard and I truly believed that I would be able to face these new unwanted challenges. I was also a fast learner. Therefore, I was sure that I would be a valuable employee at Uncle Joseph's company.

Monica and I had two weeks of leisure before her father came back. During that time she helped me get to know the area where we lived. We also went shopping, which meant that she did the shopping and I followed her around. It was a real pleasure to get to know her. I admired and looked up to her. Her beauty and the way she held herself kept me entranced. I wished I could be at least a bit like her, so I tried out some of her make-up techniques and was quite happy with the results. The most important fact was that we got along perfectly.

At the end of November, Uncle Joseph was back and my "training" began at once. He acquainted me with a totally different lifestyle from what I knew. My simple life transformed into an affluent one within days, and the ugly little frog became a princess.

He was very relaxed and very kind to me but I remained quite uncomfortable in his presence. He continuously kept his focus completely on me. His gallantry was very flattering and at some point I started to loosen up a little. I had never known anybody like him before, and no one had paid as much attention to me as Uncle Joseph did.

It felt good to sit in his beautiful black Mercedes Benz every day. He took me to restaurants and presented me with expensive chocolates, which were heavenly. Had I entered a fairy tale? Everything was new to me and happened with lightning speed.

He shared his business plans with me, and kept feeding me with promises of how my life was about to change into something I'd never even dreamed of experiencing. Day after day I heard nothing but stories about him and his successes, and after a short while I couldn't think straight. I began to think highly of him and felt proud being in his company, which was a new sensation. He made me believe that I was the luckiest girl alive—thanks to him of course—and I followed him like a puppy. After all, I was so much of a country girl that my grandparents hadn't even had a bathroom, and now I felt myself sucked into Uncle Joseph's seductive world.

But as time went by his attentiveness became overwhelming. I started to feel uncomfortable again, and vulnerable. It was also hard to deal with the attention we drew wherever we went. And the total loss of my old life frightened me to no end.

Day by day he pulled me deeper into his life, which also meant that it was time to learn some business methods. He took me to one of his photography stores, where he introduced me to the manager, who was a very pretty lady and another long lost relative of his.

She was in charge of my training, but most of the time she did nothing else but complain about everything. Since she had worked alone in the store for the last few months, she'd had no time for her family or any other personal matters, but with me there now, she grabbed the opportunity and escaped from her photo store responsibilities. From the second day of my training I was left alone in the store.

Her ten minutes' instruction, though, wasn't enough, because I knew almost nothing about what to do and how to manage a photo store. And even though I wasn't happy about the fact that she left me in the lurch, I said nothing to Uncle Joseph. I didn't want to start my blossoming career by making an enemy of her, so I just dealt with the responsibilities myself as well as I could.

CHAPTER 9

THE STORE WAS CONNECTED TO a hair salon in which a very lively woman named Greta worked. Ever since the photo shop had opened she had been interested in it and learned quickly. She took me under her wing and helped me gain my confidence. Whenever I needed her, she was there for me. In a way, we managed the store together.

Her energetic personality drew the customers' attention away from my trembling hands. And thanks to my new friend and my courage, I overcame every obstacle. Only a few days later I was comfortable managing the store by myself. Reaching that stage of my career was pure success to me.

Meanwhile, Monica and I grew closer. She was really a fascinating young woman. It amazed me how hard and well she worked to succeed in a foreign country, despite speaking quite broken Hungarian. She seemed to have no cracks in her self-esteem, but knew who she was and what she wanted, and did not hesitate to go after it.

On the evening of December 23, she took me to a nightclub. It was my very first time going to such a place. The club was buzzing, and as we entered, every single head turned toward Monica. She was welcomed within seconds and the circle of people around her just kept widening. It seemed that everyone in the club was in her vicinity while I was standing around all by myself. I couldn't have been more invisible; nobody noticed me.

The people were drawn to Monica so while I was able to reach her, I quickly apologized and told her that I was leaving. I could see that she was disappointed and sad but I simply had to get out.

On my way home I could barely keep my tears back. That few minutes had seriously shaken my confidence. The ghosts of the bullies came back to me with full force. *What was I thinking?* I couldn't possibly belong in a nightclub or any other place like that. It just wasn't my world. And obviously the big city wasn't my home either. I had never liked my home town but I was desperately homesick now.

When I arrived at the apartment it was close to 11:00 p.m. I opened the door with the key I had been given but to my shock, I couldn't enter: the door was chained. I rang the bell several times, my depression growing with every ring. *Why was I locked out?*

A few minutes later, which seemed strangely long, Uncle Joseph opened the door. I gave him a quick look and told him that the evening hadn't worked out so I was back early, sorry. I noticed that he was wearing a bathrobe and his hair was tousled, but after that I didn't waste another second on him. I was too upset about the unpleasant evening.

He led me into the dining room, which by now was furnished from Canada, and shut the door on me. I just sat there by myself, thinking about how miserable and lost I felt. And since it was right before Christmas, I felt even worse because this was the first Christmas I would be away from home. I had been in Budapest for only five weeks now and I was already drained. I didn't even care about my parents' attitude toward me; I just wanted to go home.

I had sunk into my unhappiness when Uncle Joseph entered the room. He had a bottle of wine in his hand and went to get two glasses from the cabinet. Then he suggested that we drink a toast to my calling him simply Joseph instead of Uncle Joseph. Because of the thirty-four year age difference and other reasons, I would have preferred to address him as I had been doing, but he insisted that I just call him by his first name. I didn't feel too comfortable about the idea, but he had the final word about it. Since I never drank, I took only a sip of wine, innocently kissed his cheeks according to the Hungarian tradition, and then I excused myself and went to bed. I wasn't in the mood for any chit chat.

The two beds were still in the same room and I had to change quickly; I was very nervous that (Uncle) Joseph might walk in on me. With record speed I occupied my side of Monica's bed. Then Joseph came in and went to his bed, right next to mine. I tried to relax but couldn't. His presence unnerved me. It was the first time in my life that I was alone with a man in the same room in the dark, and I didn't like the situation at all.

The air felt so thick that I had difficulty breathing. An unfamiliar fear started to grow in me. I listened nervously to his every little movement and breath, hoping that he would fall asleep quickly.

Darkness and total silence surrounded us. Then he moved suddenly and I froze. "Do you want to come to my bed?" he asked. My breath was stuck in my lungs; I didn't dare to exhale. I pretended to be asleep but felt a crippling fear crawling up my spine. I had never been so afraid in my life.

Unfortunately, I wasn't a good pretender because he kept asking the same question over and over again. I knew I had to say something otherwise he wouldn't have stopped. "No, just let me sleep!" I said.

I hoped that my firm answer would settle the issue but the next second he was in my bed, pressing his cold body on me and rubbing himself against me. He was touching me everywhere. I wanted to jump out of bed and run away but he sensed my intentions and quickly lay on top of me with his full weight. I begged him to let me go, telling him that I'd never been with a man.

I had no experience whatsoever but had some idea of what was about to happen, and I was beyond terrified. I kept begging him, "Please, don't hurt me; don't do this to me!" He couldn't have cared less. My lungs were already burning for air but I didn't know how to get him off me.

When he forced my underwear down I became frantic. I started to yell louder and louder for him to stop what he was doing, while I twisted and squirmed beneath him to get away, but I was hopelessly pinned. "Shut up!" He yelled at me. "Don't you dare make another sound!" I kept struggling under him but my efforts were in vain. He was much stronger and heavier than I was.

Then I felt an excruciating pain that racked my whole body. At that point I just wanted to die. I shut my eyes as if that would end the terror. The feeling of him inside of me turned my stomach. With his every movement I felt like my organs were being torn out of my body. I could actually feel the damage.

Nausea kept welling up in my throat, and I had to gather all my remaining strength not to throw up. With each and every passing second I felt dirtier. I just waited for the disgusting horror to be over. When he was finished and drew back, he yelled into my face, "You lied to me! I felt nothing there. I knew you weren't a virgin!" He kept accusing me of being a liar and demanded that I promise not to lie to him ever again. I mumbled an "okay", hoping that he would leave me alone. I had no strength left to argue with him.

CHAPTER 10

AS I LAY IN THE bed, I felt nothing but the throbbing pain in my body and a sense of emptiness. My hard work of building myself up, my confidence, and my self-worth had been destroyed within minutes. *I was destroyed.* I felt deeply violated and used. He had not only racked my body, he had wrecked my whole world. My mind was numb and my emotions were dead. I knew what had happened to me but didn't understand it. *Was this the* real *Uncle Joseph? What was next? What should I do?*

Then my thoughts drifted to my parents. *What would they say if I told them? Would they believe* me *or the man they thought highly of and respected?* I knew they trusted *him* blindly. And now that man had robbed me and hurt me terribly. He had forced himself into me, knocked down and defaced all my boundaries. He had ground me into the dust and there was nowhere I could turn.

Here, in Budapest I hadn't known anybody long enough to share such a disgusting secret, and my parents never listened to me or paid any attention when I really needed them, so I didn't believe they would help me in this situation either. I wasn't even sure that they would believe me if I told them. To my mind, confiding in them would be the worst move. Besides, Joseph was now my employer, who offered me the one and only chance to improve my life. If he fired me after three weeks, I was sure that my parents would confront me with disapproval and probably blame me for ruining my once in a lifetime opportunity, as well as for what had just happened.

I wasn't a child anymore but certainly felt like one now: a lost and helpless child. My mind was spinning with all of these thoughts and questions as a real battle ensued within me. The more I thought about what had just happened and about my relationship with my parents, the more certain I became that I was alone in the situation, which also crushed my hope of going home for Christmas. I couldn't possibly visit my family in this condition.

He was watching me, knowing what a big storm was raging inside of me. Although I tried hard to conceal my emotions, I wasn't able to hide everything. I knew that my face mirrored my feelings, and whatever he noticed made him smirk with self-satisfaction. Then he invited me into his bed. It wasn't a question of whether I wanted to or not; I had to. Besides, I was far too afraid of him not to obey. I was afraid that he would do the same thing again.

The following morning I wasn't able to look into Monica's eyes. She undoubtedly got the picture. "It's not my business," she told me. She wasn't angry with me but rather helped me by breaking the ice and being the warm-hearted friend I already knew she was. But nothing could wash away the mortifying shame I felt. And then there was the physical pain that tortured and reminded me of every detail for days.

Joseph of course acted as if nothing had happened so for my own sake I decided to put aside the whole incident as much as I could. The next day I went to the store, and did my job as always. But I had to keep myself extra busy. If I let my guard down, my mind and my aching body took me back to the horrible event.

My self-made peace didn't last long, though, because the store's ex-manager stormed in. "Are you aware that I am involved with Joseph?" she demanded. Her question was like a slap. "No, I didn't know that," I mumbled. "I was there when you unexpectedly came home. We were together and you interrupted us." She was fuming. I didn't understand why she was angry with me. *What did I do?* Then she told me that they were planning to have a child together, which was another shock for me because supposedly she was happily married and had two children. I didn't even know what to say or how to react to the astonishing news. *What kind of mess had I been forced into?*

Then the sudden realization hit me: Joseph had had sexual intercourse with her just before he forced me to do the same. I could only hope that he at least washed himself before he took me, although I wasn't certain of that. He hadn't bothered to use protection either. The thought itself made me nauseous but I had to keep it down because I was standing in front of this woman, listening to the insults pouring out of her. She was offended and jealous. I was the one to blame; I was the guilty one in the situation. I just didn't know why she had come to *me*. A couple of weeks ago I had been determined not to make an enemy of her but still she had become one anyway.

She was so absorbed in her own feelings that she didn't care whether she was rightfully accusing me or not. In her eyes I couldn't have been anything else but a slut. *How many other women were involved in this degrading situation?* I wondered. There were already the three of us, including his wife. I was unspeakably ashamed of being a part of such a situation but felt hopelessly trapped.

All of this happened right before Christmas. What a wonderful present. Plus, my cat had died. Christmas had always been my favourite holiday but this time my spirit was broken and I wasn't able to pick up the pieces. Joseph invited my parents and despite everything else that had happened, I was happy to see them.

We went out to the mountains and I hoped that spending some time together would give me the chance to nurture our relationship, but as the day advanced I had to realize that they were still in total awe of Joseph; they still worshipped him, as always. Witnessing my parents' devotion made me realize that I had been right not to say anything to them about the recent events.

We spent the whole day together, yet I felt awfully alone. My parents, though, were joyful and I really didn't want to ruin their mood. They were extremely respectful, polite and humble toward Joseph, and were even modestly laughing along with him. Joseph was very pleasant and thoughtful toward them, like a real gentleman. Even when they left they were still in good spirits; only I felt devastated.

I tried to forget and just go on. Within a week the physical pain was gone, but the emotional pain burned into me. Joseph continued to act as if nothing at all had happened. He was kind to me, too kind. However, I wasn't the same person anymore. To me, his seduction was endangering and had lost its magic.

Somehow, everything seemed to be upside down around me. Just after Christmas a very ugly argument erupted between Monica and her father. I had never seen them like that before, had always thought that they got along pretty well. At the end of the quarrel Joseph went out, while Monica packed her bags and was ready to leave the country for good.

At that point I felt responsible for her. Why? I didn't know. Maybe because I was afraid that if she left, she would be leaving me as well.

So, I tried to convince her to stay. "At least talk to your father. I'm sure he would be very worried for you if you just left the country without a word." She was determined and I was desperate. I did my best to comfort her. Then she opened up a little. "You know, I never finished high school because my father brought me here. I always wanted to be a chef. That was my dream. But he robbed me of my dream. Because he has no son, he treats me like one. He forced me to come here."

I was too dumbfounded to say anything. At twenty, I tried to be a solid support for her, the protective adult, and although I wasn't fully sure anymore that I was doing the right thing, I convinced her to stay.

Monica's emotions brought out some of mine. To clarify my situation a bit, I apologized and told her that I had never wanted to get involved with her father and was extremely ashamed. "I don't blame you. I know it wasn't your fault," she said, and we comforted each other like two lifelong friends, our pain and misery undoubtedly bringing us even closer.

No matter what, though, nothing could erase the ugly aspects of the incident. She moved her bed into the living room and eventually moved out. But while she was at the apartment, and even after that she was always very nice and friendly toward me.

1991
Who cares?

CHAPTER 11

THE YEAR 1990 HAD ENDED with the most horrific experience I could ever imagine. Within a few days, trauma after trauma had rocked my world. At this point, I didn't think that I could take more. But the irony of the whole situation was terribly laughable; my bright, safe future, my once in a lifetime opportunity had just begun and my lucky star had already fallen out of the sky.

After December 23, I felt condemned, as if I had a sign on my forehead saying that I was now his. When he took me to visit his relatives, I felt like a trophy that he proudly carried around, and in return I was welcomed with moderate respect wherever we went.

But life went on. I continuously did my best at work and didn't let myself be affected by the burden I was carrying. At least, I tried not to. I kept myself busy all day, every day. By now, I was officially the manager of the store and I enjoyed the privilege of being in charge.

Although the store's location was rather poor, it reached the top of its capacity for the first time since it had opened—under *my* management. I was very happy, and proud of the result I had achieved, sharing the glory with Greta because she was there every day, either to help me out or just to keep me company. Her friendship was invaluable.

I worked ten, twelve hours a day and I truly enjoyed every minute of it. That store became my sanctuary. Joseph paid me ten times more than I had earned at the bookstore, just as he had claimed he would, which meant my salary was now 30,000 forint, about $560CAD per month! For the first time in my life I had good money in my pocket and was very excited about going shopping. To celebrate my well earned money, I went out and bought two pairs of shoes at once!

Then one day, a well dressed couple came to the store with a beautiful bouquet of flowers to thank me for my services. I was deeply touched. Knowing the rules, I didn't want to accept the flowers but

45

they wouldn't leave until I took them. That bouquet was an even bigger reward than my increased salary. The fact that my work was highly appreciated by customers lifted my spirit, because no one had ever expressed gratitude toward me.

When I arrived home Joseph had a guest. Ignoring that, he threw a jealous fit about the flowers, demanding to know everything. "Where did you get that? Who gave those to you?" He was extremely angry with me. I had wanted to share my happiness with him, but now I was surprised and frightened by his reaction. After all, they were only flowers, albeit very beautiful.

Then he might have realized that he had overdone because he changed the subject. "Where were you? It's late and I was worried." I told him that I had had to go to the photo lab to drop the films off, which he knew very well. I had spent some time there, then I came home. I also explained to him where the flowers came from. He gave me a long lecture about not accepting anything from anybody except him. But he could have said anything by that point; my good mood was already ruined.

And the changes were unstoppable in my life. The next thing was that he forbade me to do any things *I* liked. He forced me to give up all of my interests. He forbade me to read books, listen to music, or watch movies. If he caught me reading a novel, he berated me. In his opinion, everything I loved was bad and stupid. These things only had a bad influence on me, and I couldn't possibly learn anything from them. "I am the only one who can educate you," he told me many times.

In one of his memorable "educations" he firmly held out his right hand, with his palm facing me, and told me to put my hand against his. Then he started to push. I automatically resisted the force of his hand and pushed back. But that wasn't right. He pushed me with even more force until I dropped my hand. "See," he said, "if you push me I have to push back with more power. Don't let that happen! And don't forget, I am much stronger than you anyway." He told me that the right thing was to let him push me; otherwise he couldn't do his job, which was to educate me.

I thought that he was talking about business so I followed his instructions as well as I could. Despite all the obstacles, I still believed that I could manage the challenges *he* had for me. I worked harder and harder to meet his requirements and demands. I tried to show more interest in his work and to please him in every way I could, because I still wanted his recognition for all I had done. I even made myself believe that our airtight connection was love, that *I* was actually in love with him. And while I was working on bringing even more out of me, he was also working on keeping me under his spell.

While my life remained colourful at the store, I didn't have much excitement at home. After twelve hours of work I wasn't permitted to rest or enjoy any free time. I wasn't even allowed to have my *own* time.

For some reason I was never asked to pay any rent; therefore, it seemed common sense that all the household chores were my responsibility. This wasn't easy because Monica and Joseph were the messiest people I had ever encountered. Really, they were in need of a maid.

Monica had enough clothes to change every day for months and her father took his laundry to his wife in Canada. To me, wearing black solved the problem. But the dirty clothes piled up anyway.

Yet after living there for a year or so, they still had no washing machine. It was entirely up to me to reform their household, which included convincing Joseph that yes, we were very badly in need of an automatic washing machine.

Chores or no chores, I still couldn't have one minute for myself; I had to be ready for him whenever he was in the mood. Early morning or the middle of the night, he woke me up and took what he wanted.

Sex thus became a regular thing between us. Of course, his only goal was his pleasure, for which he used my body. I wasn't sure whether or not it was supposed to be the way he did it, but I didn't know any better. In the movies everything was different, so full of love and passion, but at the same time tender and beautiful. But my reality couldn't have been further from that. I assumed that this beauty, which I had never experienced, existed only in the movies.

Despite all this, I wanted to experience a sense of togetherness. I had never known that special feeling of really belonging *with* someone in soul and body. My emotions were so overwhelming that I wasn't able to keep them at bay. I wanted to express my love and devotion for somebody. Since Joseph was the only person there, I wanted to share my feelings with him, even if he didn't return them. And I honestly thought that I would make him happy with my emotional outpourings.

He still took me out to dine, and came to pick me up from work each day like a true gentleman. And he started to call me "sweetheart". (He also addressed his daughter and wife the same way.) Then one day he surprised me with six rings. He said that some of the rings were real diamonds, and they were all mine. That gesture made me feel a little better. I had never had such jewels in my life and it felt good to receive them, even though he just threw them in front of me as if throwing a bone to a dog, valuing neither the jewels nor me.

CHAPTER 12

THE ONLY PLACE I COULD relax was the store. There I felt independent, free and happy. But when Joseph decided that I had had enough fun there, he took me out. After three short months, that was the end of my independence and my salary.

He stopped paying me entirely, explaining that if I was his, I didn't need any money. After all, he was the provider and he would get everything that *he* considered to be good for me, which was nothing but perfume. Within a short period of time I had perfume coming out of my ears. When I asked him to stop giving them to me because I already had enough for the next hundred and fifty years, his response was, "I know what you need and what's best for you. Don't forget that I'm smarter than you are."

Joseph's new idea for me was that I would train employees across the country. He had already found a replacement to manage my store, and I had only a few days to train the new manager, who like me on first arrival had absolutely no idea what to do. Luckily, he was a willing student and we had lots of fun during those few days. Then I was on my way to train others.

Leaving the store made me very sad and self-conscious. I lost my sense of security, my shield, my sanctuary. Plus, the idea of traveling by myself frightened me because I had never done so before.

It wasn't an easy task to train others because I was still learning myself. Sometimes I needed help and advice, but whenever I asked Joseph he just shook me off, saying, "Your work is so easy that even a three-year-old could do it. Besides, you're a well-read person, you shouldn't have any problems." That was all the help I got from him.

I worked very hard to earn his appreciation, or even just a praising word, but nothing that I did was good enough to win his heart. I needed to hear that he was satisfied with my efforts, I needed a few encouraging, warm words, but he deemed that I wasn't worthy of any.

I knew that wasn't true. I knew that I was a good employee, because I worked harder than I had worked at the bookstore, and there the boss had been satisfied with my efforts. I was striving to achieve what I knew I deserved—a kind word, if nothing else. Ironically, the more he criticized and mocked me, the harder I worked to live up to his limitless expectations. I struggled tirelessly for what I thought was rightfully mine.

Traveling by myself to another city to train a new store manager happened only once. Now, he wanted me to be around him all the time, even if that only meant sitting beside him while he worked. For a short time his neediness was flattering and I tried even more to adjust to his demands. I wanted to be loved, and was doing everything I possibly could to earn it. I even took the situation to be normal, but my soul began to rebel.

As time went on, I started to feel like I was nothing more than another part of him. He wanted to change me into someone who would please him with every movement, who would live and breathe only for him. My individuality had vanished and I felt my already small world shrinking until eventually it was completely absorbed into his. There was nothing left for me, and nothing else could exist but him and his business. I had to find all of my interests and purpose in these two. I wasn't living my life anymore—I was living his.

And I was working around the clock without any rest or help, which started to take its toll on me. I seriously needed some time on my own but that was out of the question. Even if I managed to steal a few peaceful moments for myself and my needs, when I was caught, he always ordered me to be with him instead. That became my job and my obligation. He literally disposed of my life and kept me busy 24/7 in whatever ways he wanted. From time to time, I protested against the way he treated me but he was always clever enough to smooth over my rebellion. Then everything went on as it had before, at least for a while.

At one point he gave me one of the monthly newsletters for his Canadian business—in English of course—and forced me to read it, even though I hadn't a clue how to begin. There wasn't one word I could understand and I had no idea how to pronounce them either.

Joseph told me to underline every word I did not understand, but that meant underlining the whole text. Not being able to read it made me feel like I was illiterate. It was a complete waste of time. He expected me to run to him for the translation of every word, but when I went to him he never had time and I had had enough of this pretty quickly, losing any interest in learning the language.

In the spring of this year, Joseph decided to hire my parents. He gave them a store in the large city where my godmother lived, and which was a good hour's drive from our hometown. Of course, they were delighted. I knew I would have to train them, and was really looking forward to spending some fun time together. We hadn't seen each other for four months now.

So in April, we went to help my parents start up their new store, which was a few weeks away from its grand opening. While we were there, Joseph made sure that my parents got the message: he had free access to me, and they clearly understood it.

I could feel the air around us turning very heavy and icy. My parents' reaction to the unspoken words was unmistakable. They were shocked to their core. Their faces showed disgust, and their eyes were full of anger and contempt as they looked at me. I had to gather all my strength to continue the training as if I hadn't noticed anything, but they refused to talk to me, while remaining very respectful and humble toward Joseph. Their dismissive behaviour made me feel guilty, although I knew I wasn't. At the end of the day I was so exhausted that I had developed a blinding headache. For seven days and nights my head throbbed and no medication could ease my suffering. But at least my father felt sorry for me.

Then a week or so later Joseph announced to me that his wife was coming to visit him, and I had to move out of the apartment, as if I'd never been there. This was so unexpected that I didn't know how to handle it; I just cried. Instead of feeling relieved that I could finally get out, I felt miserable and humiliated. I packed my two suitcases, and since there was no other place for me to go, I went home to my parents.

I could tell they weren't too happy to see me, and when I told them why I was home they only shook their heads, looking at me with ever so much contempt. They never actually told me what they thought about me or the situation, or why they were so hostile, cold and uncomfortable around me. Nor did they ask me what was going on or what had happened. They had received a certain message from Joseph and that was enough for them to believe that they actually knew the truth. Either they never wanted to know or simply weren't interested in their own daughter's side of the story.

But I didn't think they would believe me anyway and because of the false ideas Joseph had planted in their minds, our relationship became awkward and forced. We communicated only because it was unavoidable, but our buried pain spoke for itself.

Chapter 13

I HAD BEEN AT HOME for a week when one morning my father came to me, looking as if he had just seen a ghost. He told me that Joseph's wife was there to see me but she refused to come in. I was quite shocked that she had actually come to me. What now?

She was stunningly beautiful and very nicely dressed. She was also very friendly and uncomfortably polite, asking me to come out to the street, so that no one would hear us. First, she courteously accused me for being with her husband in order to get their money. She also told me that my efforts were useless, because they would never give up what they had achieved together; they would never get divorced. Then she asked me to leave Joseph alone.

Although she was very nice, she made me feel like a cheap whore. And maybe I was one at that moment. But I was so certain about my feelings for Joseph that I told her not to worry about the money, because I had no intention of taking that away from her. When I told her that I loved Joseph she couldn't conceal her surprise. Her reaction made me feel strange about my unexpected confession. After that she didn't say anything more, just acknowledged what I had said and left.

After her departure I felt very proud that I had had the strength to stand up for myself. My hopes and senseless love had given me the courage. But when my heartbeat slowed down and I could think more clearly, it was impossible to miss the point of this confrontation: she was more worried about losing the money than losing her husband. And that put a huge question mark over my self-made love for him.

A couple of hours later I didn't feel all that proud anymore, but was very tired. Ever since Joseph had walked into our lives, *my* life was always on other people's plates so they could chew on it. That really hurt. Just because I was the youngest female in the family, the "grown-ups" were treating me and my life as if it was nothing but a joke. I was the one everybody pointed at and judged. I had remained the black sheep of the family. And if the morning's event wasn't enough for one day, in the afternoon Joseph turned up out of the blue with Uncle Mike, while their wives kept each other company somewhere else.

Joseph came to my room and I told him what had happened in the morning, what she had said and how I had responded. Although he listened politely, it was obvious he already knew everything. I was amazed at how quickly the news had traveled, but I said nothing. But I didn't know how much of the information given to him was true and how much of it was made up, which was perhaps why I wasn't entirely happy to see him. Regardless of my emotional turmoil, Joseph seemed quite happy about my morning performance. Even Uncle Mike was pleased and satisfied that finally I had managed to have a man in my life.

Throughout the evening he wouldn't stop his teasing and dirty comments about me. He thought he was very funny and Joseph joined the game as well, but I just wanted to scream. That evening I hit my breaking point and wasn't able to take the pressure any longer. I fell to pieces and started crying uncontrollably.

I went into the other room and let everything come out. Between my sobs, though, I could still hear the men joking around, laughing and wondering what on earth was wrong with me. I heard Joseph saying that I had no problems at all, that I was only hysterical and all I wanted was to get some attention.

My mother was at my side, but was obviously very embarrassed about me being so out of control. I wanted to stop crying but my body wouldn't let me. The tension had been piling up for months now and it had to come out. My mother and Uncle Mike's wife, who arrived later that evening, were pressing me with questions I couldn't answer.

When I was finally able to calm down, I washed my face and went out for a walk without saying a word to anyone. I just wanted to get away from all of them, even from myself. It was already pitch dark outside and the streets were so peaceful. I longed to be alone in order to clear my mind and sort out my feelings, but this privilege wasn't granted to me either, because Joseph followed me outside and refused to leave. He told me that he wanted to be sure I was safe in the dark streets. His presence was such a burden, but he wouldn't let me shake him off and I had no energy left to argue. But instead of just walking quietly beside me, he kept pestering me with questions. Why was I crying, why wasn't I happy, why this and why that. Finally, I had to persuade him that I was all right, just to have a few seconds of stillness.

About half an hour later we went back to the house. Everybody was relieved to see that I was back to normal, and they began praising and thanking Joseph for doing such a marvellous job of calming me down. Then for the rest of the evening I remained withdrawn. I had never been so tired in my life.

But every day is new, and after fourteen hours of sleep I felt much better. I was ready again to face the challenges of my life, which had gotten noticeably harder. And when Joseph's wife left the country, my obligation was to move back to Budapest and pick up where I had left off as if nothing had happened. One thing changed though: my leash got shorter, and almost simultaneously he started to hurt me more and more.

In the early summer Joseph bought an old factory building from a bankrupt industrial business, which was on the outskirts of the city with nothing but other factories around. He temporarily put his head office there, and at the back of this building he set up a big photo lab, which he shipped in from Canada. With that came three of his employees who knew how to install the huge machines. Joseph's idea was that they would stay in Hungary to run the lab, but even I understood that they had absolutely no intention of staying any longer than necessary. So Joseph had to find a few English-speaking, Hungarian technicians who could work with the Canadian guys and eventually manage the lab.

He searched for the best, and with his promises he was able to lure two of them away from other photo companies. They worked on the big lab along with the Canadians, who had to stay in Hungary for several months because there was always something wrong with the machines and they remained the only ones able to fix them.

While they were there, they lived with us and I had to look after them. Joseph wanted me to be an entertaining hostess but mostly I served them in silence because we couldn't communicate. I was very uncomfortable around them because they knew Joseph's wife and I felt quite ashamed about being his...whatever. My role in life made me feel very low—I couldn't even name it—and Joseph made sure he put me even lower. Fortunately, the guys were really nice and friendly, plus throughout the last few months we got used to each other, so the agony about my role lessened eventually.

At the end I had a lot of fun being with them; if nothing else we would eye each other and just laugh. And of course when Joseph wasn't around, it was much easier to relax. Even the guys seemed more loosened up, and although I never understood any of their jokes, their laughter was always contagious. They used the word "stupid" quite often, which caught my attention and it didn't take me long to figure out what it meant.

When Joseph was around, though, I could never relax. The guys would still joke around but now Joseph was in charge of the laughter. And his behaviour made me feel that I was the subject of his jokes and derision, like when he pointed to the guys' laundry piles, which were growing. Joseph told them not to worry because I would happily wash their dirty clothes. It was obvious that they were very uncomfortable with that arrangement, but Joseph—as their and my employer—insisted, and there was no room for disagreement; he expected me to do it.

I always had to stick around, no matter how uncomfortable he made me feel. I had to be there and smile 24/7. When I forgot to do, he always reminded me: "Smile! You have absolutely no reason to be sad. If you don't smile they will think that I don't keep you well. Smile! That is your obligation."

He also told me repeatedly to be very nice to his men because they were the best of his workers. Sometimes it felt like the only thing I didn't have to do was to spoon-feed them. And my duty was never done. So although I had no problems with the guests, I couldn't wait for them to leave.

CHAPTER 14

WITH THE PURCHASE OF THE new building my role was switched again. He didn't even want me out of his sight now. To make matters worse, he humiliated me regularly in front of other people: it was impossible to mistake the tone of his voice when he spoke to me. He made me feel like a total idiot. Every time I behaved like a normal, independent person with her own mind, he got extremely angry.

He made all decisions for me and remained full of ideas. One of his new ones was that I had to be the bookkeeper for the operating stores. I hadn't had the slightest idea what I was supposed to do and I told him that I wasn't the right person for the job. "Don't forget who's the smartest!" he told me. "I'll explain to you how you do it. It's nothing else but adding. You can add, can't you?"

I didn't know much about bookkeeping but I knew that it was more than simple adding. For the first time I seriously doubted that he knew what he was talking about. And when I tried to tell him that it wasn't that easy, he berated me in front of the other people present, who had told him the same thing. But he was the boss and right or wrong, I had to do what he told me to. He showed me which number to add to which, and it had to be done.

Joseph loved being the center of attention and had many meetings in which he described his plans, pulling more and more people in. I was never a part of these gatherings; thus I just stayed aside.

One day, I was in front of the building talking to a woman while Joseph was in the office surrounded by people. All the doors were wide open, so I could see that he was very busy. I wasn't expecting him to notice my absence, and I was totally taken aback when I heard him bawling after me, "Erika, where are you? Who are you with?" The circle around him opened up. He was seething with rage. "Get back to my side immediately!" he roared.

I felt so humiliated. All the people just stared at me as I obeyed Joseph's command. Ignoring everyone he started to question me about where I had been and what I'd been doing. I told him that I was just outside talking to someone. His response was, "I didn't give you permission to go outside and talk to people. I need you here. Don't move from my side! Listen and learn." For the rest of the day, I was at his side like a faithful dog. He never even looked at me again, but I was sufficiently mortified not to risk another humiliation.

After that incident, I was always on edge when it came to socializing. I no longer knew when I was behaving well enough not to be scolded. I liked being with other people but was afraid of the consequences...

In our private life the situation was still manageable. I did my best to cooperate with him just to keep the peace, but he was always up to something that challenged my efforts: he wanted to take pictures of me in my lingerie. I didn't like the idea. It actually frightened me; thus I refused to comply. After a while, though, he wasn't asking anymore, he was demanding. I begged him to abandon the idea because it made me feel very uncomfortable, but as always, he ignored me.

He ordered me to sit on the bed and told me how to pose. I could see that my discomfort and shyness gave him extra pleasure, as he grinned at me, and that offended me even more. "Smile! Smile! SMILE! Beautiful!" His oily voice and that avid smile made my flesh creep. I was so relieved when that was over. But the next time, he caught me while I was taking a bath...

He remained very strict about my social life. I wasn't allowed to make new friends and he also forbade me to keep contact with my old ones. When I received an invitation to my high school reunion, I didn't even dare to think about asking his permission. I also didn't have the opportunity to respond to the invitation. What could I have written, anyway? How could I have explained my situation?

Then one day I received another letter from the same person, in which she was very offensive and angry with me. Her every word was like the stab of a knife; I had never read a letter with such a tone. I struggled with the idea of writing back to her, but my circumstances stopped me. I wasn't sure that anybody would believe or understood my explanation, and I didn't want to bring more disgrace on my head. I felt ashamed enough already that my life had turned out like this. But when *he* got an invitation for his elementary school reunion, we had to be there.

I had to stick to his side all the time and the only people I was allowed to speak to were those who he chose for me, from whom he thought I could learn to smile or to be kind and friendly, or just to have some general knowledge. According to him I had a lot to learn and only he knew where I could find such much needed "wisdom".

It was utterly exhausting to take the constant humiliation from him and I reached a point again when I couldn't take it anymore. I needed some comfort, and where else could I find that if not from my parents. Despite their terrible track record, they were always the first people who came to mind when I needed solace. I never gave up hope that one day they would understand me, even love me enough to care.

By now they lived in the new city and were deeply involved in their store. Because of this, my dog had to be put down. Nobody wanted the poor thing. So even though they gained something, I lost again. I knew they were excited about the new challenges and I was happy for them. I had no intention of ruining their joy, but I needed them, badly. When I was free of Joseph's supervision for a few minutes I grabbed the phone and called them.

My father picked up the receiver and I asked for my mom. I tried to tell her what was going on and how I felt, that I couldn't take living like this anymore and I wanted to go home. She didn't even let me finish. "It was your idea all along," she shouted. "You wanted him, you chose him, so it's your problem now! Don't cry to me about him! You're always so smart and independent, so deal with it."

My breath stuck in my lungs. I was already crying quietly, but my mother's hateful words made me cry harder. *What was she talking about? I hadn't chosen him.* I was choking on my tears as I begged her to help me, to allow me to go home. I wanted to get away, to leave, and to go back to them. But she just kept screaming at me. Finally my father took the phone from her and said to me, "Don't upset your mother! She has enough to deal with. Just do your best! Good-bye!"

I was devastated, and so shocked that I couldn't believe what I had just heard. I had no idea what was best to do in these circumstances. It was very hard to take that my own mother, in such a serious situation, had not just ignored me but blamed me. Her reaction made me feel like I was nothing more than a chased-away dog. After hanging up I just sat there, staring. I despised my life so much and didn't want to continue living like this. I felt I couldn't go on, but I didn't know what to do. I didn't know how to escape the misery.

Greta was the only person I knew who wasn't transfixed or intimidated by Joseph. If I couldn't contact her, she came to me. I felt safe and confident in her company, even in Joseph's presence. However, since I had been taken out of the store, Greta and I hadn't had many opportunities to get together. Fortunately, Joseph went back to Canada regularly, which gave me some space to breathe, and one day I took Greta home with me. Since my parents refused to help me, I tried to help myself.

Even though it was only a one-day trip, we had a marvellous time. In the last few long months I had forgotten what it meant to be free and have fun. It felt wonderful, although I was aware that my freedom would be over even before Joseph came back.

His latest idea shocked my whole being: he wanted a child with *me*. First, I thought he was just joking. After all, I was only twenty-one. It was only about six months since he'd made me sexually active, and now he wanted me to get pregnant?! The only excuse I was able to give him was my age. I felt far too young and inexperienced to take on the responsibilities of a baby. One day, yes. At this age, though, I felt nothing but sheer terror when he brought up the subject.

Whatever I said or tried to say, he dismissed me. "You don't have to worry. Children are pure joy." He could've said anything to me: the idea frightened me so much that after awhile he dropped it. But the seed of fear had been planted in me and I knew that sooner or later he would bring up the subject again.

Chapter 15

EVEN THOUGH JOSEPH HAD GONE quiet about the child he wanted me to bear, the thought of it constantly occupied my mind. Since we were distant relatives—as it turned out, he was the son of my paternal grandfather's sister—it didn't make any sense that he would want a child with me. I was afraid. He, of course, was very confident: he knew the answer to everything at all times, no matter what came up or what *he* brought up. I was beyond trusting his answers, though. I needed to know the facts, but not from him. I had to see a doctor about this.

The appointment was very useful, at least for calming my nerves. The doctor said that a baby would have every chance of being perfectly healthy. Good news, but that didn't make me any more ready to be a mother. And there was something no doctor could help me with: I in no way believed that Joseph was the right person to father my child...

But life went on, as it always did, and soon after the first building had been purchased, Joseph wanted to extend his territory and bought another building at the front of the same industrial area, close to the main road, to which he then transferred his head office. Beside the office he located the head store, where we could meet with our customers, store managers, and franchisees. At the back of the building were the storage areas, while the big lab remained in the old building. Our responsibilities grew daily, and with all of these changes my role was switched yet again.

Instead of being the bookkeeper I worked everywhere: in the offices, in the new store and even in the warehouses. I answered the phone, and at the same time I was the sales clerk, plus I took in the negatives for processing, and trained the new franchisees, which was how I met my future obstetrician, Dr. Lane. When the store was empty, I priced catalogues—which meant writing the prices of items beside their pictures—and everywhere, and all the time, I had to be a smiling doll who unconditionally offered her services. Then, at the end of each day, I had to clean the floors and toilets; in addition I was his personal secretary, along with Monica. And as if all of these tasks weren't enough to do, he made Monica and me responsible for feeding his increasing number of employees so they wouldn't waste their time leaving work to have lunch.

Joseph wanted to open one hundred stores and about two hundred franchises in Hungary. As he opened one store after another, potential employees began to flow in, including long-lost relatives with whom he had never kept in touch. And those who failed to contact him, he went after. He tried to charm his older female relatives into the business as well, but they refused his offers. After the fall of Communism, hundreds of thousands of people lost their jobs. Joseph thus had the power to play god in our tiny country. He even hired an ex-mayor as his adviser.

This new man was very unsympathetic, with his icy blue eyes. Even when he smiled I couldn't see him being a good, kind man. He watched me like a hawk all the time, as if I was nothing but a walking piece of meat. And this man wanted to be the brain of the company next to Joseph, who had lived in Canada and had no experience whatsoever about life in Hungary.

Despite this, his business kept growing rapidly. Only the bookkeeping was out of order. Fortunately, the ex-mayor's godson, who was an actual bookkeeper, was hired to clean up the mess. This young man was honest, conscientious, and diligent—and absolutely horrified when he saw the accounts of the last few months. Joseph of course pushed me immediately into the middle of the whole accounting problem: "You couldn't even add two numbers correctly?!" He was so angry with me that the bookkeeper rushed to my defence, explaining that the problems didn't start with the adding, which was correct, but that there was much more to it. He could have said anything, but to no avail—Joseph insisted everything was my fault. When I reminded him that he had instructed me in what to do, his respond was simple: "Don't be smart with me!" So, although he had made mistakes, I was the one he castigated. He was already my keeper and now he became my punisher.

I buried myself in my work, which helped me to escape from reality, if only temporarily. I kept my mind on my tasks and not on how my life was going. I hoped that he would just forget the baby issue; after all, we had enough to do.

To supply the stores, he shipped in countless forty-foot containers from Canada and Asia. Sometimes there were two or three containers waiting in line to be unloaded. We were still short of men so the four of us—Monica, Joseph's half-brother, Joseph and I unloaded them. Occasionally even Uncle Joe, who was around seventy years old, was there to help. Often we worked late into the night, but nobody complained.

I worked like a mule, with no reward whatsoever, not a paycheque, not even an appreciative word, although I knew I deserved either or both, actually.

Just because Joseph had never valued my work didn't mean there weren't other people who did and some were amazed by my work abilities. Once, when a man praised me to Joseph and told him that he wanted to "steal" me, I hoped that my boss would get the message and begin to appreciate my work a little. Instead, Joseph just laughed and said, "Oh, no. She's mine. Besides, you wouldn't like her if you knew her." Thanks.

When he hired a couple of extra men to work in the warehouse, I was ordered to work with them. I was also told to keep an eye on them so they wouldn't steal from him. I worked like two men with these guys and I truly enjoyed it, mostly because I was out of Joseph's sight and with that my leash got a little longer. I was free to talk and joke and laugh. Plus, these people appreciated me and my work. It felt extremely good to be acknowledged at last. I liked them a lot; they were good people, but Joseph merely criticized and belittled them, along with everybody else. His approach was: "We hire people, learn what they know, then kick them out."

But even when I was working away from him, I had to watch my back, because one of his favourite games was to sneak up on me at the most unexpected moments. The warehouse was the best place for his "hide and eavesdrop" game. I was always alert, though, and caught him hiding behind the boxes, listening to our conversation before he came over to us; I would indicate this to the other person, then we just pretended not to know that he was there. His shadow usually gave him away, but let the "kid" have some fun, right?

Since he continually checked on me, I became more and more

aware of his games, so he could rarely surprise me. And when he was busy or out of the country, his trusty ex-mayor took up the role, but at least he didn't hide.

At home, after all these hours of work, I always had to fulfill my womanly obligations to him. The whole action took about five agonizing minutes, and then when he was done he fell asleep within seconds.

I had no friends, no family, no salary, no breaks, not even a few minutes for my own needs. I was only there to serve Joseph and his people. Had I any reason to complain or not be happy? Joseph didn't think so. In his opinion I had every reason to be delighted with my life.

Chapter 16

THE BIG LAB STILL WASN'T working properly so Joseph installed a mini lab right beside the store area. As the experts explained, the machines were old and run down, but in Joseph's opinion the experts were incompetent. He blamed every single problem on them, despite the fact that he didn't even know how to turn the machines on. As a result he ended up bringing back two of the Canadian guys, who stayed with us again.

Then another couple of people were hired: one for the cleaning and one for the store. The cleaning lady, Joanne, had previously worked at the bankrupt company before coming to us. I liked her instantly. She was very unaffected and friendly, and had a good sense of humour, but since I wasn't allowed to make friends, I had to be very careful. I had already learned that if someone dared to be friendly to me, that person was punished with Joseph's insults. Even though he never swore or used foul language, the way he talked to people, the words he chose and the tone of his voice could shake anybody's confidence. He could be so cruel and brutal that he made full-grown men cry.

I didn't want Joanne to get hurt, thus I told her or rather warned her about being on guard if we wanted to be friends. She wasn't really convinced, though, until she'd experienced what I said.

Losing my position in the store saddened me a great deal because after I had trained the new employee, another long lost relative, I was stuck in the office with Joseph.

One day for some reason, he was overwhelmingly insolent and I snapped. We were yelling back and forth at each other when he suddenly grabbed my arm, shook me violently, then shoved me hard against the office cabinet, bawling into my face. Although I was still shouting back at him, I was shocked by his physical strength. I had of course already experienced how strong he was but that was in a different context.

When I was able to tear myself out of his grasp, I stormed out of the office, slamming the door behind me with such vehemence that the glass in it cracked. I knew that the whole place had heard the yelling and perhaps even the brawl, but I also knew that nobody would have dared to intervene.

Gasping for air, I sat in front of the building. I replayed the incident in my mind over and over, as if that would help me to understand what had really happened and why. I debated with myself what to do next. I had no money; he made sure of that, and no parents on whom I could rely, and of course no friends. I had no one, nothing, and nowhere to go. I felt myself trapped yet again. I simply didn't know what I should do in such a situation.

I examined my feelings and considered myself possibly insane for ever believing I loved him. Only my delusions and naivety had kept me in such a daze. After all, whatever I did was wrong, whatever I said was nonsense. Not even my youth and devotion were enough. The magic was utterly gone, replaced by desperation and doubt.

I wanted to get away so much, to live like other twenty-one-year-old girls. I wanted to be free to discover my life and who I was, to study, go further, and achieve my goals and dreams because yes, I had some too. I wanted to be loved and appreciated by someone special. But my life couldn't have been farther from that.

So why was I here? What was the purpose of my life? Just to be his doormat or the target of his sick games? Was I here to live in fear and suffering? That just didn't sound right! And how could I ever possibly think that I loved him?

It was shocking to realize how much I detested being me. The pain was deepened by my parents' ongoing betrayal. Why wasn't I important to them? Why didn't they love me enough to care? I could never understand this.

And I felt that even time was against me. The clock was ticking, somehow much faster than it was supposed to. The pressure in me was building rapidly, and the fear of him and of what he wanted from me kept me in constant agony because it was only a matter of time before he came up with the child issue again. He never let anything go.

In September we entered a photo expo. Monica and I represented the company, staying there all day long, while Joseph remained at his office. He was busy expanding his business, even making a deal with the chief of police. His offer was to process all their films in exchange for free promotion at their dance, which was held in October. Because of that, of course, we were invited.

Meanwhile, there were so many people to meet at the expo. I could almost smell the fragrance of freedom. I even had an opportunity to accept a kind young businessman's lunch invitation. But I felt guilty about it and I didn't let this new relationship blossom. Either I was a young woman of integrity or just incredibly stupid. Anyway, I didn't take the chances that were offered to me. I didn't dare. I was too afraid of Joseph's reaction because he definitely made it clear that I belonged *to him*.

After two weeks, we were back at the offices, and the world was closed off from me once again. It was becoming harder and harder to fake my non-existent happiness. And my cravings for someone in whom I could confide, for a noble soul who didn't kick me aside and didn't trample me down, who also wasn't about to hurt and despise me daily, were just too strong. I tried not to cry after that gentleman at the expo.

Finding this special someone was much harder than I thought, because everybody I knew was under Joseph's influence and on his payroll. Besides, I was kept under strict supervision. But I did my best at this treasure hunt, anyway.

Mac was a new employee at the company, a handsome, funny young man with a caring heart. We became friends, then a little more, and my world suddenly was colourful and exciting. Just one glance from him was enough to tell me I was loved and cared for.

We had only three or four months together, but he became the most significant human being in my life to date because he saved me from total destruction. He was there for me at the right time and gave me something special, something precious—a memory of love, which helped me to go on.

It was hard to admit, but I always knew that this relationship was hopeless and wouldn't last. That vulture, the ex-mayor was circling and regardless how careful we were, suspicion arose around us. With some assistance from him, Joseph became fully informed about my friend and me.

After that Joseph was always on Mac's back. He was removed from the offices and given an outside job that took him far away from me, then Joseph slowly eliminated Mac from the entire company.

And once again, the baby issue was back in full force. I was still horrified about it. I came up with everything I could think of, but nothing brought him to his senses. "Oh, don't worry," he boasted, "I can make only healthy babies."

That scared me even more and I became desperate. I begged and cried, "Please, try to understand me a little! I'm too young for such responsibilities. I'm scared and I don't feel at all ready to be a mother." But every word of mine was in vain. He didn't listen, he didn't care and he didn't stop pressuring me. So I was the chosen one for that role after all. Perhaps I should have felt honoured—certainly in his eyes—but instead I was beyond mortified.

He had several ways of approaching the issue, which included attacking my heart: "Having a son is my dream," he said. "I already have five daughters because my wives weren't able to give me a boy. I love you so much and I know you're the one." Somehow his confession didn't touch me. I didn't want to be the lucky one!

Then he started to insult his wives, saying how stupid they were and how much they had disappointed him by not giving him a boy. In his eyes, it was entirely their fault that they'd not borne a male child. I could only shake my head…

Then he approached the issue from another angle. "I am too old [he was fifty five at this point] and I have no time to wait. I still want to enjoy having a son and teaching him how to run my business." Of course. That was the main reason for everything: he and his business, and everything else had to adjust to him. Whatever way he approached the issue, though, I couldn't comply.

CHAPTER 17

HE WAS ANGRY. ALTHOUGH HE held back his rage, his frustration was obvious to me. It seemed that that was the only feeling he had had toward me lately.

I had thought a lot about having the baby he wanted; actually, the issue dominated my thinking. Unfortunately, there was more fear than excitement in those thoughts. When the time came, I wanted to be a very good mother to my child, but not just yet. That didn't matter, though, because Joseph had planned my whole life for me, just as he planned his business affairs.

I knew that the discussion about the baby wasn't over. If one method didn't work, he came up with another. There was always a plan "B", a plan "C", even a plan "G", and I didn't have to wait long for the new one, which was to take me to Canada. I was sure that he wanted to impress me enough that I would be willing to get pregnant.

He had already taken my father and Uncle Mike to Canada for a fishing expedition on his boat, paying all expenses for them. My father was very happy that he'd had a chance to go on such an adventure and I knew he also felt privileged. But that was my father and he didn't have to get pregnant. I wasn't impressed with Joseph's idea and despite the fact that I had never been overseas, I didn't want to go there.

It really bothered me that his gesture wasn't honest. I had already learned that there was always an ulterior motive behind his kindness. And I didn't like his sneaky surprises. It also occurred to me that he wouldn't have suggested taking me to Canada if *I* had wished to go. So, when he made the offer I just politely declined.

Joseph rebuked me at once: "You're not permitted to say 'no' to me. It's your obligation to follow me wherever I go. Even if I jump out the window, you must jump with me." That was the end of the conversation. He left no room for questions or reasoning.

He took me to Vancouver, Canada in October of '91. That was the first time I had traveled by plane, which made me rather uneasy, but he found my fear very funny. I couldn't eat or sleep on the plane, so when we arrived I was exhausted, and the nine hour time difference didn't help me at all either. But I was hopeful that my very first visit to Canada would be special. Unfortunately, he didn't make any effort to be the least bit kinder to me than he had been at home.

He showed off his empire and introduced me to several of his people, then left me there alone with them. He knew I didn't speak English, yet still he insisted that I ask questions and learn. I asked him, "How am I supposed to ask questions if I don't know the language?" "Don't say 'I don't know' to me," he said. "I don't want to know what you don't know."

His pushiness and unsupportive attitude brought back the familiar feeling of being dumb and inadequate. He always found a weird satisfaction in my discomfort and embarrassment. And now, being in a foreign country so far from home, I felt very insecure and lost. He made me cry every day. Although I realized that Vancouver was a beautiful place, I could hardly see it through my tears.

During the three week visit he praised everything about Canada and slandered everything about Hungary: the food, the air, the water, the buildings, and the people. This really offended me. But whatever his plans were, they failed. His wealth and everything else he was feeding me with didn't impress me enough to want to get pregnant.

The only positive event was that I had the pleasure of meeting Myrna, Joseph's most faithful Philippine employee. She had worked for him for about twenty years and was also a friend of his family. She was beautiful inside and out, always kind and patient. Even though we didn't understand each other, we bonded very quickly. She made me feel welcome and well-liked, and I never noticed the slightest hostility toward me, not even a judgmental look. What I admired about her the most was how she could handle Joseph's insults and mockery, because he didn't treat her any better than the rest of us. He always made sure that everybody around him knew who was in charge.

After those miserable weeks, I was happy to be home even though the hard work and the even harsher treatment continued. He was crueller to me than before, and since he always got or rather took what he wanted, I knew more was yet to come.

On top of everything, people around me were clearly envious of my chance to visit Canada. But no one knew what price I had to pay every day for being that special. My parents and Uncle Mike's family thought I was one of the luckiest girls and expected me to show my gratitude. But no matter what others wanted from me, I wasn't happy and that was noticeable.

My sadness was considered disrespectful and I was said to be ungrateful. "Show some respect and be grateful for the enjoyment he offers you!" was the advice I got, but again, nobody was interested in what was going on inside of me. Nobody thought that I might have any reason to be unhappy.

Joseph's behaviour was unambiguous: I owed him obedience after what he had done to me and for me, although I had never asked for any of it. I had never wanted to go to Canada, not to mention my moving to Budapest and working for him. And since I still hadn't obeyed by becoming pregnant, he switched tactics again. Now he started to threaten me. "If you don't get pregnant, I'll fire your parents and make sure that no one will ever hire them again."

That was a huge blow below the belt. He had the nerve to use my yet-to-be-conceived child as a weapon against my family and me. I was totally taken aback by how inhuman and self-seeking he was. He respected nothing and nobody. It was also hard to believe that he would go that far. Was this a cruel joke? But his eyes answered my unspoken question.

He switched the roles nature intended and made me responsible for my parents' well-being. If I gave myself up entirely, then there was a chance that he would leave them alone. But if I preferred to consider myself, my future child, and what I thought was right, my parents would be in the streets within minutes. They detested me enough already, so what would they do if they ended up unemployed because of me?

For weeks I debated the choices, but could get no closer to a solution. I felt that either way, I would lose. But I was very concerned about my parents too, and although I never really reached a final decision I began skipping my birth control pills. Then I started taking them again. I kept myself on and off of the pills for the next few months. I was simply too afraid to make either choice.

In the meantime, the two Canadian guys had left but another one had arrived. Luckily he was a Hungarian man so I could communicate with him. It was close to Christmas again and Joseph invited Uncle Joe and the ex-mayor to visit us. We went out to dine and the ex-mayor got drunk. After we arrived home, he started to chase me around the apartment. He even wanted to help me to take a bath. Joseph found the situation very amusing, but I really freaked out.

The bathroom had two doors and one of them wasn't lockable. I didn't even dare to use the toilet because I was afraid he would pay me a visit there. And since Joseph didn't care to help me out, I asked Uncle Joe to keep the ex-mayor occupied. He gathered the Canadian guy and Joseph together and the three of them sat around the guy, keeping him company while I looked after myself.

We also had a guest for the holidays. Joseph invited his dentist friend from Canada, who was also Hungarian speaking. The same day he arrived, I received a small package from the USA, containing some fine lingerie. At any rate, Joseph gave the package to me on the same day. I had ordered these items with his help, so he knew very well what I had just received.

He and his dentist friend were having a great time together, so I grabbed the chance and tried to sneak out of the room with my package, but Joseph stopped me. "Don't go! Stay and show us what you got!" His request made me instantly uncomfortable. *What was on his mind now?*

I didn't want either of them to see how nervous I had become, so I just ignored him. But Joseph didn't give up. He kept pushing me even though I remained reluctant. Finally, his friend tried coming to my rescue: "Let her go, Joseph!"

But Joseph didn't listen to him either. I knew he just wanted to show how much power he had over me. I also knew that the more I refused to obey him, the angrier he would get. I started to worry that Joseph's frustration would grow out of control, and I didn't want to end up in a huge fight over some lingerie.

I looked at the guest. He seemed to be a decent guy, so I opened the box. They both admired how beautiful the lingerie was, but that wasn't enough for Joseph. "Try them on and show us!" "You've already seen them!" I interjected, and packed everything away. But he just kept pestering me. Obviously, he didn't want to lose face in front of his friend. "But that would be more interesting and even more beautiful."

I could see that he was enjoying himself. Maybe he thought he was funny, but to my mind he went too far. He also made me feel cheap, so it didn't matter how smoothly he ordered me to obey, I stood my ground.

That was enough for him. His face turned red and I knew that in his opinion I had humiliated him in front of his guest by not obeying. The changes in his mood were obvious. His friend also noticed it, because he came to my aid again. "Let her go, Joseph. I'm just a stranger to her, of course she won't try the lingerie on, and she's right."

I thanked the friend for his common sense, but remained very nervous about the consequences of my "disobedience". Fortunately, Joseph's friend was able to calm him down and turn his attention to something else, so in the end I wasn't punished.

1992

My hopes never cease

CHAPTER 18

THE YEAR 1992 STARTED UTTERLY dismally. I remained stuck between two choices and still didn't know what to do. In my heart I wasn't able to let my parents lose their new lives, although I was sure that they didn't care as much about me as I did about them. Meanwhile, as I was struggling with my life, Joseph continued to extend his territory.

Next to the already-owned buildings a whole factory ground was for sale. There were about four warehouses, two halls and workplaces, and a four storey office building, which was right on the main road as well. The entire district was filthy, noisy, depressing and removed from regular civilization. That was what Joseph wanted, all of it. Only he had no money, so he had to take out a huge loan. But since he had no Hungarian ID either, he wasn't able to get a penny. He needed someone to get it for him. And who else was handier than I?

On our way to the bank, Joseph and the ex-mayor explained that I was expected to sign papers so Joseph could get the money. He needed 40 million forint, which was about $629,000CAD at the time. And all of that was about to be borrowed in my name! Officially, it was my loan!

My first reaction was *no way*. Forty million forint was more than most people in my country could ever imagine having. I was horrified by the idea that I would be legally responsible for paying back such an amount. I would be the one to rot in jail if something went awry.

I thought seriously about not signing anything, but then I would be in danger of Joseph's wrath. It was a catch-22. So what would be better, jail or his revenge? He had already threatened the livelihood of my parents, and now I would be the one everybody blamed for not supporting Joseph's noble ambitions, his dreams to save the Hungarian people from themselves.

After all, he was already successful in Canada, so why wouldn't he be in Hungary? And he was the perfect gentleman now, well dressed, charming, but modest. I had never seen him act like that. The ex-mayor was his spokesperson, telling the bank workers (all women) who Joseph S. was, what he had achieved already, and what he wanted to do with the money. And of course, the ex-mayor didn't forget to mention that he had been mayor of one of the northern counties, and to talk about how much he supported Mr. S. Then he told them how much this young lady (me) was honoured to help Mr. S. borrow the money and make his dreams come true. With that, the women's jaws dropped.

To make the seduction process more effective, the ex-mayor started to flirt with the bank ladies, whose number had been increasing as they gathered and hung on his words like flies on a honeyed string. They were giggling, blushing and nervously buzzing around, while I just stood there motionless, saying nothing and feeling quite sick.

All of the bank workers were amazed by Joseph and his ambitions, so much so that they began trying to persuade me about the whole process, how safe and manageable it was. They never questioned his intentions. At least seven people were staring at me with huge expectations and growing impatience. I felt like I was facing a firing squad.

When I finally signed the papers with a trembling hand, I could hear the ex-mayor sigh with relief, then start to chuckle. Good girl! Everyone was over the moon. I was the only one not smiling, saddled with huge doubts and worries about Joseph's future performance.

It was all too much. I was almost suffocating under the various burdens put on me. Then in April my own debating ended. I was pregnant.

When I heard the news, my whole body was suffused with a warm, surprising joy. Every problem I faced had vanished. There was a baby, another life inside of me! I wasn't alone anymore. I had somebody to love and care for, somebody who might love me as well. I had never felt so happy.

When I told Joseph the big news, he shed tears. *So he isn't that heartless after all,* I thought. In that moment I felt hopeful that everything was going to be all right. *I can do this, and maybe he will like me a little.*

But my hopes ended right there. His demands became absurd: he wanted a boy and *only* a boy. I wasn't allowed to bear a girl. That wasn't love, that wasn't what I thought would happen. Had he lost his mind?

So the new subject of my fear was the sex of my unborn child. He forced me to go to the doctor more often than I was supposed to and took me for ultrasound twice, because he wanted to know as soon as possible whether or not I was carrying a boy. He wasn't even interested in the baby's health, only what was between its legs.

My pregnancy didn't make Joseph any more caring about me; instead he started to drive me harder. Besides overburdening me daily, he also took me on every business trip, all over the country. I sat in the car, then in his meetings for long hours, and my back was killing me. We returned to Budapest late at night, but instead of going home he took me to the offices. His faxes were more important than anything else; they just couldn't wait until the morning. At 11:00 p.m., I just couldn't take it any longer and asked him very softly to take me home because I was very tired. "You can't be tired!" he scoffed. "You did nothing but sit. Only *I* can be tired. I drove the car and talked to people all day long. Besides, you're not the only pregnant woman in the world."

I felt as if he had just hit me right across the face. I had no doubt that he was tired; I never questioned that. But I hadn't expected such a reaction to an innocent and understandable request. His insensitivity broke me into pieces all over again.

My whole body was stiff and I would have preferred at least to stay in the car, but I was ordered to go into the office with him, where I had to sit in an uncomfortable chair in front of his desk, watching him as he went through all his faxes and messages. But after fifteen or sixteen hours, without realizing it, I fell asleep sitting up; only the sense of falling woke me before I hit the floor. That happened twice in a row, but I didn't wait for the third. I was dizzy and felt like I was about to lose consciousness if I didn't move. I had no energy left to worry about his reaction anymore, whether he would get angry at me or not, and told him that I didn't feel good at all. I don't know how I looked but one glance at me made him jump out of his chair and help me out to the car. Finally he cared. Finally he understood me. But not before he had totally worn me out.

Chapter 19

THEN ONE DAY *HE* DECIDED that I needed some maternity vitamins so he took me to Vienna because in his opinion, nothing in Hungary was satisfactory, not even the vitamins. The trip could have been a romantic getaway, but the word *romance* wasn't in Joseph's vocabulary. That was the first and last journey we made that wasn't associated with his business but was a nest for his sexual satisfaction.

In the early summer I learned that I had a boy under my heart, a very big boy who was—thank God—perfectly healthy. I was overwhelmed with happiness and relief from the fear that had haunted me for months. Once again, I hoped that this great news would make Joseph melt a little toward me, that maybe he would treat me a little better. After all, I was the very first woman in his life who was giving him a boy, his life's dream.

I flew to him with the ultrasound pictures, hoping for a positive reaction. He looked at them, congratulated me, and with that I was excused. I felt painfully disappointed. I had to realize that no matter what, Joseph was never going to like me.

His dreams, though, were becoming realities. Step by step, he got everything he wanted. He had the baby boy (through me), and he had the money (through me) to buy the land and buildings. I had signed the papers, he got the money, and then he was overjoyed by his *own* achievements. He took credit for everything.

From then on he was the "master of the castle" and wanted to spend every minute at the new place, which meant that he wanted to live there while still keeping the downtown apartment. He moved his head office to the third floor of the office building, quickly put together a living area on the same floor, and moved us in.

I absolutely loathed that place. The offices were filling up, and there were more and more people in the lab and the warehouses. My brother was among the new employees. But while others went to work there, I had to actually live there, and that made my life an open book to them. I wanted to move back downtown, but there was no way I could convince him. He told me that our living at the workplace was a good example to all the employees, a proof of our dedication.

And there were other people from whom Joseph wanted the same thing, like his half-brother, who was the head of the warehouses. He and his family moved into the second floor, becoming another "good example". At least he didn't have to pay rent. But the rest, who weren't family and had their residences within the city, or even a bit farther out, had no intention of abandoning their homes.

No wonder. The factory grounds were filthy and always noisy. Across from the main road went the goods train, the suburban train and the tram, and the traffic was very heavy on the six-lane thoroughfare. I could actually feel the building shake. As a workplace it was okay, but as a home it was hell itself, not the sort of place a pregnant woman needed. And if it wasn't healthy for an adult, it was definitely not healthy for a newborn. So, these new circumstances just added to the constant stress.

But of course, I was the only one concerned about the situation because he was busy hiring eighteen- and nineteen-year-old beauties, who I had to train while he flirted with them in front of me. His behaviour was disgustingly obvious and I knew his goal was to make me jealous, but instead I felt humiliated, as well as ashamed for him. He also used them to put me down. "Look at her!" he'd say. "She's pretty and smiles all the time. She's friendly and smart. Go spend some time with her. Maybe you'll learn some kindness from her."

Ironically, though, he was right, because these girls were truly like a soft breeze. They were enchanting and carefree; their biggest problems were what to wear and how to apply their makeup. Besides, they had friends and loving families—of course they were smiling. I could have smiled in their position but our lives were completely different. I was imprisoned here and kept in what may as well have been chains. I felt like an old matron compared to them, even though there were maybe only three years between us. My heart ached every time I was with them because they reminded me of my stolen youth.

But as time went by my sadness was neutralized by my pregnancy. I loved my condition. I had no morning sickness at all, and surprisingly

I became a vegetarian, mostly because the slightest thought of meat made me sick. Not eating meat, though, didn't slow down my baby's growth at all. For my thin frame, he was becoming huge and I began to experience an excruciating pain in my left leg because—as my doctor said—the baby was pressing on some of my nerves. At this point I could only hope that the pain would go away with the baby's birth.

Besides the pain, my blood pressure dropped and stayed down at 90/60. I was always on the edge of fainting and couldn't be left alone, so Joseph assigned one of the young girls, Mandy, to be my assistant. She regularly took me to my doctor, and wherever else I wanted to go under the camouflage of my appointments. Suddenly, I was quite free, and even was given some pocket money! I wasn't sure about Joseph's intentions, but it worked out perfectly.

Mandy was a very sweet person and being with her made me feel I was just another carefree girl myself. It felt so normal and so right. Her cheerful spirit lifted mine and relaxed me enough to talk about things I hadn't been able to discuss before. She admired my strength in enduring what I had to, day after day, although she didn't understand how I could live like that. Neither did I. Regardless, we had a marvellous time together which Joseph never knew about, and that was just right.

But there was a downside as well. It wasn't easy to go to the doctor's office because the waiting room was always filled with loving couples. The fathers-to-be and moms-to-be were patiently waiting together, holding hands and talking softly. Their love, their silent excitement and expectation about the future life they were carrying together, filled the whole waiting room and once again reminded me of what I didn't have or know: something so simple and precious, so wholehearted and natural—something like pure love and devotion.

CHAPTER 20

ALTHOUGH THE BUSINESS WAS EXPANDING the big lab still didn't work the way it was supposed to. In fact, it never had. Joseph therefore brought in Myrna, who had to stay for three months and produce nothing less than a miracle. Myrna worked eighteen to twenty hours every day, giving her very best; she was devoted and conscientious. Unfortunately, no matter what she did, the machines weren't cooperating. Thus she was ordered to stay another three months.

Despite the ultrasound pictures and the doctor's opinion, I remained constantly worried about my baby's health. I needed Joseph; I needed him to be there for me. I wanted to be close to him; I wanted to spend some valuable time with him. I was longing for love but all I received was hard work and harsher treatment. And even though Joseph knew very well how much I suffered from the unexpected pain in my left leg, he still enforced his demands on me in every aspect of life.

Once, when Joseph came with me to my appointment, my doctor warned him, saying that I really needed to rest, that he had to spare me because the consequences could be fatal to the baby. Joseph's response was, "Of course, no problem. She can rest as much as she needs." But when we left he said to me, "That doctor's stupid. He has no idea what he's talking about. I know what you need and I'll take good care of you."

In his care I was still driven to work ten to eleven hours a day. My belly was getting bigger and heavier, but I continued running one task to another to keep him from being mad at me. Still, his demands escalated.

He appointed me the office manager and held me responsible for training the ongoing flow of secretaries. I shared a big office with Mandy and took over all the mail that flew in, plus I worked hard to put everything in order for him. But no matter what I did, nothing was good enough. Although I didn't understand his purpose in overworking a pregnant woman who was carrying his son, as always, his dissatisfaction drove me to please him even more. *I can do this! I'll show him that even in my present condition, I can do everything he orders me to do.*

My desperate attempts, though, frightened the other women. "You must be careful!" they warned me. "If you keep pushing yourself so hard, you will lose the baby." In the back of my mind I knew they were right; I had to slow down. I owed that much to my baby and to myself. The only problem was that it wasn't up to me; I simply wasn't allowed to slow down, let alone stop. And because I didn't have a caring partner or a supportive family behind me, my situation felt quite hopeless.

But I tried, and I took risks by asking his permission to take time out so I could have some well-deserved rest. His response was: "In Canada I have many female workers from the Third World and they work throughout their pregnancy. When the time comes, they run to the hospital, push the baby out, put the baby on their back and run back to work." Well, I had no idea whom he was comparing me to, but I wasn't from the Third World. My whole body was screaming for some rest, so he generously let me sit down in his office…

Times like this usually left me looking at him as if he unhinged, and I couldn't react in any other way than being ironic: "I would really like to know how many children you've borne."

My disrespectful behaviour made him angry. But since I didn't have many opportunities to laugh, I enjoyed it when he made a clown of himself with his overstated remarks. So maybe that was the reason why I was kicked out on July 21, when I was five months pregnant.

"I can't tolerate you around me! You can go back to the downtown apartment and shelter yourself there. Get your stuff right now and get out of here! Your brother can take you back."

His words sank in very slowly. He had actually kicked me out. I wasn't laughing anymore and although I should have been happy, I felt devastated. I had worked for him like an animal—without a single paycheque for over a year. I pleased him in every way I possibly could and now my reward was to be kicked out—pregnant!

I was too deeply hurt and confused to say a word. When I walked out of his office, I was well aware of the other people's pitying glances. Clearly, they had heard everything. I felt like a beaten dog but I packed my bags and my brother took me back downtown.

The apartment had been unoccupied for the last couple of months. It was so empty and deserted that my steps echoed. In that total silence, the humiliation finally hit me. My tears, held back so heroically, now slowly streamed down my face. I'd never felt so alone in my life.

But I tried to cope. I told myself that it was much better being alone than being tormented by him every day. After all, wasn't this banishment a wish come true? The only problem was, though, that I was too afraid to be alone. I simply couldn't imagine how to handle my situation totally by myself and without a penny. What options did I have?

As before, I wished I could go back to my parents. But I pushed that thought away as quickly as it entered my mind. Sadly, that was clearly hopeless. And if there was any other way, I couldn't figure it out. Joseph had cut me off from the world and I had no one to reach out to, no one but him.

It was getting dark and my fears began to pile up. *Was he really my one and only chance?* It seemed that way, but I didn't want him to be. I paced around desperately, reassuring myself that everything was going to be all right, when I felt something strange in my tummy. *Did my baby just kick me for the first time?*

I stopped walking and waited. Then it happened again. Yes, my baby was kicking. My agony was forgotten and I started to cry again, now with happiness. I was overwhelmed with joy. My baby had reminded me that I wasn't alone after all. Such a mesmerizing feeling! I was talking and singing to him for quite a long time, and in answer he kept kicking me again and again.

But my joy was roughly disturbed by the demons of reality and our uncertain future. I had to do the best I possibly could for my baby, no matter what that entailed. Even though I wasn't sure what the best thing was, I knew for certain that I wouldn't be able to take the present situation much longer. So I gathered all my strength and, with trembling fingers, dialled Joseph's office number.

I had never been so afraid of him as in those seconds while I waited for him to pick up the receiver. With each ring my fear increased. I was horrified that he might reject me. When he answered the phone, his voice was so icy that I was sure I had made the biggest mistake of my life by calling him. But again, there I was, pregnant and all alone. What was I supposed to do?

I felt so defeated that there was no pride left in me. I openly cried into the phone and begged him to take me back. First, he totally refused my plea, which made me even more desperate and frightened to let him push me away. I begged him as if my life was at stake. He listened to me, then he listed all my sins to prove how bad and unbearable I really was.

After tormenting me for an agonizing fifteen minutes, he allowed me to go back, but not before I promised that I would always be obedient to him no matter what; after all, he was the only one who knew what was best for me. By then I was emotionally drained, so numbly I promised him everything he wanted to hear.

When I was back I worked hard to keep my promise, but I only succeeded for a few days. I simply couldn't manage his mind games and provocations. Although he didn't kick me out again, he continuously drove me hard, remaining as merciless as always.

Then in mid-August, when I had another doctor's appointment, I received the devastating news: "You are very close to losing the baby. I can feel his head." And I wasn't due until the end of November!

CHAPTER 21

PARALYZING FEAR AND RAGE SWEPT through me. I blamed Joseph for not caring about us and for not allowing me to look after the baby and myself properly. I cursed him to hell right there. Because of him I had ended up with a high-risk pregnancy. He had endangered my unborn baby's life and for what? To punish me? Was he really willing to sacrifice this baby just to get his way, to annihilate me?!

My doctor said that I had no choice but to spend the last three months in bed, either at the hospital or at home. Since he knew me well enough, he didn't push me into the hospital but I was ordered to stick to bed at home. He didn't have to tell me twice. I was going to remain in bed no matter what Joseph did to me.

When I told him what the doctor said he made a fuss and ordered me to bed right away. His reaction was very weird; he didn't blame me, but somehow made me feel like I wasn't even able to be pregnant properly. My endangered condition, though, didn't change anything between us.

He went back to Canada—as always, business came first—but that was more than all right with me. At last, I could have the rest and peace prescribed by my doctor. Before leaving, he assigned Joanne to help me out for a few hours a day, in addition to her duties. This worked perfectly both ways. I had some company for a short time and Joanne could have a well deserved rest, since she was the one and only cleaning lady for the entire premises.

She was like a mother to me, a mother whom I missed very much. I loved her tremendously and was very grateful for everything she did. It also felt good when other people came in from the offices to say hi; sometimes even Monica came in, although my pregnancy had made her a little distant. In the end, though, Joanne was the only one who was really there for me.

And I caught up on lost sleep, although keeping time on my side so my baby would remain safe was very stressful. I was afraid to get up even for a minute. If I had to pee, and I had to go often, I always pressed my legs together as I inched toward the bathroom, as if by doing so I could keep the baby in his place.

When Joseph came back, I tried to confide in him. Of course, he didn't share my concerns. All he wanted from me was his portion of sex. It didn't even bother him that I was as big as a whale and couldn't move; he used my body to empty himself.

To him, his being entertained was always more important than I was. Like when he wanted to take pictures of me, naked. Nausea washed through me and I had no intention of obeying. I was far too pregnant to be humiliated like this. I told him over and over again that his idea made me very uncomfortable. But the more I protested, the angrier he became. "If I tell you something, you do it without a word!" he yelled into my face.

I could see that he wasn't going to let me get away. His commands became more and more angry but I was still unable to move. Then he grabbed my wrist so violently that I felt he was about to crush my bones. I cried out in pain as he squeezed my wrist and forced me to get undressed, ordered me to pose and, of course, smile. When he had gotten what he wanted, he left the room in total satisfaction, while I was shivering uncontrollably, cold inside and out, feeling deeply humiliated.

When I was back to the safety of my clothes, I checked my wrist and could already see the marks caused by his fingers. I didn't even know what or how I felt anymore. And the disgrace didn't end here. While I was bed-ridden he was busy taking women out to dine. Although it was a relief not to have him around me, I also felt a bit of envy. Why couldn't he be nicer to *me*?

Lying in bed 24/7 started to be a little too much. I became restless and had to fight the urge to get up for longer periods of time, but I remained determined. I also wanted to read a novel so badly but I already had learned that I wasn't allowed to do such things. So to calm the storm between Joseph and me, I asked for some product catalogues to keep myself busy. Unfortunately, the catalogues made me terribly bored and sleepy, so I then asked to take over the incoming mail.

Some letters were pretty interesting. For instance, one woman offered a castle for him to buy plus the glass factory in her town, so they would be saved. Seeing this made me wonder what people assumed about him; how much power did they think he had?

I enjoyed answering the letters, but as my due date approached, I felt myself longing after my mother again. I thought that mothers were supposed to be with their almost-in-labour daughters. I needed her help and support; after all, she had already gone through the whole process. I also needed her guidance to help me look after my newborn, for a few days at least. And I wanted to share my joy and fears with her.

I told Joseph that I would really like my mother to be with me, but he quickly dismissed my request, saying, "I don't think that she would be good for you or the baby. After all, look at what she created." He pointed at me, laughing condescendingly, and gave me no time to express my whishes. "When the time comes, I'll hire a certified nurse who will know what to do."

To me that sounded like a threat, as if he wanted to replace me as a mother. I didn't want a stranger looking after my son. I didn't want to be substituted. I wanted to do everything. After all, I was the baby's mother. So whenever Joseph mentioned hiring a nurse, my whole being weakened with fear, which was much stronger than my fear of labour. It even made me call my parents to ask for the impossible.

My hand shook when I dialled the numbers to their store, because I remembered very well what had happened last time, but I thought that my condition or the future promise of my child would soften my mother's heart a little. I told her how much I wanted her to be with me, at least for one or two days. I wasn't at all expecting her response to be so cold.

"You don't need my help!" she shouted. "You didn't ask for it when you made that child. You brought this situation upon yourself, so handle it!" Even before she had finished her accusations I was already crying. I'd thought that my little son would melt her heart, and for his sake she would at least try to be a bit loving and caring. I felt so hurt that I yelled back with full force, "How could you be so cold? You're my mother! Why do you let me down every time I need you? For once, you could be here. For your grandson, at least!"

The whole argument didn't make any sense to me. The conversation wasn't supposed to go that way. I could hear that my mother was out of control and I knew that she hadn't heard one word I said. Then my father took the phone. I begged him to make my mother understand how much I wanted her to be with me, that I truly needed her. My father's response wasn't much better either: "Try to understand your mother. This is too much for her to handle. Give her a break! Maybe she'll change her mind. Just don't burden her!"

So that was that. At the end, I felt totally exhausted. But I was also angry with myself. *Twenty years wasn't enough to bring you to your senses and learn that you couldn't count on them?!*

Chapter 22

Joanne was my only comfort during the day. She helped me and encouraged me, kept me going, tried to calm my fears and agony; thus all my love and trust which I wanted to give to my mother but couldn't, I gave to her. I also told her about the phone conversation and she didn't understand how a mother could be so heartless.

Every night, though, my worries got stronger and then Joseph was the only one to whom I could turn for some solace. His supportive words were: "These days labour isn't a big deal." *What was that supposed to mean?*

He also remained persistent about hiring a nurse, and even asked for my doctor's help in finding one. Although Dr. Lane didn't share his opinion, and said, "The mother is the best caregiver for her baby," he felt obliged to find one. I guess money speaks volumes.

I stayed in bed until the end of October. For the rest of the time I was allowed to stay up and do what I had to do. I was tireless when it came to my baby. I was also calmer now and very proud that I had been able to keep my child out of danger.

In November, out of the blue, my father came to help me set up the crib and a changing table in the downtown apartment's only bedroom. We were coming back here after the baby was born. It was a great relief that I wouldn't have to take my son to the offices. Living there was a nightmare, since I never felt at home.

I had missed my parents all my life, despite them always being emotionally unreachable. Thus I wanted them at least physically close to me. I mentioned this to Joseph repeatedly but he refused my wish every time. So it really shocked me when I learned that he had given them jobs at the main store and would move in with us into the third-floor living quarters, for as long as we were there. I thanked him wholeheartedly for his understanding and kindness, and told him how happy he had made me.

On November 20, around 5:30 a.m., my water broke and the pain started. It was time to go to the hospital but I wasn't able to move because the water was pouring out of me. Soon the pains started to strike every five minutes, but still I couldn't move. And in the middle of my agony Joseph told me that Myrna was there to say good-bye to me; after six exhausting months she was finally going home. Somehow I managed to wave to her, then I was engulfed in pain again.

In the meantime, somebody called my doctor but only about three hours later did I manage to stand up. Joseph and, of all people, my *mother* took me to the hospital. Dr. Lane had already been there, waiting for me a long time. "I thought you'd end up giving birth at home," he said with noticeable relief.

Little Joey was born around 1:00 p.m. When I could finally hold him I couldn't speak, just laughed. He was so beautiful, so perfect and huge—almost ten and a half pounds. I had never been so happy in my life. I didn't even feel anything when my doctor stitched me up with at least twelve stitches. And when he asked me how I felt, my answer was, "I'm starving!"

At the hospital everybody was very nice to me. Their praise and friendly words were like healing balm on my beaten soul. I was praised endlessly, perhaps because I hadn't screamed and cursed, or maybe because I simply deserved to be. Since I wasn't used to being treated so nicely I was deeply moved and touched by all of them, especially by my doctor, Dr. Lane; he was my angel.

He rolled me out of the delivery room to where my mother and Joseph were waiting for me, praised me again, then left us alone. They had already seen Joey. My mother was choking on her tears as she told me how beautiful he was. Joseph congratulated me then rushed off to get some food for me. I was surprised at how quickly he disappeared, and interpreted his action as a new sign of hope that things would be fine between us.

My mother continued to praise my little boy. "He's a huge baby and he's so perfect. It's hard to believe that he was just born." I drank her words in. It was so rare for her to speak to me like that. I wanted her to stay longer but after Joseph came back with a huge sandwich, they left.

I was given a separate room with its own bathroom. Obviously

Joseph had paid them well. But paid or not, everybody remained nice to me. For once, I was being treated well and that felt amazing. News of the huge baby spread very quickly across the hospital, and from time to time, people stopped in to congratulate me. I thought I would burst with happiness and pride. I was actually appreciated and acknowledged; these strangers gave me exactly what I wished to get from my parents and Joseph.

But once again, my joy didn't last. The next day, Joseph brought Monica in to see her new sibling. She was terribly pale and obviously very uncomfortable. I could sense instantly that she wasn't there of her own free will. Even though the ice was very thick, I really wanted to break through. I tried to share my joy with her, but she remained unmoved. Then I asked the nurse to show Joey to her. I hoped so much that she would thaw a little when she saw the baby.

Monica hardly looked at him but whispered to me that he was cute. She didn't smile, didn't even seem to breathe. Her face was like a stone. She was suffering, poor thing, and it hurt me to see my friend like that. And it didn't help at all that we were surrounded by happy families. I was so envious of their being joyful together. Not like us. We were tense, our faces stern. My happiness turned into sadness and disappointment, then full-blown anger.

Just the day before I had been lying on the delivery table and I was still in great physical pain. Standing there, watching Monica's discomfort and Joseph's rigid face, all I wanted to do was scream. There wasn't even a trace of a smile on his lips. I couldn't take the icy silence anymore and turned to him with total exasperation. "Look around you. Look at the other people. They're so happy and excited about the new life that's arrived. They're proud and full of joy. Why can't you be a little like that? Why can't you say something nice to me? At least you could smile! And why did you bring her in? She doesn't want to be here. Look at her, she's literally suffering from being here. I don't need this!"

With each word I got angrier. Then I just turned and started to walk away, but Joseph grabbed my arm. His face was contorted with anger. "You can't just walk away from me. And you are not allowed to behave like that," he hissed.

What did I do wrong again? We had a heated argument right there. But I didn't care anymore. I poured my heart out. It didn't move him but at least I told him what I wanted to say. Then I just left them. As

I dragged myself away I could feel his sharp glance on my back but I didn't turn around. I wished that I would never see him again.

In my room I just cried, letting my sadness, pain, fear, disappointment and anger flow out. I was afraid to go home. I was afraid for my baby. What kind of life was awaiting him with such people in his family?

CHAPTER 23

THE NEXT DAY JOSEPH BROUGHT in my father and brother, acting as if nothing had happened the day before. My father brought me a basket of strawberries, which was nice of him. He was ecstatic about little Joey but also tense, and my brother looked rather uncomfortable as well. Everybody and everything seemed so unnatural: their actions, their smiles, their words. Then Joseph took some pictures of us, posed for some, and that was the end of the visit. It was utterly impersonal. Even the hospital workers displayed more warmth toward me than my own family.

On the fourth day we were taken back downtown. I was very excited about my new tasks but also frightened by them. I wanted to be a very good mother, and was willing to work hard to learn everything about my baby and his needs.

Joseph went to the office daily and stayed there all day long, which gave me the opportunity to get some rest and peace because it was more tiring to be with him than to look after my newborn. Every day I had to gather my energy so that I would be able to deal with him when he got home. His presence distressed me a lot and nothing got any better.

Since he had no chance to hurt me during the daytime, he didn't hold back in the evening. If the baby so much as squeaked, he bit my head off. "Don't make him cry! You're making that child neurotic." When I bathed Joey and he cried, Joseph stood over me, shouting, "Hurry up, you're too slow! He's cold. And don't talk to him! Just shut your mouth and move. Quickly, quickly!"

This went on every day and every time he was home. I simply wasn't allowed to soothe my baby when Joseph was around. And of course when he was raging over our heads, Joey cried even harder. But that too was my fault. Actually, everything was my fault.

Whatever I did with the baby was unacceptable. In his opinion, if a baby was well looked after, it never cried. And since Joey cried, Joseph blamed me for not being a good mother. When I told him that this was how the baby communicated, Joseph's response was, "This is only your stupidity! You're a bad mother to him. You don't even know what you're doing. You do things instinctively, like an animal. He needs an expert."

As a new mother I was nervous enough about doing things right, and what I needed were a few encouraging words from him, not this ongoing verbal torture. It was impossible to bear Joseph's raging. He made me afraid of my own child's cry. When I told him that most of the time his constant yelling made Joey cry, he jumped on me. "Don't be impudent!"

He picked quarrels with me about everything, and continuously criticized whatever I did. But of course, he never bathed or changed Joey and my mother never came to help me either. There was no assistance and no encouragement from him, only torment. So one time I offered Joey to him. After all, he'd already had five children. "Okay," I said, "if you know so much about babies, show me how to do it right." He flinched but didn't take the baby from me. "Don't be insolent!" he snapped and left the room.

Joey and I had some long nights together but most of the time I jumped out of bed as soon as he cried, looking after him and trying to keep him quiet as much as possible so that we wouldn't disturb Joseph's sweet dreams. But inevitably he sometimes was awakened and immediately would start to yell at me in the middle of the night to silence the baby because he had to go to work the next day. When I dared to tell him that I needed some sleep as well, his answer was, "You're home all day long. You can have as much sleep as you want." Well, I was home all right, but if I had slept, who would have looked after Joey? Besides, Joseph had given me a bunch of catalogues to price because he was worried that I would get lazy, since I supposedly had nothing to do all day.

Well, this was how we spent the first weeks of my motherhood. Daytime, when we were alone, Joey and I were like a normal family. We had peace and quiet and joy! But every evening when the breadwinner came home, all hell broke loose.

He also hired the certified nurse, who turned out to be a young girl with no experience; she honestly admitted that she couldn't be of much help to me. But she was a very kind person and we became friends.

Joseph never learned to tolerate Joey's crying so every time the baby made a sound, he ordered me to feed him. If he cried every five minutes, I had to nurse him every five minutes. Of course, that didn't solve the problem. Joey was quiet while his mouth was full, but when he was done he resumed crying. He wasn't a fussy baby; still, he had his own issues. And since the constant feeding didn't silence him, Joseph attacked me again. "Your milk isn't good enough. *You're* not good enough to him. That's why he cries all the time." Well, he cried a lot when Joseph was home, that much was true.

The next time the paediatrician came to check on Joey, he was shocked and told me to stop feeding him so often. When I told him what the problem was, he just said, "He's very healthy and your milk is obviously very good. So good, indeed, that he's gained quite a lot of weight just being nursed."

Oh, I was so happy and proud that the doctor was satisfied with me as a mother. When he left, I had every intention of following his advice, but of course, Joseph didn't let me. When I told him what the doctor had said, his answer was, "He's stupid. He doesn't know what he is talking about. You must listen to me, only me, and do what I say!"

I was always nervous and tense around him. Now, with each day, the tension increased and my strength lessened. When I heard Joseph arrive home, my stomach lurched. As the entrance door opened I already knew that I had to brace myself against whatever he had in store for us.

It became an everyday scene to have Joseph on one side yelling at me and Joey crying desperately on the other. I tried my best to ignore Joseph and focus on Joey's needs, but Joseph shouted over the baby so that it was impossible not to hear him.

I worked very hard to keep up with his demands, but still I wasn't always able to be on time with his dinner. When I tried to explain why I was late, he wasn't interested. "Don't make excuses!" he said. "And don't think that I'm ever going to adjust to suit the two of you."

It took a few seconds for his words to sink in. I wasn't even sure whether I had heard him right. I simply couldn't comprehend his being so selfish that his needs were more important than a few-week-old baby's.

My little boy's first Christmas was both miserable and memorable since nothing reminded me of the holidays except the date itself. But he slept well; thus Christmas Eve was unusually peaceful. Joseph was watching TV and I decided to join him. I wasn't expecting him to watch porn, though. When I told him that I'd like to watch some comedy, just for a little while, he refused to change the channel, instead inviting me to watch the porn with him. When I refused and called him a pervert, he just laughed. All I wanted was a couple of hours of fun, because I could scarcely remember the last time I had really laughed, but he wouldn't allow that. I couldn't stay with him in the same room so I went back to my sleeping baby and just sat in the darkness.

1993
Sweet motherhood

CHAPTER 24

SIX WEEKS AFTER HIRING THE nurse, Joseph became furious about her being there and ordered *me* to fire her. He also refused to pay her full wages and this too I had to handle. With that, I lost another friend, and even though I had done nothing wrong, I felt ashamed.

Since Joey was such a big baby, my recovery from the delivery took about two months. In January I was still in the process of healing, and that was unacceptable to Joseph. With each day he became more and more impatient. "Hurry up!" he said. "The temptation at the office is too big," and he started to list the women who supposedly were after him.

Although two months' recovery was a long time for me too, I was relieved to keep him away. His list made me think, though, that it would be much better for me if he found someone else. But unfortunately he remained totally devoted when it came to tormenting me.

Day after day he nagged me about being ready for sex. If he was in a bad mood, he accused me of deliberately not wanting to heal just to push him into another woman's arms. "Do you want me to find someone else?" he asked. Inside I was screaming *"YES!"* but in reality I thought better of it and did not open my mouth. "I can't help it," I said instead. "The doctor told me that the healing would take a longer time than usual, since Joey was so big. Besides, I had about twelve stitches, because the little one pushed his way out."

Oops! I already knew I had said too much because his eyes lit up. "Stitches? What stitches?" Obviously, I had never mentioned them to him. "Where are they? Show me!" he demanded. At first, I was just too dumbstruck to say anything. It took some time before I could answer. "They were removed. There's nothing to see," I said, pretending to be more confident than I really felt.

I had such a bad feeling about the next few minutes and my

stomach twisted. I had no intention of obeying his sickening demand, but he also had no intention of leaving me alone. "You know that you're not allowed to say 'no' to me. There are many women who want my attention, you know, but you're the lucky one."

Even though I just shrugged at him, I was afraid. I really didn't know how far he would go. I was sitting on the sofa, unable to move. "Okay, show me!" he repeated. I could hear in his voice that he was losing patience, that my time was up, but I couldn't even look at him. Then he snapped, "Enough of this! Stop wasting my time. Show me right now!" In the next minute or so I just wished that the earth would swallow me up. I'd never felt so mortified in my life.

When he was finished, I sucked my breath in and with all the mockery I could gather, I asked him, "Satisfied?" He didn't seem to notice my lack of respect. "Okay, just take care of yourself. I'll be patient," then left the room. I stayed where I was, sitting there for a long time, wondering how much deeper into shame I could sink. I didn't even feel human anymore.

But my challenges never let up. Joseph remained cruel toward me and impatient toward his son. I really wanted to know why he was acting this way, so although he hurt me unceasingly, I started to assess him. I was shocked to discover that he was jealous of his son. This I wasn't expecting at all and didn't know how to handle.

My baby was everything to me. He was my whole world, my source of vitality. I was very happy to be a mother and felt proud because I knew I had accomplished something remarkable, something special. My feelings were bursting from me and I so much wanted to share them. I knew that Joseph wasn't the right person to confide in, but there was no one else. For whatever reasons, I really wanted him to be a part of my joy and not to be excluded. But instead of sharing the joy with me, which was supposed to be a mutual happiness, he was only concerned about himself. "What about me?" he asked. "I want you to take care of me just as much as you take care of the baby." I didn't really get this. Was he joking? "I want you to pamper me, hug and kiss me as much as you do with Joey. I want you to love me just as much as you love him." Well, in the last two years I had already tried that, hadn't I?

I knew that we were on a very sensitive topic, and I had to be careful how I answered him, but a picture in my mind really bothered me. "Would you want me to wipe your butt and change your diapers as well?" He answered me without hesitation, "Yes, if that was necessary, yes."

My stomach twisted as I searched his face in the hope of finding a trace of humour there, but he remained serious. His expression was so set that the possibility of his request scared me and I could actually see my whole life stretching dismally before my eyes, starting and ending with him. I didn't like this game of his and just to keep him calm, I quickly said, "Okay," then turned my whole attention to little Joey again.

By February Joseph's inhumane treatment had left me physically and emotionally drained. To *him* my milk still wasn't good enough, so he started to force formula on Joey. Being replaced with a bottle hurt me a lot and my milk eventually dried up. I was overwhelmed by the loss, feeling so inadequate. I wanted to give my best to my little boy, but felt I had failed by no longer being able to nurse him. Joseph of course remained cold in that matter too. "That's not a problem. He doesn't need it anyway. There are formulas that are much better than your milk." Now that was painful. I couldn't have been more disappointed in him.

As the time went by it was harder and harder to pretend that I was head-over-heels in love with him. His insensitive behaviour had killed off any good feelings toward him that I had once thought I felt. And he just kept lecturing me about how I was supposed to look after the baby, yet he never even fed him after enforcing the bottle feedings.

One day, though, he wanted me to take some pictures of him feeding little Joey. He was dressed up in his business suit, already one leg out the door, but took a few seconds to pose. I was quite shocked to see that even after having five children he had no idea how to hold the bottle at the correct angle so Joey wouldn't swallow air...Then, when everything was picture perfect, I took a few photos of the devoted father.

A short time after that, as I was looking after my precious baby, Joseph casually walked into the room and said to me, "You don't need this baby because you're too young. He'll soon be annoying to you, since you want a younger man. I'll take him to Canada to my wife. She is very happy to help me out, you know." I stopped breathing and the room started to spin around me. I had to sit down. For a while I wasn't able to say a word as my thoughts started to run away. *What on earth is he talking about?* I shivered. *He wants to take my baby away? Moreover, they want to take him away from me? Is there a conspiracy behind my back? But I'm his mother! I've done nothing wrong. Was this why he "helped" me to be unable to nurse? I did my best to look after Joey. I don't deserve this.*

My voice trembled as I replied. "*I* am his mother. He lived in my body for nearly nine months. He is my life. You can't just take him away from me." Then my fears turned into anger. *How dare they?* "You know what?" I said. "If your wife wants a baby, she can have one herself. Joey is my baby! *I* am his mother! And don't forget that I'm not a rent-a-mom!"

I sounded pretty confident but that was only on the surface. In reality, my whole world was rocked. I couldn't shake off the fear and the possibility that he would do something like that; the idea haunted me everywhere. I didn't know what he might do to carry out his threat. I didn't know how many days I had left to be with my child.

CHAPTER 25

TRAVELING BETWEEN THE OFFICE AND the downtown apartment started to annoy him; thus in April he moved us back to the office building, onto the fourth floor now, where he had formed a larger living area out of several offices. With this our freedom was completely gone.

After we moved out of the suite, Monica moved back in and created for herself a little mansion there, so that when her mother came to visit her she had a decent place to stay. On one occasion I was there too, and Monica's mom and I had a short conversation about the events that went on around us. Her final statement on the subject was: "He requires lots of patience."

I knew that already but it also showed me that she didn't have an easy life with him either. Plus she told me that she would never take my son away from me. I was his mother and his place was with me. That had just been Joseph's sick idea to keep me in fear, but she had never agreed to it. Whatever the truth was, it remained disturbing. I didn't trust *him* no matter what his wife said.

Then when she left, Monica expressed her mother's unspoken words: "My mother is very happy that you took him off her hands." Yes. The curse had definitely been passed on and I was struggling to cope with it. However, I was a mother now and my crying became secondary, at least to my mind. My responsibilities were enormous, which I liked very much because they took my attention away from all that I was deprived of having in my life with Joseph.

The loss of freedom was a terrible hardship. While we had lived downtown we could go out for a walk. But now, our whole life was narrowed down to that filthy factory ground. There were no parks, no playgrounds, not even a grocery store nearby. There was absolutely nowhere to go. That building was our prison and the real world had slowly faded away.

I had great difficulty getting used to living in the workplace again because my life was once again like an open book. I dreaded the thought that people were chewing over the details of my life and now my son's as well. And if they didn't know the facts, they created rumours, poisoning Joseph even more against me.

To compound the situation, the newly created apartment on the fourth floor was liveable only until it started raining. Then the roof began leaking like a sieve. There were twenty-three buckets, basins, pots and pans throughout the apartment. The whole mess drove me over the edge and I couldn't do anything but cry for my little boy and for myself.

When the rain stopped the damage became even more visible. Along the supporting pillar and the main beam the wallpaper was rotten and mouldy, and the wall was soaking wet, as was the carpet, which was stained and reeked from the rust-laden water. The living room looked like a shipwreck. And the troubles didn't end there.

There were problems with the electricity and the water pipes. Joseph said that he was an expert at fixing things, but his so-called expertise just caused more damage. I had to chase down the real experts to fix up our place and they noticed immediately that someone had made a botched job of it, so one of them asked me to keep the boss away from everything. That was easier said than done because if I ever questioned Joseph's knowledge about anything, he lectured me mercilessly.

And now that we were living at the workplace again, he began to push me to be with him in the office instead of letting me look after my baby. "While he's asleep, you can come down and help me. Make yourself useful!"

I didn't want to leave my child alone, but Joseph demanded it. Fear crept up my spine again. "How can I leave a six-month-old baby alone? What if he has a bad dream or something else happens? I have to be here for him." I tried to come up with every possible reason, fact, and excuse to make him understand that I couldn't possibly leave the baby alone. But Joseph just became angrier and angrier. So since reasoning didn't work, I started to beg, then I asked him calmly, then I yelled in frustration. Nothing moved him. "Your explanations are only cheap excuses. You're only saying that because you're a lazy pig."

His office was on the third storey and I began a senseless race between the two floors. I went upstairs as much as I could manage, which greatly depended on him because I had to ask his permission to check on the baby, and there were times when he simply forbade me to go up to him, which kept me in constant agony and worry over my little boy. I did nothing else but clean up after Joseph, file, price his catalogues, and feed him. Sometimes he just ordered me to sit there and watch him work, while Joey was all alone.

I knew that he enjoyed my pain. I felt utterly helpless, though. Ever since he had forced himself into me, he had been in charge of my life and now that extended to my son's life as well. Plus, each and every day Joseph verbally attacked me, taking any opportunity to humiliate me. He pushed me into miserable situations of his own creation, then put me in the middle of them and placed the blame on me. He never missed a chance to shame me in front of other employees or his daughter. "You are nothing but a reeking skunk," he would say. "Nobody wants to be around you, because wherever you are you stir up hatred. Just to let you know, nobody loves you."

I remembered, though, when I worked at the bookstore, how many people had liked me and valued my work. But here, Joseph made me feel worthless and ineffectual. I worked diligently to please him in every way I could; still I wasn't able to earn his approval. I couldn't count on him, not even when it came to something as simple as saying a few nice words. Like the bullies at school, he never got tired of his own games. One time I was a skunk, then the next time he would call me a rotten apple, or a mould that spoiled everybody and everything. Each word stabbed me like a knife. I would just stand there, frozen, as he shouted obscenities into my face even while Monica was standing right beside me. This is what I got for wanting to be a conscientious mother.

Making humiliating remarks became his habit and whenever there were people around us, they became the audience. That happened when a bunch of us went to a restaurant. I was eating quietly when unexpectedly Joseph said, "Don't open your mouth so wide. People might think that I don't feed you." At first I didn't even know that he was talking to me, although everybody else at the table was looking at me and bursting into laughter. When I glanced over at him he repeated his remark, chuckling uncontrollably. I felt so ashamed that my appetite vanished at once. For the rest of the lunch I didn't even dare open my mouth to eat, because I thought the others were watching me.

But after several weeks of tremendous humiliation, he seemingly stopped bothering with me. From that time on, I could go upstairs whenever I wanted to and he didn't say a word. So even though I was still in the offices, I felt calmer now because I was free to check on my little boy anytime I felt it was necessary. This new free access to my child helped to improve my focus on my tasks, and I knew I did a good job there. Even Joseph showed some signs of recognition of my work. "Finally, you're able to do something good, by chance." Notwithstanding his tone of biting sarcasm, that was more than I could have hoped for from him.

He didn't need me there, though, that was obvious. He had a secretary and his daughter, who worked for him all day long. I was only useful to him when he couldn't find something and then could blame that on me. Any problems that occurred were my fault. He needed a scapegoat and kept me at hand. Other than that, I was worthless to him. Because of that he brought over from Canada his youngest daughter, who was supposedly much more capable than I. But she was assigned to look after little Joey while I had to remain at the office.

One day when I went upstairs Joey was screaming desperately as she sat right beside him, reading comfortably. I took the whole scene in within moments and felt my anger rising. "I don't know what's wrong with him. I did everything," she said innocently. What was wrong with him? He was swimming in his poop! That's how good she was. Needless to say, that was the end of her supervising Joey and her staying in Hungary.

After that, every time I went upstairs to check on Joey, I stayed a bit longer, then I simply didn't go back to the office. I also no longer showed any interest in Joseph's business or what he was doing, or where, or with whom. I was tired of being a yo-yo and a public punching bag. After all, my son needed me more than Joseph did. I lived only for my little boy, and my joy grew along with him. What surprised me, though, was that Joseph let me stay upstairs without even mentioning my absence.

It was around this time that Joseph imported a Cadillac Eldorado from Canada. Since I was so proud to be a mother I asked him if I could put a "Baby in the Car" sticker on the back windshield, but he wouldn't let me. "We're rich and very important," he said. "People are hunting us. If they learn there's a child they'll kidnap him, and maybe you too." Then he started to laugh. "How much do you think you're worth? Should I pay your ransom?"

That became his new joke about me: being kidnapped. He said that the kidnappers wouldn't even demand a ransom for me after they learned how worthless I was. "They'd soon regret taking you. They would realize they had made a huge mistake. They wouldn't be able to tolerate you," he laughed. Still, he gave me a hunting knife and told me to keep it under my bed so that if we were attacked I could protect us. He kept filling my head with such possibilities and I started to feel like a live target.

And something had changed again. Now that he had a car that no one else had in Hungary, he took us to visit my uncle and my grandparents, even though we had visited my home town only a couple of times in the last two years. I was very happy to see my favourite uncle, hoping that I could steal a few minutes to relax and laugh with him. Our relationship, though, wasn't the same anymore. When I saw him, I felt his distancing himself from me instantly and that stopped me from throwing myself into his arms. His remote behaviour hurt me very much, and whatever I tried, I couldn't bring back the familiar uncle who I knew and loved so much.

CHAPTER 26

CREATING A HOME AND MAINTAINING harmony and peace were probably the biggest challenges for me. But if we were destined to live on a factory ground I at least wanted to create a nice home for us. I had always liked to decorate, to make my environment more beautiful. I knew Joseph would never appreciate the home I created, so I simply did everything for my son and myself, and in a way for my parents, even though we barely saw them. They were working hard to make Joseph more successful and to fill his pockets. I believed that he paid them quite well, but he also robbed them as human beings. They weren't appreciated either, nor were they happy about living and working at the head offices, but they had been ordered to do so.

From time to time they would complain to me: "We were so stupid to come here. We should have stayed far away." I knew that they believed they were out of options, and tolerated many humiliating situations because in their minds they had nowhere to go. They were certain that there were no job opportunities for them anymore or anywhere. I never understood their mentalities. They were free! They could have broken the chain if they really wanted to. But of course, "What would people say if we just left you here? What kind of parents we would be?" So it seemed that this was also my fault. I was the cause of their agony.

I wanted to leave as well. I told Joseph many times that the place wasn't healthy or appropriate for raising a child. I asked him for little Joey's sake, thinking that maybe this would move him to create better living circumstances, and he finally agreed to look for something outside of Budapest. But the house hunting was entirely about what *he* preferred, his desires and not ours. Since he loved water he wanted a house near it. We visited the Danube branches, which once again were away from civilization. There were only ten or fifteen houses, mostly weekend cottages, and some areas were under construction. The neighbourhood was obviously on its way to becoming more inhabited but it just wasn't the place I was longing for; I didn't want to be more isolated than I already was. But my job was to adjust to him—always to adjust.

He patiently kept searching for something that would fit into his fantasies: not just a cottage, but something big that represented prestige. It was his luck that he found one such place there for sale. The house was far too big and ostentatious for the neighbourhood. It reminded me of a cold fortress rather than a habitation. But for Joseph it was perfect because he had always wanted things that were conspicuous and bigger than whatever other people had. (Talk about making us a target.) He also constantly criticized, belittled and despised others for their efforts and accomplishments. Everybody was lower than he was.

My parents worked their tails off so Joseph could buy that house with cash. He paid the owner 300,000 forint, about $5,000CAD, under the table, then signed the house over to Joey but kept the right to enjoy the house until his death. He was satisfied, but I couldn't like that house. It was unfriendly, downright ugly, and the layout of the rooms was very uncomfortable. The atmosphere was dismal and depressing. I didn't enjoy a single stay there, even though we had numerous gatherings at the house.

Joseph had an inflatable boat, which was his main item of entertainment. He loved it; therefore everybody else was expected to enjoy it. My father and Joseph's half-brother were very cooperative when it came to boating but the women were reluctant. "It's not safe," I told Joseph. Brushing my concern aside, he said, "Don't worry! You're always safe with me." And I had to be on that boat along with my baby.

There was no place to sit except the edge of the boat and the only thing I could hold onto was a piece of rope. I was clutching Joey with one hand while I was grimly hanging on with the other, but still I was slipping. Joseph, not interested in my struggle, joyfully increased the speed of the boat until it was flying across the water. His guests were utterly impressed, while I was holding on for dear life, afraid of losing my balance. Then my fear changed into anger. "Slow down! I can't hold on any longer!" But to Joseph that was rather amusing and his dangerous overconfidence made everything more frightening. Oh, I was so mad at him for endangering us that I felt my blood boiling in my veins… But I couldn't complain, could I? I had gotten what I wanted: a place outside of the factory grounds.

Joseph loved meetings, as they emphasized his importance, so he had meetings every week for the supervisors and section managers. These were short, maybe two hours long, but for the entire time he insulted the attendees. He also had monthly meetings, which were held on the last weekend of each month. Every store manager throughout the country had to be there, along with the supervisors and those who had leading positions at the head office. That meant about 300 sandwiches each month, which Monica and I had to make with occasional help from Mandy and another office worker.

These meetings lasted for more than six hours, were extremely boring, and drained the people completely every time. I knew that everybody loathed each and every minute of them—except Joseph, of course—but no excuses were accepted: everybody had to be there if they didn't want to lose their jobs. Even I, with little Joey, who was only eight or ten months old, had to sit there for long hours so that he could learn the business. Sometimes, though, Joseph let my mother look after Joey so I could attend with my full attention.

For these meetings Joseph wrote long newsletters, but he was never on time with them. Thus I was ordered to work on his papers the night before, which kept me up late. The next morning, he would drag me out of bed at 5:00 or 5:30 a.m. to type up the rest of the newsletter, even though typing wasn't my forte at all. My mother was a typist, but I was directly at hand.

He kept making notes until the very last minute, then all the stress and responsibility of putting it together ended up on Monica and me. The meeting would already have started, but we would still be working on his newsletter. We copied the pages, then stapled them together at the *right* angle, of course, making it all look professional. And if his message wasn't ready—which was almost every time—we were the ones to blame. He drove us like a maniac to catch up on the time *he* wasted.

Joseph kept me busy both emotionally and physically. I juggled Joey's needs and Joseph's demands, trying to manage both simultaneously so neither would complain although when their requests crossed each other, my son was the priority. That his father couldn't tolerate.

His new command was for me to prepare his breakfast at 10:00 a.m. and his lunch at noon, served in his office. He even instructed me in how to cut the bread, cheese, meat, and fruit into bite-sized pieces. When I had to look after him—and he always had to come first—he didn't care whether Joey screamed. He was in his office and couldn't hear it. I had difficulty comprehending how a father could push aside his own son so that his demands would be fulfilled first. Joseph treated Joey like an opponent, which saddened me a great deal. I had thought he would love his son. It was also very hard to keep up with his senseless games. Many times when I hurriedly took him his meal, he held me back with meaningless excuses, even though he knew that Joey was alone upstairs and needed my care.

And dinner was to be served at 6:00 p.m., even though Joey's bath time was at 6:00. "Change the child's bath time," Joseph said. "He won't know the difference." But I had no intention of changing Joey's bath time. Ever since he was born, I had always bathed him at 6:00 p.m. Our routine was like a well oiled machine. To lighten the situation, I prepared Joseph's dinner as he requested: his meal was on the table at 6:00 p.m. sharp. But then instead of accompanying him, I went to look after the baby. This plan didn't work, though. "I don't want to eat alone," Joseph whined. "I'm sorry," I said to him. "I told you, I can only sit down to dine at 6:30. But since you wanted your dinner by 6:00, there it is. And now I have to look after Joey. It's important that I maintain his schedule." After that, dinner time was changed to 6:30 p.m.

In all that madness, it never came up that I might have had some needs of my own. I already understood well that he didn't regard me as a human being. I felt like a slave, day and night, with him as my owner and tormentor. And he kept us hermetically isolated. We had no places to go and no friends to be with. I started to believe that this was to be my life, that this was what I deserved. Nobody told me otherwise.

1994
Around the world

CHAPTER 27

THIS WAS THE THIRD YEAR of my life with a man who had never loved me, only used and abused me. Yet still I was naive enough to hope that one day I would be able to win his heart. But I was getting smarter and more experienced about the life I was seemingly destined to live.

As the years went by, I started to compare them, hoping to discover at least one year I could describe as *normal*. But it felt that with each passing year Joseph became more aggressive and intimidating. He dominated us entirely, and I was constantly being punished, although I didn't know what for. I started protesting against his treatment more often, wanting him to understand how much he hurt me day after day.

Our conversations were invariably vicious fights. I wished to hurt him just as much as he did me, but I was no match for him. He was strong physically, verbally, emotionally and financially, and always had enough energy to cause pain, whereas I was usually drained. I had to do something, and urgently, because I didn't feel safe; the circumstances and the atmosphere Joseph had created were clearly destructive for us, and I didn't want my baby growing up in such a milieu. He deserved better, much better, and so did I.

My desperation was overwhelming. I was scared, helpless, and alone. Since he kept us totally isolated, I lost my sense of the outside world and had no idea what was going on beyond the factory ground.

I also still wasn't allowed to watch TV or read a book, or even listen to music. As he always said, I would only learn bad things from all of that. I wasn't allowed to have any other interest except what he liked or considered smart enough.

Joseph was becoming a complete stranger; I didn't think that I had ever known him and certainly didn't want to now. He was so unpredictable that I was afraid of him, not knowing from one moment to the next what was going to happen. I simply couldn't keep up with his mood swings. Ironically, though, the farther I felt myself drifting from him, the more he stated that we belonged to him. He still addressed me as "sweetheart" but by now the expression made my skin crawl. He also used the diminutive of almost every noun when addressing me, emphasizing his opinion that I was nothing more than an idiot.

I had never really heard my inner voice before, but now it became undeniably audible: "Leave him!" I knew that would be the best thing to do but also difficult, if not impossible. Fear was my heaviest chain of all—I feared his anger and punishment. Besides, I had no one and nowhere to go. To my parents who lived on the third floor? The situation seemed totally hopeless but the voice kept nagging me. "Leave him! For your child's sake and for yours, leave him." I had absolutely no idea what I could do to save my son and myself from total destruction.

My mind was filled with the sweet thought of freedom. I wanted at least to go home for a little while to be with my grandmother, who I had barely seen in the last few years. But we weren't allowed to go anywhere without Joseph, and going home with my parents was also out of the question. Hence, my grandparents couldn't be a part of their great-grandson's life, just as my parents couldn't either—and they lived right below us.

I often asked Joseph about going home but he invariably refused, saying, "That wouldn't be good for you, going back among the plebs. You'd just sink back to what you were, and then all my efforts at fixing you would be in vain." Other times he just whined for me not to leave him alone because he needed me to look after him.

Canada remained a constant big issue between us. He still praised it endlessly, while decrying everything about Hungary and its people; he simply looked down on the whole country. Many times, he brought full suitcases of canned foods, macaroni and cheese, even frozen salmon from Canada. And he went back regularly because while his business was booming in Hungary, in Canada everything was sinking. In his opinion everyone was incompetent, that was the cause of the problems. Whatever the reason, it was all right with me. If I couldn't go where I wanted to at least he was gone from time to time.

Monica and I remained close in spite of all the difficulties we were facing. I knew very well that she wasn't happy either, chained to her father/boss against her will. Their relationship was so cold it froze my blood. She had to work thirteen to fourteen hours a day and come in on weekends as well. She wasn't even allowed to call in sick, although she was quite often ill. Her well-being was clearly fading, but that made no difference to her father.

She lived independently, and although Joseph was still able to control her life, it was easy to understand the reason she put up with all the abuse. She had an inexhaustible supply of resources, with or without her father's knowledge…

There were times when the two of us got together for a few minutes to cry on each other's shoulders. She had her own story to share. "We lived in fear," she said. "Each time my father got home from work, I and my two sisters hid or pretended to be asleep so we wouldn't have to meet him. Year after year, he ruined our Christmases. He constantly hurt our mother, always yelling at her and calling her names. He tortured the whole family with his rages. And he hated my grandmother, who practically raised us because he wouldn't let my mother look after us; she had to work with him. Then one day he walked in with a young woman and introduced her as our new mother. That's how we lived."

Monica's words shocked me deeply, not just the horror of what they had had to go through and what a heavy burden she was carrying, but the familiarity of the story. I was more certain than ever that I didn't want my child to grow up like her. Anyone deserved better than to be at the mercy of a maniac's mood swings. I had to tell my parents. Hopefully they would understand the seriousness of the situation and help me find a solution before it was too late, if for no reason other than the safety of their grandson.

My mother's reaction was totally unexpected. "Don't believe her!" she said. "She's just trying to stir up problems between you and her father. We all know she isn't happy with your relationship and now she has a rival, your son. She simply doesn't want to lose her share of the inheritance."

Heavens! Had she heard me? "I have no reason not to believe her. I'm already experiencing what she said. I don't want to live like this, and I'm afraid for my son's well-being and happiness." Monica had no way of knowing the details of my life, but she knew what was going on, from her own experience. I said as much to my mother but she remained immovable. "You should be kinder to him."

Her answer was like a slap across the face. So the help I hoped to get from my parents was once again denied. I had to face the reality that I was all alone with my problems, as I had always been. But Monica's story gave me extra strength to fight for my son's best interests, even if that meant I had to stand up to Joseph all by myself.

CHAPTER 28

LIKE TWO CASTAWAYS, MONICA AND I had formed an unbreakable bond through our life experiences. Against all odds and parental advice, we didn't hide how well we got along. It was therefore rather disturbing when Joseph came to me one day saying that Monica was complaining about my being rude. I couldn't recall any incident between us, but Joseph was so upset and convincing that I almost believed him. The more he pressed the issue, the more disappointed I became because I felt betrayed by Monica.

Thus, the next time I saw her I confronted her as calmly as I could. She didn't get upset at all. "Don't be so quick to believe him! He's doing this on purpose. He says something to you, then he says something to me so we'll get into a fight. He likes to drive people against each other, then he just sits back and enjoys the show. But we're too smart for his tricks." Now that was just unbelievable. I humbly apologized to her and said, "You know, Monica, I feel like I'm trapped in kindergarten." It was simply incomprehensible to me that a grown man would do such things, but Monica's warning made me more aware of Joseph's games. I had to keep my eyes and ears really open to avoid walking into his traps again. This event, though, took me back to Mandy.

The last time we had run into each other, she hadn't even acknowledged me. I was hurt by her coldness and didn't understand what had caused the change in her. When I tried to talk to her, she just snapped out a few incomprehensible words. That was our very last "conversation" before she quit or was fired. I never learned the truth. Had he done the same thing to destroy the relationship between us? Had I lost her friendship because of his lies?

The more I thought about it, the more certain I became that he had been behind her animosity. The changes in her had happened far too suddenly and I believed her to be too young to recognize such disgusting mind-games. I, on the other hand, learned to understand things I had never even known of before.

Now that I realized he was deliberately poisoning relationships between people, I warned my father, who was constantly complaining about Joseph's half-brother. I told him that even if there were some disagreements between them, he had to be aware that it might be Joseph who was stirring up the problems by manipulating them. Unfortunately, my father was just too upset to consider this. I wanted to help him clarify the situation, but instead he remained stuck in that hostile relationship.

However, my father's reluctance to hear me was so strong that I started to doubt the facts: maybe the brother really wasn't nice to him. But I also watched more closely Joseph's actions and his reaction to the enmity between them, and I could see how satisfied he was when the two of them were at each other's throats; he was clearly enjoying the war. And if the existing chaos wasn't enough, he wanted to draw in all my relatives, and got to my godfather, his wife, my uncle, and my first cousin's family. He even approached my maternal grandmother.

My godfather and uncle came to work for him in the warehouses but they didn't last long—Joseph's constant criticism and dissatisfaction with them and their work drove them away. My godfather said he was too old to be treated like that, since he had worked for decades for the same company without any complaints against him.

My brother, who had already been involved in this mess for years, was also an everyday target of Joseph's insults. It didn't matter how hard or how many hours he worked, he was never good enough. Plus, Joseph condemned him for loving motorcycles and having tattoos. In his opinion, my brother was a useless person and a permanent bad influence on us.

Still, I knew that my brother appreciated the opportunity to work there. He worked hard, so hard that he twice developed a hernia. While he was recovering Joseph called him lazy and wanted to fire him. What saved my brother's position? The possible legal consequences, I guess. Although Joseph was never bothered about whether his acts were legal or not since he was a law unto himself.

In his eyes, I and all of my family were "useless pigs from the pigsty", and now we were trying to take advantage of him instead of being grateful. He despised us so much that he seemed almost sick of us. Unfortunately, I was the nearest, so he made *me* pay constantly for our "sins". "And don't forget that I make more money than all of your relatives together ever made or will ever make."

Thankfully, Joanne remained a part of my life and also a good friend of steadfast loyalty. For as long as I had known her she had always been there for me, and now that I had little Joey, she was there for us.

We still kept our tradition of my inviting her to visit us when Joseph was out of the country. She worked so hard all day, week after week, and I knew very well that Joseph paid her only the bare minimum. I couldn't raise her salary, but at least I was able to give her some peace of mind and a few minutes of rest.

Every time, the second he left, I felt myself coming alive. I could sleep, I could even eat. With his departure I literally felt the burden lifting from my soul. I could actually breathe. But even though I was free to go out, I didn't really want to; I just wanted to savour the peace and quiet of our home.

Enjoying my so-called freedom was one thing, but actually having freedom was another because Joseph's spies were everywhere. I never knew whether the person I was talking to would report me to him or not, although I started not to care about that anymore.

Once he returned, he again ordered me back to the offices from 8:00 a.m. to 3:00 p.m. and there was no running up to check on my little boy. The only time I was allowed to go upstairs was when I prepared his meal, and maybe had a bite myself. But if he thought that I had been upstairs for too long, he cursed and shouted at me.

While I was in the office, Joanne looked after Joey. I was lucky to have her with my baby as I trusted her and knew that she would do a great job. But still, as a new young mother I was longing to be with my son and look after him myself. After all, Joseph could easily afford that. Again, there was no reason for me to be at the office, since I was still only a rotten apple who made everyone around her miserable. He simply wanted me to suffer. Keeping me away from my baby was the harshest punishment for me and he knew that very well.

My desk was in his office and whenever somebody came in for an interview or to see him, I was there to listen and learn, right? But what I had to witness was him shamelessly flirting with every woman who walked in, making young girls blush and stammer at his suggestive remarks. Then from time to time he would joke around with the men, making me one of the butts of his jokes. I was very humiliated, feeling clumsier, dumber, and uglier than ever, and I withdrew into my shell even more. As if that wasn't enough, he continuously blamed me for every problem that came up.

But since I had to be there, I wanted to do a good job, at least for my own satisfaction. Unfortunately, that was pointless as well. I created a filing system with his guidance, but then he didn't like it. He was unable to manage his own papers, so he simply dismissed the whole system as if it didn't exist. And he didn't keep one of the many variations. All my work, time, devotion, and sacrifice were flushed down the toilet. After that I was certain that he deliberately kept me busy on something he had no intention of using just to keep me at his side and away from my son.

At the offices the tension was always palpable and many people couldn't take it for long. Employees came, then left before they were kicked out. But I envied them all. They were free and had privacy, plus a salary. Even if Joseph treated them badly, they could go home and lock the door behind them, while in my case, when I shut the door I was locked up with him.

As an added insult, he kept me on the payroll—for tax benefits— but I never saw one penny for my work, never saw a pay cheque or an envelope filled with well-earned money. My only reward was the tax refund, and my so-called income was the government child allowance, which was 2,000 to 3,000 forint, about $50CAD!

And now, *I* couldn't take the pressure at the office any longer, so I made a deal with him: I offered to work for him in the apartment. Surprisingly, he agreed. I stayed upstairs and he hired a young girl to work at my desk and at his side.

He gave me a bunch of catalogues to price. It was such an embarrassing task, but I was willing to do anything just to stay with my son and get out of his office. To make my job more interesting I used different coloured pens and wrote the numbers with extreme care. I was almost drawing them; I wanted him to see how beautifully I could write. But that lasted for a short time only; although I had every intention of doing a precise job, it became extremely boring. At that point I just wanted to get it done, and then I simply stopped doing it, telling Joseph that I had no time for his catalogues because I was busy with Joey and had to look after him as well. With that I was released from that monotonous job.

Occasionally, though, there were some funny moments when I could only laugh at my miserable situation. A couple of times Joseph changed his appearance by shaving off his moustache or growing a beard. That second change didn't work out too well, as it only enhanced the thirty-four years age difference between us, and Monica's remark made this makeover hilarious: "That's great! Now he looks like your grandfather." And the beard was gone.

CHAPTER 29

THIS WAS A VERY BUSY year. In May he took us to Canada and began to plan for our lives there. Those were a frightening few weeks. I certainly had no intention of living in a foreign country where I understood nothing. How would I look after my son properly? I didn't speak the language and knew nothing about life in Canada. Besides, I felt like an intruder. Whether he took me to Toronto or Vancouver, I felt that I simply didn't belong and I was always very happy and relieved to be back in my homeland, despite the constant challenges I faced.

In July he took me to Romania, where he was looking for more business opportunities. Then in October it was Hong Kong to attend a photo expo. Through these trips he deliberately separated me from Joey for weeks and had me entirely to himself. Although it was rather difficult, I tried to view these trips from a different angle. After all, I was seeing the world, right? Hong Kong could be a very exciting and interesting experience. I wanted the trip to be something special, and watched my own behaviour very closely so that he wouldn't find fault with me.

It didn't work. Throughout the whole trip he was cruel and insensitive to me. He forced me to go and ask for information about certain products. Even though he told me what to say or ask, I was so nervous that I couldn't speak. I felt dumb for being inadequate. My shaky self-esteem was rocked all over again, as he bad-mouthed me right there, making me cry.

Joseph often wanted Joey and me to accompany him on his business trips around Hungary as well. These events were anything but enjoyable. We were stuck in the car for hours and our only entertainment was him and his lectures. I would have loved to listen to music while we were on the road, but first I had to ask his permission to turn the stereo on. Nine times out of ten, he refused. When Joey turned it on he would let us enjoy the music for a couple of minutes, then in the middle of the number he would turn it off, and we were forbidden to turn it back on.

But I tried to take advantage of the opportunity of being outside of my prison. When we walked around in the cities or towns and I saw a church, I would slip away into the sacred silence and peace, as I was always drawn to the house of God. Those heavenly few minutes were truly revitalizing, and temporarily washed away the terror I was living in. For that short time I felt completely safe.

Unfortunately, though, the constant stress and pressure started to show. I had never had an extra pound on me, and now I was losing weight rapidly. The people around me told me that I looked like a ghost or a shadow. Monica said that I had already been see-through and was now about to vanish. Only Joseph found my condition funny.

I was always unacceptable in his opinion and now I was surely undesirable, of which he made sure I was well aware. He compared me to famine victims in Africa and had great laughs at my expense. But even though I looked like a skeleton, he was ever so persistent when it came to sex.

I felt so uncomfortable because I knew I looked quite awful. Actually, I was extremely ashamed of my body. He of course didn't miss a beat and even during sex put me down. "What do you want with these two pieces of skin?" he said about my breasts. His words hit me so hard that my breath caught in my throat. After four years of constant bullying, he could still hurt me that deeply. I had always been self-conscious about my looks and he made this even worse. His remark remained with me and echoed in my head every time he took me. I felt weak and defenceless against him, and sank into a state of being neither dead nor alive. Although I functioned, I felt lifeless.

Then one day I stopped in front of the mirror and looked deeply into my own eyes. I could see nothing but pain and sadness. What shocked me the most was that my eyes seemed dead; there were no sparks, although I knew I used to have them. I kept staring at myself, hoping to discover at least a tiny glint in my hollow eyes. But there was none. At that moment I felt that I could just slowly sink away if I let myself. Instead, I tore myself away from the mirror and every time I was in the bathroom, I deliberately avoided looking into my eyes because I was too afraid of what I might find or not find there.

And the tension didn't ease. Just because I was allowed to stay in the apartment didn't mean I could do anything I liked, not even if I was done with all my duties. When Joey slept I was a clear target for Joseph. So, since there was nothing else left for me, the household work became my escape. I had to be busy with responsibilities and chores every minute of the day, otherwise I was sworn at. I was even afraid to sit down to eat. When he saw me busy with my everyday duties, he didn't bother me too much. But sometimes it was inevitable that he found me sitting, and then he called me a lazy pig and useless.

He also wanted his dinner at 6:00 p.m. again, and now I couldn't convince him otherwise. He forced me to switch the baby's schedule instead. And I cooked everyday because he refused to eat leftovers, except when he prepared something. Thus, I had to cook just the right portion so as not to waste food. But then he started to invite some of his employees to dine with us or even to stay overnight, without first telling me. He just showed up with them unexpectedly. I couldn't hide my disapproval and when he did that repeatedly, I was certain it was deliberate. Because of his arrogance, most of the time I refused to eat with them. I knew that I was impolite, but I was just too mad at him to sit at the same table.

There were also times when I didn't eat so the guest could. That usually made the guest uncomfortable, which put Joseph on the defensive. He was never openly angry at me at these times, but the situation itself was humiliating enough. Of course, he recovered himself quickly; after all, he was the perfect gentleman. He threw together macaroni and cheese, opened a can, and dinner was served. Despite my unease in these circumstances, I also felt sorry for his guests.

For him, though, it wasn't enough that he wrecked my days; he had to ruin my nights as well. I made sure dinner was ready at 6:00 on the dot, but more often now he simply didn't show up. Hours went by; nothing. When he finally came in, he refused to eat alone, so at 11:00 p.m. or even later, it didn't matter; he dragged me out of bed to keep him company while he had his dinner. I had to sit with him and watch him eating.

He also didn't let me sleep unless his demands were fulfilled. I was obligated to give him a massage then have sex, even if I was half asleep. If I dared to refuse my services, he became extremely angry and started to yell at me in the middle of the night, not bothering that he might wake little Joey up. Because of his constant disruptions I slept only two to three hours a night, month after month.

Then it came to a point where I simply wasn't allowed to sleep if he wasn't sleeping. Whenever he found me asleep or just resting, he came to me whining. "How come you went to bed without me? You're not supposed to sleep without me!" I knew what would come next, and nervously listened to his every movement in the bathroom. The seconds ticked by, and then he was there pressing his cold body to mine, touching me everywhere. It was time again to fulfill my obligations...

After some time I simply didn't dare to fall asleep, knowing he would disturb my rest and complain. Thus, I just lay in bed, listening to every slight noise, fearfully waiting for the door to open. Sometimes I tried to pretend that I was asleep, praying that he wouldn't bother me. But the time never mattered to him when he wanted something from me. He totally ignored my needs and me as a person; I was expected to be willing and eager. Afterward, he fell asleep within seconds, but I always had a hard time even relaxing. I felt sick and disgusted by how he treated me.

CHAPTER 30

ONCE AGAIN, HE HAD HAD enough of my withdrawal from his business, and assigned me to look after the store on the main floor. He wanted me to be there for some time to analyze people's work, then report back to him. Since the store was under my parents' management, I didn't object. To be at the store was surely more interesting than pricing catalogues. Besides, it was also a rare occasion for me and Joey to be with my parents. Even if they didn't really want me around, I wanted to be with them.

So I went downstairs diligently, carrying little Joey with me, and worked along with my parents to improve the store. My parents weren't afraid to work hard, and took great pride in their work, always striving to reach above the average. And it was good to be there. We actually had fun working together, cleaning, decorating and organizing. The store sparkled. We were proud of the results and quite certain that Joseph would be satisfied, maybe even happy with our work.

But when he finally came down all he did was complain. Our efforts were totally unappreciated. Joseph was and remained dissatisfied, finding only mistakes in nearly everything we had done. Needless to say, his attitude crushed our enthusiasm.

And the game rules were always changing. Here and there, I still had chances to socialize, to talk to people, even if it was only a part of my assignment. But when he decided that I had had enough socializing, he ordered me not to speak to anybody except when he wanted me to learn something from the young girls he hired and continued to select for me as role models.

"Go and spend some time with her," he would say. "Maybe you can learn how to be kind and pleasant instead of annoying and intolerable. Go and learn from her how to smile." He also told me that people were constantly complaining about my being unfriendly, which showed how seriously I needed *his* help and guidance.

I desperately hoped that my little boy would not notice or understand the situation we were in. Then one day as we were browsing through parent magazines, Joey kissed and caressed every baby picture. I interpreted this as my son's longing for companionship and I felt my heart sink. I had to do something.

I started by asking his father several times to let us go out to a playground. We only had the dirty factory ground, without even a green spot where we could at least sit down. Cars and trucks were coming and going constantly. The noise and the pollution were driving me crazy. Yet if I wanted Joey to have some "fresh air", that was the only option Joseph allowed.

Ignoring my experience with him, I approached Joseph again. "Joey needs to meet other children. He has to be *among* children. It's very important for his healthy development." But Joseph always dismissed me by saying, "I'm his friend. He doesn't need anybody else." And that was how it was. We really had nobody but him. He even told me the same thing: "I'm your boyfriend, your girlfriend, your parent, and your grandparent. I'm everybody for you. See how lucky you are?"

For all his claims to be Joey's friend, Joseph never bothered to look after the child—didn't teach him, didn't play with him, didn't even feed him...apart from one time.

On that particular evening, we had another unexpected guest and were all sitting around the table. Joey had his own meal but his father insisted that he would eat some of our dinner. I told Joseph that the food we were having was far too heavy for Joey's little tummy, but since everything I said was nonsense to him, he ignored me and fed him some of our dinner, regardless of my warning. Two minutes later Joey threw up.

The only thing he did was show the child off, gaining the glory while I did all the work. I wasn't allowed to take Joey out to be with other people, but he could do it. I wasn't allowed to sit down to watch TV, but again he could. He controlled even the simplest events of our life.

There was a period of time when he came up to dine on time, then sat down to watch the news. But of course he didn't even want to watch TV alone, so he took Joey to accompany him. It didn't matter that Joey was already in bed—he woke the child up just to sit with him. And if

Joey was still awake, his father simply took away his toys or took him away from me if we were doing something together.

I didn't think that all the bombing and shooting that poured out of the TV was what a two-year-old needed, but as always I was just a stupid person who didn't know what she was talking about. He was the head of the family, and of course, he was the smartest. So smart, indeed, that the continuous disruptions he caused made Joey very fussy and upset, but of course it was my fault as well that Joey didn't want to watch the news with him. "You raise him to be against me. That's why he doesn't want to watch TV with me." That frequently started the evening fights. "Do something else with him," I suggested many, many times. "The news isn't for a two-year-old child. Why don't you play with him instead? Join him in playing his game." But that was way too much to ask. He never sacrificed a minute of his time to be with his son. Never! To learn his business at the age of two, that was what he wanted from him. I fought Joseph endlessly to prevent him taking Joey's childhood away. Although I was powerless against him, I was determined to find a solution for my little boy's best interests and happiness.

Then he bought a PlayStation system so they could play it together. Although Joey had the controller, Joseph was the one who told him what to do, where to go. Actually, he didn't tell him but rather shouted at him. Poor child, he wasn't able to enjoy one minute of those games. But again, why did a two-year-old need videogames anyway? Of course, the game itself provided the entertainment, thus Joseph didn't have to make an effort.

So, the next time as we flipped through one magazine after another I came up with the best solution I could. I knew beyond a doubt what I was going to do. If Joseph forbade Joey to have friends and prevented him from being among other children, I would give him one. I swore to Joey that I would give him a friend: a sister or a brother. I didn't care that Joseph wanted to destroy me or how much he wanted to hurt me; there was nothing that could stop me giving what I wanted to my son. It was my decision, mine alone.

Since Joseph never used protection with me, I was sure that I could get pregnant again easily. My goal gave me an incredible strength. Giving a friend to my son was my ultimate mission. Then he would have someone to play with, to laugh with; someone he could love and who would love him back.

So I told Joseph that I wanted another baby but gave him no explanation. He wasn't overjoyed by my idea, although he graciously offered his services. "I don't need another child, but if you want another one, I'll help you." The way he said it made me wonder whether I was expected to bow to him and kiss his feet to show my gratitude. But whatever he'd said wouldn't have made any difference to my intention because my mind was set.

CHAPTER 31

I TRIED HARD TO COPE with our situation, but that became more and more difficult. Because of all these limitations on our life, even shopping for groceries was a special event. The grocery store was our only connection with the outer world. But then, we were deprived of even that when Joseph opened his own market in one of the hangars. With that, he closed our last door to the real world.

Joseph had never valued my opinion on any aspect of life, but when he opened the Dollar Item store beside the discount food outlet, he asked what items I thought would be the most marketable in my country. That was a difficult question because of the isolation he kept me in. I had no idea what went on outside the four walls that confined me, so I could hardly give him a useful idea about what he should order. But there was one thing I definitely knew: Hungarian people highly valued excellent quality. However, Joseph ordered in container after container of cheap, low-quality items. Some were so inferior that to me as a Hungarian citizen, it was humiliating even to look at what he wanted to sell. But he thought he could sell anything in Hungary, because in his opinion my country was stuck in the primitive ages and the citizens were nothing but barbarians.

While I tried to get pregnant, he came up with a new idea for me. I dreaded his ideas so much because they always turned my whole life upside down. This time, he wanted me to have my own company. Since he knew that I was interested in fashion design, he thought that a company selling clothes wholesale was just what I needed. I had no idea what I had done to deserve such a privilege but I wasn't particularly eager to take advantage of it. In normal circumstances I would have jumped at the chance to have my own business, but not with him in the picture.

His intentions always served him and in the end hurt me. The more he pushed me, the more suspicious and nervous I became, so I told him that I wasn't interested. My answer didn't please him. After all, I wasn't under any circumstances allowed to say no to him. The only permissible response was, "Yes, sweetheart." And he didn't let me escape; what he wanted, I had to want too.

He said he would give me one million forint, about $15,000CAD. He hired a couple from somewhere who already had great experience in fashion merchandising, and when he thought that everything was ready to get started, he said to me, "This is your company. You're the boss, you control the people. I'll let you do your best." That was his blessing. To me the most important sentence was the last one. I believed that he meant it, and that fired up my courage and desire to create something that even he would be proud of, since everything would be happening under his roof.

I had no experience at all of what it meant to have my own business, nor did I know how much it cost to launch a new company. It was an enormous blow when the registration fee took off 30% of our capital, which was a lot compared to what we had been given. One million forint was a huge amount to me, but as I learned, it was absolutely nothing when it came to starting a business.

Anyway, we gave it a try. I was full of ideas and plans, but I had to rely on the couple's experience and knowledge, which turned out to be fine since we became good friends. They were very special people and it was an honour to work with them. To me they were my partners, never my people who I had to control. Together we started to plan the future of my new company. Their expertise showed the way and I began to believe that we could actually succeed.

Enthusiasm was high. Our dream was to create a high quality store with plenty of goods to satisfy all of our customers. We wanted to have the latest fashion clothing in a wide and colourful variety. But again, the free hand promised by Joseph was never actually given to me. He was there at every step, nosing into everything we did, criticizing my work, insulting my partners and, of course, me. He constantly humiliated me in front of them, trampling my dignity without remorse. (And I was supposed to be the boss!)

Within a short time, difficulties started to occur, one after another. Our biggest problem was that the money wasn't nearly enough to make the company strong and competitive. We never had enough stock to offer. In my partners' opinion, for a successful business we needed at least ten times more start-up capital.

It was my duty to ask for more, which I knew was a dead end. I told my partners that Joseph wouldn't give me one penny more. Their answer was, "If he honestly wants this company to be successful, he has to invest more into it."

I didn't want to let them down, so I attempted the impossible: I asked Joseph for more money. He hardly listened to me before responding, "Those people are just after my money. I'm a great businessman, I know how much money is needed to start a business, and that amount is enough." (Yet he had started his company with forty times more.) "They just don't know what to do or how to do it. I'm not giving you more." For once he didn't blame me, but since it was my company, it was my failure.

And then it was Christmas again, which drifted past almost unnoticed. At least we had a tree, which I enjoyed decorating, but ever since Joseph had been in my life, somehow I had never had a real Christmas. Still, it was my favourite holiday and I wanted to amaze my little Joey with a dazzling tree. However, the mood was tense and rigid through the holidays. And the fact that another frightening year was on the doorstep also overshadowed my mind. I had no idea what the next year had in store for me. It felt like I was heading toward the unknown abyss of my life and I was very afraid of the gaping darkness.

1995
In full circle

Chapter 32

In January, Joseph brought my parents and us to Canada, even though the problems between him and me were getting uncontrollably worse. This journey was entirely unforeseen, and I didn't understand why he would make such a nice, generous gesture.

Rather than being happy, though, I was suspicious and nervous. I knew there was something hidden behind his gallantry which would eventually backfire on us, and felt that it was only a matter of time before we all learned the true reason for this trip.

While Joseph was in Hungary, he entrusted Myrna to look after his apartment building and his flat in Canada. After a while he allowed her to move into his apartment, giving up her own, which was right next to Joseph's, to her family. When all five of us unexpectedly showed up—she didn't seem to know about our arrival—she immediately had to move back in with them.

She was very pregnant and had no time to prepare or get help. Although she did her best to grab her stuff and leave, there was just too much. (She had moved in completely.) My mother helped her while Joseph stood yelling at her but never offered a helping hand. She couldn't conceal her tears, crying openly in front of us, and my heart cried with her. I wanted to help her, but I also didn't want her to leave. So all I did was look after Joey, who had to witness this heartless scene. I simply don't remember what my father did.

I already knew what it meant to be pregnant and kicked out. I could feel Myrna's suffering. It was clear that she was exhausted but she also appeared to be in physical pain. She moved out within a few hours and despite not speaking much Hungarian, she was extremely grateful to my mother for her help.

A few days later Joseph was looking for something but couldn't find it. He turned the apartment upside down, but the items were nowhere to be found. He was sure that he had left them in the closet at the entry door, but they weren't there.

Myrna was his first suspect. Ignoring her condition, he verbally attacked her with full force. I didn't understand what he told her, but Myrna's reaction was unambiguous: she had no idea what he was shouting about. Thus, the whereabouts of the missing items remained unknown. Still, he did not doubt that Myrna was guilty.

Then, a few days later, he found the things he was looking for—as it turned out, he was the one who had put them away. When he next saw Myrna he just laughed, saying that he had the items but never apologizing for falsely accusing her of stealing.

Having my parents around us didn't make any difference as he didn't even try to restrain himself, but provoked me endlessly and picked arguments about every tiny thing. Since he didn't like the fact that I applied moisturizer to my face, he forbade me to use it. When I didn't obey, he punished me by not talking to me for three days. He looked through me as if I didn't even exist. Although his behaviour was rather offensive and childish, it didn't bother me that much because at least I had some peace. Just to be left alone, I would have happily applied the whole jar to my face.

He also liked to cause unpleasant surprises, so he invited or ordered his wife to pay us a visit. She was supposedly managing his Canadian business line and there were a lot of losses and problems; obviously his company was sinking faster and faster. So he blamed all the crises on her, raging, yelling and calling her names right in front of us, so brutally that she burst into tears.

I felt very uncomfortable and was worried for my son, who again had to witness a cruel scene, but I didn't even dare to move. My parents were equally uncomfortable while diligently examining the floor. I was getting angry, though, and had the urge to step in and stop his flood of obscenities. But then I thought otherwise because I didn't want to make the situation worse, if that was still possible. I was also too shocked. I had never expected him to speak to his own wife that viciously. Besides, this event was a clear reflection of my life and very difficult to witness. So, Monica had been truthful after all—my mother could see that clearly now.

The whole scene left us trembling. I tried to understand why he had to humiliate his wife in front of us. His inhumanity didn't win my respect and love for him, that was certain. But if he wanted to freeze us to our seats, then he succeeded. I was sure, though, that he wanted to teach all of us, including little Joey, a heavy lesson that he was the boss. Yes! He was the master of making our life a living hell.

It took some time before all of us were able to calm down a little, and communicate like normal human beings again. Then, at Joseph's insistence, his wife spent the night there with us, sleeping on the couch. But before that she wanted to go out to pick up some dinner for herself. That gave Joseph the idea to have me accompany her. "Go and make friends," he ordered. For him it was only a game, which he seemed to enjoy very much. He not only liked to turn people against each other, but found pleasure in forcing people together who didn't want to be in each other's company.

I didn't want to go and she didn't want me to go with her, but we both knew it didn't matter what either of us wanted. So I went along and had a polite but forced conversation. The tension between us was almost razor-sharp; this friendship just wasn't meant to be. I was sure that she was as relieved as I was when we finally could go our separate ways.

In those five weeks I not only experienced but also witnessed his brutality, as did my little boy and my parents. I felt sorry for Myrna and the wife, I was also seething. None of us deserved such treatment. *How dare he treat people like that? Where did he get the right to be so inhuman toward others?* If he was half as decent as he stated himself to be, at least he could have dealt with the situation in private. But no, he had to involve everybody, so he could tyrannize all of us at once.

We went back to Hungary at the end of February and I already knew I was pregnant again. At least something good had come out of the trip. Joseph hardly acknowledged the fact, but that was all right with me. I was happy about successfully accomplishing the first step of my mission.

My company was still surviving under the management of my partners. I trusted them fully, knowing they were doing their best to make something out of the impossible situation. And since I was aware that I couldn't be of much use to them, I invested my time in my little boy and in my new pregnancy.

After my first one I had weighed about 150 lb (68 kg), but starting this one I was only 110 lb (52 kg), which was far too little for my six-foot height. Thus, I considered the second pregnancy to be a lifesaving opportunity to gain back what had been eaten off me by him.

And now, there I was with a small boy and a baby inside me. My defenceless condition made me an even easier target for Joseph's vicious attacks. I had to be very strong, trying not to take his insults to heart or react to his provocations. I had made a promise to my son and was determined to focus on my goal. Unfortunately, it was much easier to make that decision than to actually carry it out, since my existence wasn't up to me.

CHAPTER 33

WHEN MY PARENTS LEARNED THAT I was pregnant again, they were totally mortified. Actually, no one was happy about my second blessing, except maybe Joanne. It seemed that I was the only one who truly wanted this second baby. This was satisfying enough for me, although it hurt. I knew what I was doing and why, and to me it was worth it, regardless of the opinions of those around me.

It was also rather interesting to watch Joseph's attitude. This time he didn't take me to Austria for maternal vitamins, didn't bother with whether the baby was a boy or a girl. He didn't ask me how I felt or what he could do to help me—although he never asked me such questions anyway. He wasn't even interested in what the doctor said.

Despite his indifference, I told him that I was worried about going to see my doctor by myself, that I needed somebody with me in case my blood pressure dropped again. That person wasn't him of course, but he assigned my *mother* to accompany me. I wasn't expecting such generosity at all.

She wasn't utterly happy, but that was her job now. I could feel her distance all the time we were together. Although I had to melt away a thick wall of ice between us, I was glad to spend some time with her. She did need a break from the daily grind. Thus, we both benefited from the situation, even if she didn't see it that way.

My pregnancy went smoothly until I had to undergo a test to determine the health of my baby. The reason was Joseph's age; he was now fifty-nine. When I told him what I was advised to do, he became offended. "You don't need such a test. I'm like a forty-year-old young man. I can make only healthy babies." And he refused to take me for the test.

His unrealistic confidence was overbearing as well as very frightening, showing me once again that his pride was much more important than an innocent baby's health, even one he had fathered. But that didn't stop me from doing the right thing for my child.

It was a very stressful time. I wasn't worried about the process but I agonized about the result. Joseph merely left me alone with my fears. When the result came back negative, I was utterly delighted and relieved. I shared the wonderful news with Joseph, but he remained indifferent to our unborn baby. Not only did he not take part in my happiness; he wasn't able to tolerate it either. I had to conceal my joy from him to prevent him from doing everything he could to destroy it. Against all odds—the circumstances, Joseph's malice, and the difficulties he put me through—I loved being pregnant again. I was sure that I had another little boy under my heart.

My company, though, wasn't going well. The problems just kept piling up and soon a crisis was upon us. We already knew that the company had no future unless Joseph changed his mind and saved it. But that he had no intention of doing. He only demanded some results, which we couldn't produce. Thus, we were on our own, trying to deal with the problems, but they became far too much for us. My partners were becoming tired and annoyed. They contributed a lot of energy and sacrificed a great deal of time away from their children, even putting some of their own money in, yet we came up with nothing but a huge deficit. I believe that only their loyalty kept them there until the very end.

In the summer, when our one and only employee managed to empty the cash register, the problems in my company reached their peak. We had never had much but now everything was gone. I didn't dare to tell that to Joseph, although I had no idea what to do or how to save us from the inevitable.

One day one of my partners and I were on the phone discussing our possibilities for a workable solution. Unfortunately, we ended up with nothing and knew that this was the end of my company, which should never have existed in the first place.

Somehow, we had always sensed that the company was doomed from the very beginning; we just didn't want to think about that. I should have known that Joseph never wanted me to succeed, but rather to fail and humiliate myself. And for this purpose he used two innocent and very decent people. Without them the company wouldn't have lasted as long as it did.

A few days later Joseph called me into his office and ordered me to sit. He sat down facing me. His face was like a stone as he said, "I want you to hear something." He pressed the play button on a tape recorder and voices filled his office, women's voices. First I didn't understand why I had to listen to the tape. I didn't even recognize the voices. Then it slowly sank in that I was listening to my business partner and myself when we had been on the phone just a few days before. I was glued to my chair as cold perspiration covered my whole body and the walls began closing in. I couldn't comprehend what was going on. Then Joseph started to speak to me slowly in a reserved voice. He wanted to be sure that I heard every single word. "I got this tape from the tax office, who tapped your phone," he said. "For what's on this tape I could put you in jail because you're a tax swindler. You handed over the company, *my* company, to strangers. You're a traitor and a swindler. You sold me out but now you're caught. I can put you in jail."

I wasn't able to speak. I didn't understand what he was talking about; I didn't even know what "tax swindler" meant. The only thing I knew was that my fear made me unable to move because I believed him. I believed that he could put me away.

How history repeated itself. When I was five months pregnant with Joey, Joseph kicked me out. And now I was five months pregnant with my second baby and he was threatening to put me in jail. He had brought me full circle. I could only stare at him. His face was contorted as he spoke and his hatred was so powerful that it pinned me to my chair. I still didn't understand what I had done wrong. I tried to explain the situation but he cut me off, refusing to hear me out. My mind was racing. *What did I do wrong?* My only guilt was that I hadn't shared our business problems with him.

Then my thoughts abruptly turned toward my children. I put my hand on my tummy and involuntarily caressed my unborn baby. *Oh my God, my poor children! What will happen to them if their father puts me away? Why does he hate me so much?* He noticed that I was holding my belly, and that just fired him up to hurl more threats and slanders at me.

I could no longer hear him, though. My mind was totally occupied with my children and my life. *How could my life have turned into such a hell? What did I do to deserve this?* Then something clicked in me and my attention was brought back to the current situation. I had a feeling that something was wrong with the picture he was painting. Things just didn't fit together. I still didn't know what was wrong but I could feel it, and while I sat before him my mind worked with extreme speed to find the flaw I knew was there.

First, what drew my attention was that he talked too much. He exposed himself by never shutting up. With each of his words I became more and more certain that Joseph himself was behind the whole scheme and it had nothing to do with the tax office.

When I left his office I was confident that my theory was right, and I started to ask around. I wanted to know who had installed the phones throughout the building, and I got lucky. I ran into two young technicians who I had previously met, and asked them what they knew about my home phone being tapped. They told me that the whole thing was Joseph's idea. He had ordered them to bug my phone because he wanted to know whom I had contact with and what we were talking about. I even learned that all the phone lines in the building were tapped, or at least somehow connected to his phone, so he was able to listen into anybody's phone conversation in the building anytime he wanted.

I felt disgusted by what I had just learned but decided not to mention anything to Joseph. His insolence blinded me with rage but I was far too afraid of him. He threatened me, accused me of crimes I had never committed, and lied right to my face without blinking. He actually sacrificed one million forint to bring me down. Amazing! Such love!

But then I realized that there was one thing I could do to somewhat neutralize the pain he caused me. I started to warn people about the phones. I also mentioned the recording bug to whomever called me and to whomever I called. If he was diligently listening, he learned through his own device that I knew what he had done. I understood that he was the boss, but the bugging and eavesdropping were unacceptable. I was his faithful common-law wife, the mother of his son, yet he was so spineless as to violate my basic human rights, not to mention what little privacy I had, which obviously was too much for his liking.

I really had had enough, and not even my fear kept my mouth shut. His reaction to my emotional eruptions varied. Sometimes he said: "Poor you. I'm just teaching you. You should be grateful for all my efforts to help you. Because you need help, serious help. And I'm the only one who's willing to take the trouble with you."

Other times he blamed everything about me on my parents: "Your parents raised you badly and now it is my job to fix you. Never forget how lucky you are, because I'm the only one who has the ability to make you normal. You should thank me and love me for being so good to you."

His favourite response though was: "Oh my poor little sweetheart. You're such a miserable creature. I feel so sorry for you." At these times his voice was so full of pity, it literally made me wince. I wasn't aware of being such a hopeless case.

Hearing such words repeatedly and often eventually made me think that he was right. I had always been considered stupid, so it was a possibility that no change had occurred in me since childhood. So yes, from time to time I thought he was correct, but deep within I could never actually believe it. I knew I wasn't mentally challenged, despite being treated like an imbecile.

His constant provocations and insults drove me to the edge, yet I simply couldn't escape his punishments. He threatened me daily, using my parents and my son against me. To keep me in line he told me that he would fire my parents. When that didn't work out the way he expected—I had already made that sacrifice and learned my lesson—he said that he would take Joey away from me and kick me out.

Now that worked. My biggest fear was losing my son and it didn't take much for him to realize or remember this. After all, nothing was new about it; he had been threatening me with this ever since Joey was born. Nothing kept me there but this fear and the fact that I had nowhere to go even if I did leave. When he ordered my parents to move into the office building, he had even cut off that route, despite its complete hopelessness.

CHAPTER 34

THERE WAS ABSOLUTELY NO REASON to be with this man. He was beyond being a stranger to me now. I was almost suffocating in his presence and had no idea how I would continue to manage my life like this, because I didn't want to live in constant fear, bullying, and uncertainty. I had to get out of there, had to go because I was close to losing my mind. I packed up some stuff, got Joey, and left. I didn't know where or to whom to go, but I headed toward the only town I knew: my home town.

On my way I debated with myself about whose doorbell to ring when I arrived. My final but very tentative decision was that I would go to my godfather's—a weak and rather hopeless solution, but I was driven by desperation. I knew that it couldn't be permanent but I didn't have much choice or even knowledge about what to do in my situation.

They listened to my cries, made some horrified groans, felt sorry for us, and let us stay. I was relieved that they gave us a bed to sleep in, but I still didn't feel safe and couldn't relax. I knew that it would take only a short time before the menacing shadow would swallow us up again. I became more and more nervous as the hours slowly went by.

A few days later the doorbell rang. With that I already knew my freedom was over. The owner had come to claim his property. I heard his voice as he formally greeted my godfather's wife when she opened the door, and I froze solid when he walked into the living room.

He sat down in front of me, looking very sombre. We said nothing but were eyeing each other for a while. I knew he was also aware that my godfather and his wife remained within earshot. Then slowly, Joseph started to speak to me, choosing his words carefully. "I love you so much," he said in a quiet voice. "I want you to come back to me." I had never heard him speak like that before, calmly and respectfully.

He sounded so broken. What he said could have touched me if I hadn't been shaking with fear. This unknown kindness sent chills up my spine. I didn't want to go back to him, but there was nothing else I could do. Unfortunately, for me he was the only way. "I promise that I'll be nice to you but you also have to promise to listen to me. It's very important for the peace of the family." I didn't believe him but fighting was pointless. To me his plea sounded like a death warrant. Along with my fear, I couldn't shake the feeling that he had shown up too early. How had he known where to come?

Joseph's niceness lasted until we got into the car and closed the doors. Then he started yelling at me, insulting and lecturing me for the next three hours (the time it took to get to Budapest). "How dare you leave me and humiliate me in front of all those people? You're obliged to respect and love me! You must obey me! And if you ever want to leave me again, you can go, but you're not allowed to take Joey with you. And never forget that you're nobody without me. The only reason people tolerate you is because of me." He went on and on until I felt my brain buzzing. Then he said, "Your godfather's wife called me and literally begged me to get you. She also told me that you were complaining about me. You know, I might have one percent of defects, if I have any, but you're ninety-nine percent defective."

I had been running for my life and now I was put back in my keeper's hand. I felt betrayed and sold out. I understood that the solution I had chosen couldn't have worked, because who would have wanted me, pregnant and with a small child? But at least she could have discussed the issue with me before she called him, so I could have prepared myself. After all, my life was at stake and my children's, not hers.

Sitting in his car and listening to his streams of obscenities made me believe that this was it for us. There was no way to escape. He was my destiny, a living curse on me. With one and a half babies I was defenceless, extremely vulnerable, and he took advantage of the situation and us without the slightest remorse. I knew that he believed he had the right to do anything with us, whatever he wanted, and of course, he was always right.

Joseph never paid any attention to his son, just showed him off like some kind of trophy. And now he started threatening him with a wooden spoon if he didn't behave as was expected, always putting him in the middle of the arguments he started, so that Joey was rather reserved toward his father. There was a period of time when Joseph would walk in, squat down, open his arms and call Joey in a weird, high-pitched voice: "Come here, Joey, run to Daddy! Show Daddy who loves him! Come here, Joey, give Daddy a hug!" But Joey didn't even budge. Seeing this, Joseph got annoyed and started to yell at his son.

The whole scene made me sick. Joseph treated his son as if he was nothing but a little puppy; the next thing I expected him to say was, "Prick up your ears and wag your tail for me!" I couldn't conceal my disapproval. "Don't scare him!" I said. "You can't force him to go to you. If you love him, reach out to him. Show him some affection!" That was enough for him to blow up at me. "Shut up!" he shouted. "Tell him to come to me and give me a hug!" I could never do that, though.

Poor baby! He was so scared he couldn't move. Losing all patience, Joseph went to him, squatted down, put his tiny arms around his neck, and made Joey hug him. But the instant his father let him go, Joey ran to me. "This is entirely your fault!" Joseph pointed at me. "You're the one who sets a bad example. Come here and give me a hug! You have to love me so then he'll see how he's supposed to behave. And don't even dare to raise him against me!"

After several such episodes, all I could say was, "You can't force anybody to love you."

"Don't be smart with me!" he snapped. "Your obligation is to obey me and do what I say!" Of course. What else?

And there was another version of his approach to his son. When he had no patience to call Joey to him, he walked over to his son, hugged him, and said, "You know, Joey, if you don't love Daddy, Daddy won't feed you." All the time, he said that I raised the child against him, yet I always thought that he did a very good job of that on his own.

Despite my being in the middle of this madness, my pregnancy remained problem free and that was a miracle in itself. It was also easier this time. The baby wasn't as big and heavy as Joey, although it was pushing on my lower back pretty hard. This one was also more energetic, seeming to move around 24/7. Altogether, though, it was fun. I was able to look after my little boy, who was quite surprised if not scared when I put his hand on my moving belly.

Joseph's rule of not allowing us to speak to people became his obsession. Although I wasn't allowed to socialize, I always did, even if it was risky. So whenever I had a chance to take a break, I took Joey out for a walk around the factory ground. I liked to spend time with the employees who *I* chose. Many of them were very friendly and good natured; thus I felt very sad for them when I learned how unhappy they were. They confided in me, sharing their concerns. One of them even asked the ultimate question: "How can you take this?" He was in total desperation after spending just a short time in Joseph's company. He was a very nice man and exceptionally intelligent, but his efforts were never appreciated by the boss. His question surprised me, though. "I don't have a definite answer to your question," I said to him. "I have to be very strong, that's for sure, and I do what I can." He just nodded and looked at me with open admiration.

Yes, I was able to imagine what he was being put through, and I felt for him, so I wasn't surprised when I heard that he had quit. He just couldn't take what I had to take day after day. And he wasn't the only one.

Most of the people at the company were underpaid, and also were never paid for overtime. They complained to me constantly, as if I had the power to get them a raise or payment for the extra time they spent working late into the evenings. These were simple people who only knew how to work conscientiously. Most of them had been employed by the bankrupt company and came to work for Joseph after he bought the place. They needed their jobs to feed their families.

"And whose side are you on?" Joseph asked me when I told him about the workers' rightful requests. Then he said, "Stop making friends with such low people." And that meant not to speak or even look at them. But of course the next time when we went around the factory, I spoke to the workers anyway. I just couldn't ignore them. I was ashamed about Joseph's refusal and humbly apologized to them for not being able to provide what they needed, and they thanked me for at least trying to help them.

Joseph kept taking savage advantage of his employees, constantly violating the workers' occupational distinctions as well. (He believed that he was invincible and could get away with anything.) He forced some people to work in fields that weren't their specialties. One of the electricians was ordered to do roofing; if he refused, he would be fired. To keep his job he did what he was told. But the roof gave way under him and he fell to his death. Joseph was in deep trouble. The man's family threatened to sue, but he silenced them with a mysterious amount of money, and his problem was smoothed away. That was the way he always escaped when the net closed tightly on him. (So after all, maybe he *was* invincible.)

And whatever happened, he remained true to his word, and thus kept firing people just as often as he hired them. He always surrounded himself with those who he could control and dominate at some level, or with those of whom he could take full advantage. If he wasn't able to take charge of someone or if the person was more intelligent than he was—and most of them were—he simply kicked them out.

No wonder that his empire felt so shaky. I always had the feeling that one day everything would just collapse, like a house of cards. In my opinion, one of the essences of success was to respect your business partners and the people who worked for you, and to pay them fairly. Keep your employees happy and then they will help you to happiness, right? No. He paid the lowest possible wages to his labourers, and insulted and fired people regularly. In his opinion, everybody stole from him, absolutely everybody. Even my parents agreed with this.

I'm not saying that theft never happened. I knew it did. His own brother shorted him. It was also a possibility that people tried to get revenge for being underpaid and mistreated. However, he usually accused innocent people because the real thieves were too shrewd to raise suspicion.

Living without any freedom was very depressing. Still there wasn't a peaceful, clean spot where I could take Joey, so when I had the chance, I brought the playground in. When Joseph left for Canada, I purchased a swing set. A few workers set the swings up and our playground was born. I was very happy to finally be able to introduce a piece of normality into our abnormal world.

We spent many hours there. Joey sat on one swing; I sat beside him so I was able to push him. We talked and I sang to him. It felt so wonderful, but also foreign. I knew we made a strange picture in the middle of the filthy factory ground. Cars, trucks, and people went by all the time. First, they just stared at us. It took some time before they got used to the unusual appearance of a mother and child on a swing set, placed where it didn't belong.

CHAPTER 35

As time went by I could actually feel that the whole country heaved a sigh of relief when Joseph left. Usually, his half-brother took him to the airport and he departed without generating much attention.

While he was in Canada, Monica was responsible for collecting all section managers' reports twice a week to fax them to her father. She had to write her part and of course I had to write mine. I was to give an account of *everything* we did, but I always had great difficulty gathering enough information to write at least a few lines. I had to be loving and devoted in my faxes too, otherwise his answers were hurtful and offensive. No matter how far away he was, through modern technology he could still cause pain.

Joseph also expected us—Monica and I, with Joey—to welcome him at the airport every time he returned, even though none of us wanted to be there. Sometimes his brother had to come along as well. The more people who were at the airport waiting for him, the better it looked; he wanted to have a delegation of happy family members to welcome him back. It was so fake and such a burden. We were always squirming with uneasiness, and on my part with nervousness and deep fear. Even before he set foot in Hungary, it was enough to know that he was coming. From that moment on, I could feel the dark clouds gathering over my head, shadowing my life once again. I honestly wished that he would never come back. But he always returned, like a recurring nightmare.

Our traditional greeting is a kiss on each cheek and since he wanted be welcomed by happy people who were pleased to see him again, I did my best to seem devoted and eager. On one occasion, I was flying to him for the kisses and ended up kissing the air, since he had turned away from me so abruptly I wasn't able to react in time. At that moment, he couldn't have hurt me more even if he had slapped my face, right in the middle of the arriving crowd. And after that he didn't waste another glance or word on me.

On our way back home he literally interrogated Monica about every detail of what had gone on while he was away, and we were forgotten. If Monica answered him in the right way, and usually she said what he wanted to hear, he praised her; if not, all hell broke loose.

I was eight months pregnant now and still everything was all right, at least with respect to my condition. Our family life was ever so miserable, though. Arguments dominated our relationship. One broke out when Joseph wasn't happy about the way Joey ate. (Yes, even that was an issue.) At this time, I cut his food into bite-sized pieces and he just ate with his hands. Since he wasn't even three years old, I thought I could afford him such a luxury, but that was unacceptable to his father. He forced Joey to use a fork with sandwiches, even with a piece of chocolate. "If you touch your food your hands will get dirty." Well, I didn't know that we were eating dirt, but regardless, Joey had no intention of using the fork.

We were already quarrelling above his head. I tried to convince Joseph to let the child eat comfortably but he didn't give an inch. It really bothered me that he had to intervene in everything, absolutely everything. But why was I surprised? To him I wasn't even able to water the plants properly.

I could see that the disturbance had already affected Joey's appetite, because he was only picking at his food, so I asked Joseph again just to let him eat peacefully. The next instant, he took a step and gave me a huge slap. My glasses flew across the kitchen. He struck me again. I was so surprised that at first I wasn't even sure what had hit me. Then the pain finally reached my brain. My head was rumbling. I didn't know if there was another strike on its way, and I also didn't know who or what to protect: my head, my unborn baby, or my terrified little boy. For a while I lost track of time as I slowly sank to the floor, holding my belly. I was in such spasmodic pain that I felt I was about to give birth right there on the kitchen floor.

My son's screaming brought me back: he needed me! I was in terrible pain but I had to get to my little boy, I had to get up. Joey wanted to come to me but his father held him firmly back. With great difficulty, I managed to stand up. With one hand I was clutching my tummy as if to keep the baby there, and with my other hand I tried to reach out to my son, but Joseph roughly pushed me away. That made Joey cry even harder. He held his tiny hands stretched out for me, but his father didn't let go of him.

Joseph tried to soothe his little son, tried to calm him down, but nothing worked. Then he started to explain to him what had just happened. "You know, Joey, Mommy is stupid sometimes and Daddy must help her. She has to listen to Daddy, because Daddy is the smartest. And you, Joey, you also have to learn that Daddy is the boss here, and everybody must listen to and obey Daddy." Then he turned to me. "Go get some rest and be careful. Don't overtax yourself." And he started to laugh. Ever so pityingly, he laughed at me. I felt like I must have lost my mind. I didn't even try to understand what was going on.

I couldn't look at him. My focus was on little Joey. I had never seen him that scared. I wanted to help him, to comfort him, but wasn't able to until Joseph let him go. When he was finally free, he ran to me at once. His loving arms were just as comforting to me as mine to him.

After this incident I kept myself as far away from Joseph as was possible in my limited world. He was either extremely strong or his rage had given him extraordinary power. Only two vicious slaps had knocked me down and I didn't want to experience that again. I tried to behave as ordered, entirely ignoring my needs and my personality, hoping that this would be enough to keep us safe.

Fear became my everyday partner. I woke up with fear, I went to bed with fear; my whole being was fear. I couldn't even imagine my life without fear anymore. I really was sleeping with the enemy...

Close to my due date, which was at the beginning of November, he attacked me again. First, he threw a one-and-a-half-litre bottle full of water at me, but missed. Since he'd failed to hit me with the bottle, he charged at me like a savage beast. I knew I had nowhere to hide and no way to avoid him, and running around in the apartment wasn't an option either because my condition slowed me down considerably.

When he approached me I was already covering my head with one hand while with the other one I pushed Joey behind me. But this time instead of hitting me he grabbed my wrist and tightened his grip until I felt my circulation cut off. My fingers were tingling and I had the sensation that he was about to snap my bones. My arm looked like a child's in his large hand. I tried to get free of him, but he just laughed.

He didn't need much physical effort to immobilize me.

I didn't want to yell in my pain because I didn't want to scare my little boy, but when he tightened his grip even more he caused me such pain that I cried out. After what seemed to be an endless time, he finally released my arm. I lifted Joey up and held him as close as my belly would allow. He clung to me, trembling. Or perhaps I was trembling. All I knew was that I had to protect him, to keep him safe. I didn't want his father laying one finger on him.

I was circling the sofa and the coffee table like a caged animal, trying to block Joseph's way to us. He seemed to enjoy this situation very much as he playfully chased us around. He was laughing, loving every moment of our terror. Then when he had had enough fun, he simply got to me and grabbed Joey, forcing him to let go of me. He literally pulled him out of my arms. As he did, I could already see the ugly bruises around my wrist. "Be careful," he said, "don't lift Joey, to avoid any possible consequences." I felt beaten and I felt like an idiot, because he unmistakably treated me like one.

He tried to calm Joey again and wouldn't leave until his son's breathing normalized and his shaking subsided a bit. Then he left ever so contentedly, successful once again at defeating me.

If there was any fallout for my baby due to Joseph's brutality, I wasn't aware of it. But for some reason my second baby had no intention of leaving his warm safety. (He was smarter than that.) I was already past my due date but there were no signs of labour. My doctor told me to watch my baby's movements very closely and if he stopped moving, I had to rush to the hospital at that instant.

I also had to be at the hospital every second day to check his heartbeat. During the process the nurse had to reposition the foetal heart sensor several times because my baby constantly changed his position. The nurse was rather amused as she said, "I can't believe how lively your baby is. I've worked here for twenty-three years but I've never met with such activity past the due date. He doesn't even have enough room." Yes, that was true. He kept kicking, pushing, and punching me, making me see stars. His favourite target was my left ribs, yet I was thankful for this baby's liveliness.

Everything went fine, but after two weeks and rearranging two eight-foot-high wardrobes, I was ordered to the hospital by my doctor. "We can't wait any longer. We have to induce labour whether he wants to come out or not." Then he explained the process that was awaiting me. I still wasn't sure what he meant by "induce labour", but I learned soon enough.

CHAPTER 36

JOSEPH TOOK ME TO THE hospital on November fifteenth at 8:15 a.m. and left me there. Since we didn't know when my baby was to arrive, he didn't want to waste his time. My doctor promised to call him once the baby was born.

I wanted my father to be there for us, but Joseph wouldn't allow him to get away from his work. I was left alone and felt quite terrified. No wonder. A few minutes after my arrival, the most excruciating experience began: they induced labour.

The doctors manually made me ready to give birth, which wasn't what I had expected. The pain was so intense that I felt like I was going to be ripped apart. They had to break the membranes so the water could flow away. In that instant, labour pains started. So now I was engulfed in two different pains, as they came back to check me every ten minutes until they were sure I was ready. I had to clench my teeth not to cry out but inside I was screaming. After an agonizing couple of hours, I was done and then we were waiting for Nature to take over.

I was lying on my back and the pains came regularly, so much so that after a while I was unable to move my limbs. I couldn't feel my hands and thought there was something very wrong. I told the first staff person who walked by. She checked me and said, "There's nothing wrong with you. You're just too tense." Or as I would have said, I was paralysed by the pain. It took me some time to recall the labour of my first son, when the only position I could tolerate was to lie on my side. So I gathered all my strength to change position and felt better at once.

I was staring at the clock on the wall now, while the other women behind me were screaming and cursing. It was a total madhouse. One of the women was walking around and around with her IV pole, against the doctor's instructions, and of course she couldn't keep her mouth shut. She drove the whole staff crazy but made me chuckle. When I turned on my other side she was standing right beside me, looking down at me, and asking, "How come you're not screaming? Doesn't it hurt?" I had to suck in my breath before I could answer her. "Of course it hurts. But if I scream, it still hurts." To this, she said nothing, just walked away, cursing incessantly.

She was such a miserably funny creature but I envied her, because in the waiting room she had her whole family anticipating her baby's arrival. At least ten people! And I had no one there. No one was waiting for my baby.

At that moment the emotional pain was more unbearable than the physical. I wanted to cry but my baby swiftly grabbed my attention; he was ready to come out and see me. I could feel his head. It was my turn to scream now: "The baby is coming!" Only my doctor was missing.

The nurses were shouting after him, while somehow I found the strength to worry about his absence. Then, out of nowhere, he was right at my side and my second son was born within minutes. But he didn't cry. I couldn't take the creepy silence. "Why isn't he crying?" My doctor just laughed quietly. "He will." And he did—loudly and strongly.

When the nurse handed him to me he was wearing a gauze toque because he had long dark hair. He was so cute, looking like a tiny imp in that hat, that I had to laugh. He was 8.8 pounds and there were no complications, and this time no stitches.

Dr. Lane was the very first person to congratulate me. He held my hand, kissed my cheeks and I was ready to melt away. I assumed that was how it happened in a normal family. He gave me some special moments of his time, and the kind attention that was supposed to come from Joseph but never did. He was obviously happy for me and my new son. I felt so grateful to him that my heart was overflowing with love, just as it had when Joey was born. His affection touched my heart in a way that it had never been touched before.

But there was an obligation to fulfill: he had to call the happy father. I didn't want him to, didn't want to break that special moment we shared. When he left, a wave of ice-cold air hit me and I began to shiver, which I found rather strange because there had been no change in the room temperature. The coldness that surrounded us now was the first sign of Joseph's imminent arrival; he was at our bedside far too soon.

I wasn't happy to see him, not at all. He had brought a camera and asked my doctor to take some pictures of us. He hardly noticed little Alex, as he was too busy posing himself. After a couple of minutes, he was gone and my father came in. Now I was happy. He was all smiles, with tears in his eyes. His joy meant a lot to me. He was in awe of my baby, and I could see that he loved him the instant he looked at him. But he couldn't stay long. They were both gone just as quickly as they had arrived. When we were alone again, my doctor made a shocking statement: "You and Joseph looked like total strangers." It was *that* obvious.

At this hospital the babies stayed with their mothers and we had to look after them from the very first minute. This also meant that we had to do our best to start nursing. And this time there was no separate room for me, no private bathroom, just a bed. I shared the room with two other moms, which I didn't mind a bit, although I was happy to get the bed next to the window.

I was totally absorbed in my baby. If there was nothing I needed to do, I just watched him tirelessly. But unfortunately, my fear overshadowed my joy. It always crept in. I knew Joseph would come and visit us again soon and I dreaded that moment.

Once again, he came in on the second day, bringing in Monica. He also surprised me with a beautiful bouquet of flowers! He had never bought me flowers before and I wasn't sure why he had done so now, but he brought them to the wrong place at the wrong time. My bouquet ended up decorating the nurses' station because it posed an allergy risk. It was hard to believe that he wasn't aware of that regulation.

This visit happened exactly the same way as it had when Joey was born. Monica showed no interest at all in my new baby, but I didn't take it personally now. I had learned that much in the past five years. I could also sense the thick tension between daughter and father. The only thing I wanted to do at that moment was stay away from them, before the pressure blew up.

They stayed for such a long time, though, that I had to change Alex and treat his bellybutton. The visitors had to stay behind the half-closed door, but could watch everything through a small window. That was what Joseph did, watching my every movement with critical eyes.

While I was looking after Alex, he cried constantly. I was sure that he felt my nervousness but I couldn't help it. I tried desperately to soothe him because I knew that his cry riled Joseph. I wasn't even done with this thought and he was already yelling at me: "Don't make him cry! Just shut your mouth and do what you have to do. Hurry! Hurry! Why do you speak to him anyway?"

There were several people around us but that didn't stop him from shouting at me through the half-closed door. I was so humiliated and mortified. My hands started to shake even more and I felt the blood rush to my head. I said nothing to Joseph until I was properly done with little Alex, then lifted him up, slowly walked to the door, looked into Joseph's cold eyes, and in a restrained voice said to him, "You know what? Since you're such an expert on babies, come and show me how to do it." His face got redder with every word I spat at him. "Enough of your insolence!" he barked at me, then turned around sharply and left.

After their departure I was in tears. Looking at my baby's innocent face made me cry even more. I felt beaten. *Oh my God, what will happen when we get home? What kind of life is waiting for us?* My roommates, who had witnessed everything, were very supportive, trying to comfort me, but their kind words just saddened me even more. Once again, it was a reminder of what I was missing from my life, and I didn't even dare to make a mental list of my yearnings. And nothing was better the next day when he brought my mother in.

CHAPTER 37

I WAS HAPPY TO SEE my mom and I hoped that we could have some pleasant time together. It delighted me that even though she wasn't happy about my second pregnancy, Alex stole her heart instantly. So I thought that was a good start for a pleasant conversation and then I asked her about my little Joey.

While I was in the hospital, Joey was in my parents' care and I missed him terribly. I was eager to know everything about him, but my mother seemed very uncomfortable and hardly said anything. I tried to get her into a little chit-chat, but since I had to drag each word out of her, I soon gave up trying. I was very disappointed, because I learned almost nothing about my little son. She remained so tense throughout the visit that I could hardly wait for them to leave.

And the fact that I ate very little during those four days I spent in the hospital didn't make my situation any easier. It was a long weekend. The hospital's store was closed but I didn't have money anyway, so that didn't even matter. And I wouldn't have left Alex alone either.

My roommates were lavished with delicious fruits and foods by their loved ones, but I only received mandarins and about ten litres of iced tea, which made me even hungrier. I had to rely on the hospital's menu, but the portions they supplied weren't nearly enough to silence my hunger.

I was the only one who finished the meals given to us, and I ate the last crumb but forced myself not to lick the plate. I was so grateful and happy for those few bites that the workers were astonished when I wholeheartedly thanked them. But it wasn't enough. I was so hungry that my rumbling stomach was audible. And somehow I had to feed my newborn baby.

One of the girls received so much food that she wasn't able to eat it all. Since it was obvious that I was hungry she kindly offered me what she had. I was so ashamed of the situation but I couldn't resist, and I thanked her with each bite I took. Finally, I became so annoying to her that she laughingly snapped at me, "Just be quiet and eat everything you want."

I sat in the dark corner, eating her food and thinking of my millionaire common-law, who only wanted to hurt me, if not annihilate me, and didn't bring me so much as a crumb of bread. I silently started to cry again, swallowing my tears along with my friend's food.

I seemed to spend my hours just looking after my newborn baby and expressing my gratitude. So it was a rather shocking thing when the mother next to me flipped out.

She had a beautiful, healthy little boy with a touch of blond hair. He was perfect in every aspect, but his mother refused to nurse him. She kept complaining that she had no milk or that her baby was rejecting her.

Within a short time her son stopped crying, turned bright yellow, and became seriously dehydrated. Still, she didn't care about her child, but rather was eyeing mine. "He is so beautiful," she said. "I want a baby like him." My inner alarm went off at once. She wasn't just a weirdo anymore, she was creepy. I tried not to show my panic as I told her, "Look at your son! He's perfect. He's beautiful and healthy. And he needs you. He needs you to live." My friend joined in, trying to reassure her that everything was all right and that her son loved her very much. We tried to save that little child.

Unfortunately, whatever we said to her was useless. She really spooked me and my paranoia kicked in. I didn't want to leave my son without supervision, because I was terrified at the thought that my baby would just mysteriously disappear or would end up with the wrong mother.

Finally the hospital interfered, took her baby away, called her family in, then brought the baby back to her and with the family's support tried to make her responsible.

Seeing a newborn nearly die because of his mother's stupidity was a very depressing and horrifying experience. But although this event weighed heavily on my mind, I had my own problems. My fear of going home was increasing with every ticking second. I didn't know how I would manage the life that was awaiting us.

When the time came, I felt so nervous that I was shaking. In the car Joseph kept picking on me all the way. Four days was apparently far too long for him to go without his favourite target.

We had a short argument about Alex's name. I had chosen it because it had significance for me, but Joseph was of course against it. To finish the disagreement, I said, "Joey got your name, so it's my turn now." In any event, we had a more serious subject to discuss.

Since we weren't married, I thought it was important for the children's sake that the father gave the children his surname. When Joey was born he did the right thing without any reluctance, but in Alex's case he was hesitant. When we arrived home I still wasn't sure whether Joseph was willing, but I was too hungry and had no strength to try to persuade him any further.

My mother was in our apartment looking after Joey. "I have to eat!" I said after I greeted them quickly. She made me five scrambled eggs and they just laughed as I wolfed down everything that was prepared for me. I felt quite hurt and very disappointed in them for not bringing me any food for four days, but said nothing, neither reproaches nor complaints for letting me starve while I had the responsibility to produce milk for my newborn. At least my mother should've known better. So I just thanked her for the food and for looking after my little Joey.

Two weeks after Alex was born, Joseph was willing to go to the registry offices to sign the papers, but he had one condition. "I'll sign the papers but you have to promise that you won't use that against me." I was stunned. "Why would I use it against you?" I asked him. "The only reason I want this is that Alex won't be an illegitimate child. You're doing this for him."

Then it was Christmas again. This was my sixth holiday with Joseph but it didn't get any more pleasant. I always hoped that he would respect the traditions and join in, or at least stop hurting me during those special days.

For now there I was with two little children, and I wanted to create one of the most beautiful trees I had ever decorated. I also strung garlands across the ceiling to make the room more colourful. I was proud of my work and even felt happy.

While I was decorating I imagined us, Joseph and me, beautifying our home together. In my mind that was what a real family did. And since I was yearning to have a peaceful Christmas, a real family time, I did my best to be acceptable to him, even though I felt as if I was on the edge of a cliff all the time. Unfortunately, a real family Christmas was just another unreachable dream for me. The reality remained cold and harsh.

We never decorated a Christmas tree together. He never joined me; he never even shared the Christmas spirit. Although it hurt me to see him so insensitive, I had to accept the fact that he would remain as he had been. But, who knew why, I really wanted to bring him into our family. I thought that through my joy, he would be at least a little bit moved. Instead, he made me cry again.

First, he started to insult my mother. He now blamed every fight that erupted between us on her. "Your mother is evil," he said. "It's her fault that our relationship is ruined, because she's brainwashing you. She's turned you against me."

But strangely, although he labelled my mother as "evil", he invited my parents for dinner. (My brother was never there. He was always treated as an outcast.) He invited Monica as well but she stayed away, always having some excuse to avoid family gatherings. I wished to do the same thing, because when we were all together I could cut the tension with a knife.

Still, I was glad that my parents came up to see us, since it was ever so rare. Unfortunately, they were very uncomfortable and that stretched my nerves to their breaking point. Everything seemed so forced, so fake, even our smiles.

I wasn't able to enjoy our togetherness at all. Despite all the jokes flying around, the mood remained tense, and by the end of our dinner I was emotionally exhausted. My hands were shaking uncontrollably. When we cleared the table I nearly dropped the larger soup bowl, which I emptied into the small one. When my mother noticed that, she couldn't resist telling me, "It would have been more logical to empty the small bowl into the large one." Her tone and the laughter around me made me feel like a total fool; although my action had been intentional, I felt very bad about my mother's unexpected remark, and could only mumble an answer, "I just wanted to save some space in the refrigerator."

That was one of the most miserable Christmas evenings of my life. Even though I put every effort into making it beautiful, I was unspeakably relieved when the so-called party finally broke up.

1996

Am I still alive?

CHAPTER 38

ANOTHER YEAR HAD ARRIVED. I had already stopped seeking any hope or way out of the hell we lived in. After five long years I was about to give up on everything. I had no power over Joseph's acts. I could only pray that we would be safe, and that I could protect my children if that was necessary.

In the middle of January he declared that my parents were thieves and removed them from their jobs, although strangely they could remain in the building. He also forbade us to have any contact with them. I wasn't even allowed to *speak* to my own parents! "Just walk by them when you accidentally run into them," he said. So I couldn't even greet them? But I simply wasn't able to do that, even if it meant risking my well-being.

And now of course, I had to explain this madness to Joey. I certainly didn't hesitate to tell the truth, as I had no intention of defending such insanity. But what I told him didn't make any more sense to him than it did to me; he just wanted to be with his grandparents and since I couldn't let him go, I became the bad guy in his eyes.

The humiliation was unbearable for my parents. Needless to say, the whole factory ground was chewing over this latest scandal. However my parents acted toward me, I always admitted that they were some of the most conscientious, honest, hardworking people Joseph could ever have employed, yet he treated them like garbage, neither respecting nor appreciating them. Somehow, he always hurt most those people who absolutely didn't deserve it.

My parents were devastated but Joseph's unfair behaviour toward them made all of us angry. Just a year ago he had taken us to Canada, covered all the expenses, and now this. He had held the ladder for my parents so they could climb up, and they did climb higher and higher. But now he had violently pulled it out from under them and let them fall down. And that was an entirely new experience for them. They had never been accused and humiliated like this in their entire lives.

Keeping my distance from them was impossible. Besides, Joey loved them and wanted to be with them. So when we met, yes, I stopped to exchange a few words with them. But my father was always very worried and sent us away. Although our conversations lasted for maybe thirty seconds, the spies were onto us. Whenever I dared to speak to my parents, I was reported instantly to Joseph. He always knew what I did, where I was, and to whom I spoke. Sometimes he even knew what I said.

And he remained indifferent to my needs, even after two boys. He had his dream, twice over. Still, he just did what he wanted, like organizing big family-employee gatherings in our apartment without discussing this with me first, and then expecting me to be the hostess, which I could only refuse. Regardless, on one occasion, only a couple of months after Alex was born, he invited about fifteen people plus Monica, and fortunately she was an excellent hostess.

During the party I simply withdrew with my children into the bedroom; fifteen people were way too many for me. But once again, my behaviour wasn't acceptable to Joseph, since I always had to behave in a certain way that pleased him and if I didn't, I was punished. (That reminded me of my childhood.) In this case, he berated me in front of all those people for not being the perfect hostess, serving his people, and smiling endlessly like a doll.

He still spoke to me as if I was a mentally challenged person. He dragged each word out in a tone that most people use with a two-year-old, even when he called me "sweetheart". This word became more bittersweet than ever. Every time I heard it, I felt almost sick to my stomach. I really didn't know how anybody could put so much contempt into such a beautiful expression. To him it just meant "possession".

My happiness was totally limited to my children—they were the sunshine of my life, the reason to live. They gave me pleasure and helped me to keep going. Although they deserved so much better, all I could do was keep a healthy balance between them so neither would feel left out.

Joey was happy and excited about the new baby, while his father almost never paid any attention to Alex, like he didn't even exist. But it was probably better this way, because I already knew that his "love" was destructive. Thus, I always thought that Alex was luckier. Unfortunately, though, he was now stuck right in the middle as well when his father erupted.

Joseph could lose his temper within seconds, without any warning signs, so most of the time I was totally unprepared to shield myself from him. He also turned into a sexually aggressive monster and started molesting me. It never mattered to him whether I wanted to be touched or not. It wasn't about me: it was always about *him* and what *he* wanted. I was his; therefore he could do to me and with me whatever he wanted. He had a right to, as he said. And he enforced his rights more and more often.

He already took so much from me, of me, and still he wanted more; he now wanted to deprive me of my thoughts as well. "I always want to know everything about you. What you like, how you feel, your concerns and your wishes. I want to know your thoughts. You have to share them with me all the time for the peace of the family. If you're mine, everything is mine of what you have, even your thoughts." It felt like I couldn't even take a breath without his knowledge, or rather permission. But why was I surprised? After all, slaves don't even possess their own right to consent.

Even then, I wasn't about to give up my only escape, my only sanctuary, no matter what he wanted or demanded. My thoughts were mine, only mine! I had no intention of sharing the secrets of my mind with him, because I was dreaming about a happy family life, a life that was full of love, appreciation, respect, and safety. And I certainly didn't want to tell him that he wasn't in it.

I was filled with dread every single morning, because spending another day with him was sheer terror. The thought of having to face him again made me sick. My stomach hurt a lot now, and my hands shook on a regular basis. Yet there was nothing I could do except bury myself in looking after my children and the household chores. I considered it a pure miracle when we had a peaceful day, when he neither bullied nor attacked me.

He also kept us locked away from the entire world. We lived our lives among those imprisoning four walls, so I kept the windows open just to have a sense of freedom. It was a big mistake. When Joseph found them open, he had a fit. "You can't open the windows!"

"We need some air," I said to him.

"This apartment is large enough to have enough air," he retorted. "You are not allowed to open the windows!"

And then there was the refrigerator. I couldn't even open the fridge without him yelling at me, "You can only keep the refrigerator open for three seconds. Just get what you want and close the door. You don't have to wander around in it."

Well, I opened the windows anyway, but just a bit so he wouldn't notice when he looked up at the building or was inside. And I asked him to lock the door when he left because I wanted to hear him when he turned the key in the lock, so I could brace myself before he stood face to face with me.

He also wanted to initiate family meetings, which mostly meant listening to his lectures. A few times I was educated about how to be thrifty with paper napkins. "You can use a napkin in three different ways," he said. "First, you wipe your mouth with it, and then blow your nose in it and finally you wipe your butt with it. See how smart that is?"

Very! I could only hope that he was trying to be funny, although I wasn't laughing. At the same time, I never knew what motivated him when he went to the open market and bought so much fruit for the four of us that it could have been enough for an army. It was simply impossible to eat it all before some spoiled. And that of course was my fault as well.

CHAPTER 39

JOSEPH'S DEPARTURE WAS EVEN MORE refreshing than before. His absence was like a breath of crystal clear air to me. It was literally reviving as I felt the burden lifting. At these times I had a chance to be me. I was free to talk and laugh with people around us. I didn't have to sneak around, I could do what *I* wanted and needed to do. My needs had been ignored for so long and so many times, that when I had a chance I went after what I was yearning for—I just hoped that I gave enough entertainment to the spies…

Before he flew away, he usually left us some money. Sometimes, when I was good enough in his eyes, he could be very generous. With that and my maternity allowance, I felt like a queen. I had a taxi driver who became a friend, and who I called regularly when I could afford his services.

Seeing him was uplifting after Joseph's stone cold face. He was always smiling and so understanding about my situation. He took me to my medical appointments and helped with the shopping; he was patient and faithful, a huge help and a true gentleman. (Thank you.)

When I went out I always visited my favourite boutique, book shop, and beauty shop. I also made friends with their owners. They were such wonderful people. My closest friend was the boutique owner. She was a beautiful and successful girl, and was only a few years older than I.

I was always happy to see her and the others, even though these times just increased my sense of not being "normal" and free. There was so much out there to do and to enjoy, and there was so much being taken away from me that it hurt, a lot. My heart always sank when I saw how many things were missing from my life, how many things I could have done. But in spite of this, I treasured these times because it was extremely rare for me to have healthy relationships. And when I had some extra money I shopped around, bought some clothes from my friend, so at least my wardrobe was happy about that. And when I didn't have anything to spend, we just chatted.

When I was financially punished, Monica was my source of help. At such times, Joseph either left us with a very small amount of money and I ran out of it before his return, or he simply didn't leave a penny behind. He did this more and more often now, so Monica was my only hope of getting some money to buy groceries. She helped us out several times but I always felt so ashamed when I was forced to beg for money.

There were still times when she took me on a shopping spree but as always, I was never able to keep up with her spending. Usually the whole amount that I had would have been enough for her to buy a pair of panties. So, as in 1990, I just followed her around, and was in total awe of all the beautiful and fashionable stuff she bought. As a young woman, I loved beautiful things as well. But I couldn't complain, could I? I had what I had.

When he was back everything continued as if he had never left. After all these years, things had started to become painfully familiar. I already knew that his brutality was deliberate, which also meant that he never wanted peace in the family. He couldn't stand me so much so, that he would do anything to jeopardize my life. Since my being wasn't important to him, he simply made my existence worthless.

And now he started to nag me about Canada again. He wanted to leave in April and stay there for up to six months. That was far too much for me; I couldn't even utter the words. I didn't want to go there ever again, and I told him that, but he pressured me daily, and I refused his idea just as often.

It didn't count that I technically lived with him; I was a single mother, on my own when it came to the children or anything else. I explained my concerns to him and told him how I felt—after all, he had asked for it—and I even begged him not to take us out of our homeland. I couldn't imagine how I would look after the children in a foreign country because I knew there was not a chance of his being helpful to me, and that made me very afraid of the unknown.

Fear. I had so much fear bottled up in me that it clouded my mind. And the time was ticking. The closer we got to our departure, the more desperate I became. There was no way he could move me an inch toward Canada, so he came up with a new idea. "I'll give your parents' jobs back if you come along with me."

That sounded very promising, but my experiences with him didn't let me fall for it. I was well aware that he just used us against each other to get what *he* wanted to achieve. And I was really tired of his making me responsible for my parents. I had already ignored my needs several times for my parents' sake, and I just couldn't do it again. I was a parent myself now, and my children came before anybody else. My peace of mind was crucial for my children's well-being.

Since his tactic failed, he had to come up with something else to control the situation. "I already purchased the tickets, so get ready for the departure." Well, that wasn't enough to make me budge; plus, his timing didn't fit into Alex's immunization schedule.

To me it was very important that my children were looked after properly, the best way I possibly could, and I explained this to him because he seemed not to comprehend the seriousness of it. "This vaccine is very important to Alex. It could save his life," I told him. His response shocked me. "Your concerns are simply stupidity. I know that a vaccination is not necessary at all. If I say he doesn't need it, then he doesn't need it."

But I thought differently. I actually cared. Besides, the vaccination was the only thing that could buy me some time. Since Joseph didn't listen to me, I explained the situation to our paediatrician and asked for his help in enlightening Joseph about the importance of the immunization.

I felt quite ashamed when he started to argue with the head physician. Luckily, our doctor didn't let Joseph get to him. He stood his ground firmly, and was able to convince him that it really wasn't the right time for Alex to fly. But of course, he wanted to know when we could leave, so they agreed that the end of May was a good time for our departure.

When the doctor left, Joseph was fuming. "This doctor is stupid. He doesn't even know what he's talking about." His reaction didn't surprise me anymore. That wasn't the first time he was smarter than a doctor. Anyway, the time was set, he put my parents back to work, and everybody was happy—except me.

For some reason, I was so fearful of going to Canada that it almost seemed irrational. And this time he wanted to prepare for us to live there. All I wanted to do was find a way to escape my forced obligations, but my options were less than zero. I felt trapped once again. And although my parents got their jobs back, I didn't get my parents back. Joseph was still insistent on keeping us far away from them.

One weekend, though, when I took my children out to the factory ground, we ran into them. It was Sunday so the stores were closed but they were working. They were walking back to the office building when we met and Joey asked me, then begged me to let him go upstairs with them. I knew that if I let him go, I would have to suffer the consequences, but I couldn't say no. After all, he was only an innocent child who shouldn't suffer from his father's senseless rules. Brushing aside my fears and against Joseph's command, I allowed Joey to go visit with his grandparents.

While Joey was at my parents', I walked with Alex until he fell asleep in his stroller, and then sat down on the bench that I had positioned a while ago; we were well out of sight and it was quite peaceful. As I sat there I tried to read but wasn't able to focus. I knew that I had disobeyed Joseph, had gone against his orders and broken his rules. Thus, I was now fearfully looking around because I also knew that within minutes Joseph would come to check on us.

Chapter 40

I WAS RIGHT. WHEN I saw him I froze in my seat but was still able to slowly hide my book. When he approached us his first question was, "Where is Joey?" Then he sat beside me to my left. "With his grandparents," I said as confidently as I could, but my insides were trembling.

"I told you not to let him have any contact with them." With every word that came out of his mouth I felt my blood rushing to my head. When I responded to him, I spoke very quietly so as not to disturb Alex's sleep, but I wasn't able to conceal my anger and hurt. "You can't forbid him to see his grandparents! He loves them and they love him. This is the right way to be." I might have sounded very confident, but I didn't feel that way and his response terrified me: "Once we are in Canada your parents won't be there, just you and me. They won't be able to interfere in our lives and you won't be able to run to them. That's just what you need."

Yes, I was aware of that very much, and that scared me the most: being with him, alone in a foreign country. I knew that responding to him wasn't the best idea, but my desperation broke free. "I told you already that I don't want to go anywhere with you, not even to the next corner."

"Of course you'll come," he said. "You have no choice! Your obligation is to follow me! Don't forget that you belong to me!" The more he pushed me, the more I protested. I just couldn't help it.

I could see that he was getting angrier and I knew he could smell my fear, like a predator. Then in a flash he grabbed my right arm, held me down so tightly I couldn't move, and started to pound on the nape of my neck. As I tried to twist out of his way, I saw his clenched fist. He was beating me with his forearm!

With every strike I literally felt my brain shaking and I was sure that my head was about to break off my neck. I didn't want to scream, because I didn't want to alarm my sleeping baby, so I clenched my teeth to strangle my shriek. Then the world slowly started to disappear. Only the excruciating pain and his strikes existed. I made a weak attempt to break free, but he held me in a steel grip. *He wants to kill me! He wants to kill me! My children! What will happen to them?*

I was sure that I wouldn't be able to survive such brutality. I had never experienced such power. I couldn't bear the pain any longer. His arm felt like a huge, heavy hammer on my neck. My terrified shriek broke free and Alex woke up, crying. But that didn't stop Joseph. He kept beating me. Alex's cry gave me the power to yell out to him, "You stupid maniac! Alex is crying. Don't you hear him? He needs me!" It felt like an eternity before he released me.

When I stood up my body shook uncontrollably but I felt strangely calm. I picked Alex up and held him very close to me. "I'm here, my heart, I'm here," I whispered to him. I felt myself to be moving in slow motion as I held Alex in my left arm, got my book, grabbed the stroller with my right hand and slowly walked to the building. I didn't look at Joseph, who remained seated.

As we walked away from him an unusual but powerful sense of peace surrounded us and I was more floating than walking those hundred metres to the building. Everything was blurry around us except our immediate surroundings, which were perfectly clear. Such stillness! My head was pounding and I had to focus on not dropping my baby, but I was calm, so deeply calm. Actually, I felt more than calm; I was in a trancelike state of inner peace.

When the doorman saw us, he jumped out of his seat and opened the door. I was even able to send a faint smile to him and thank him for his kindness, but found it weird that he didn't notice anything unusual about me. I got into the elevator and went upstairs to the apartment. There, I thanked God profusely that Joey had not witnessed what had just happened.

I was changing Alex when Joseph walked in. I knew that he would follow us in a few minutes because he wanted to know where I was going. I thought of going to my parents, but I also realized that that would be the worst possible idea. And it also wasn't safe for me, not after what had happened, because I was certain now that Joseph was capable of killing me.

He was in a surprisingly good mood, cheerful, smiling ear to ear, even giggling. He was talking to me about something. I heard his voice but had not the slightest idea what he was saying. My peace faded away, and by now I felt utterly empty. I wasn't angry or scared anymore; I didn't feel hatred or sadness, only emptiness. Something had shattered in me; something in me had died, again.

I was dizzy and had a headache for about a week. I could feel that my neck was swollen and very painful. I knew I needed a doctor but I didn't dare to ask for help. Since the phone was tapped, Joseph would have known that I made the call and I was certain that he would finish what he'd started. When he went into his insane rages, his brutality was endless and his power beyond human. I simply couldn't risk experiencing such savagery again.

The only person I could ask to take a look was Joanne. I told her what had happened. When I showed her the back of my neck, I heard her gasp. "Oh my God!" she whispered. "Your neck is black." She was more terrified than I was, but she comforted me, which meant a lot.

I thought that my father should know about the incident and I was hoping so much to find some understanding from him. He didn't say much, though, just heaved sighs and looked at me ever so pityingly. I had to admit that I was expecting more compassion than this. Actually, I kept dreaming of and waiting for the day when my father would stand up for me and confront Joseph, saying something like, "That's enough, Joseph! I won't allow you to torture my daughter and my grandchildren any longer!" But that never happened. He never even tried to protect or help us. It seemed their own comfort and sense of security was always much more important than we were.

I was certain that my life was in danger and possibly my children's as well, but my father didn't say anything about that, only, "Give Joseph another chance and go to Canada with him; just one more time." I wasn't sure I had heard him correctly, or maybe he hadn't heard me. He was my father, yet it seemed that he didn't care. I truly believed that the incident would wake him up. I never even imagined that he would send me away with a man who had come pretty close to killing me. My disappointment in my father was physically painful.

If nobody else, at least I had Joanne as a friend. I could always count on her. She was a great help all the time, when it came to our isolation. And we kept our "tradition" that on nearly every occasion when Joseph wasn't around, she was with us. She cooked, cleaned, went shopping for us, and looked after the children so I could break free for a little while. And she was great company. Her devotion, though, made me rather uncomfortable, because I wasn't used to being served, wasn't at all used to such extensive kindness. I always felt that I owed her. So, I tried to help her in every way I could. Joseph still barely paid her and I didn't even know whether she ever got a raise, so I wanted to compensate her for everything.

I shared with her what we had, gave her things we didn't use anymore but which were still in good condition. I asked her many times just to sit down and take a break, while I served her a coffee or a tea. Countless times I invited her for lunch. It made me happy to make her happy. After all these years, I believed that she deserved every good thing, and I was willing to give her anything I could.

She was the only person with whom I shared every detail of my life. Besides seeing my bruises, she also witnessed the verbal and emotional terrors Joseph put me through, and she personally experienced his abuse as well. So she understood...

CHAPTER 41

THE END OF MAY QUICKLY approached and it was time to pack and go. It really moved me that Joanne was actually crying at our departure. I knew that the three of us were like a family to her, just as much as she was to us.

The trip lasted for about fifteen hours but felt twice as long. The problems started right at the beginning. Joseph gave Joey a camera bag to carry all the way. "Joey, this is your bag," he said. "You are responsible for it and you have to carry it!"

That was the last thing my three-and-a-half-year-old little boy wanted to do. And I couldn't blame him. The bag was rather heavy, even though empty, and Joseph literally forced it on him. Joey began complaining and then he started to cry. I couldn't bear his frustration, so I took the bag from him. I was already carrying Alex, a bag for him, plus pushing the stroller because he wouldn't have stayed in it. I also had to manage to hold Joey's hand because he refused to be with his father. And now the camera bag was on me as well.

Joseph's only help was to get angry. He was constantly bugging Joey about the bag and about staying with him. The fact that Joey wasn't allowed to say no either, just like me, made the whole situation unmanageable.

Every time I helped Joey, Joseph snatched the bag out of my hand and gave it back to him. That happened repeatedly until Joey was on the verge of throwing a tantrum. I couldn't stand the circus. "Why are you torturing that poor child?" I asked Joseph. "He doesn't want to carry that stupid bag, don't you see that? This trip is long and tiring enough the way it is. He doesn't need an extra weight on him." When he turned to face me he was ready to blow up. "Behave yourself," he hissed at me, "or you'll get one!" That stunned me. He actually threatened to hit me right there at the crowded airport. And perhaps he would have. I just didn't know what to expect anymore when it came to his rages.

On the airplane, he fell asleep just as we took off, while I was fully occupied with the children. When they finally fell asleep on me, I was stuck to my seat for at least six hours, while Joseph snored through the entire time.

The whole trip was a complete misery. When we arrived I could only drag myself: I was beyond exhaustion. And once again, the nine hours' time difference made everything even harder.

So here we were in Canada again, four of us now, but Joseph didn't have a proper car for us, just an old white GMC van with two seats. I had no intention of sitting in that van with my children. We were already at risk without this additional hazard.

When I told him that his van wasn't safe to transport the children, he just snorted at me. "If I say it's safe, then it's safe! I drive very safely. You won't find anybody else who can drive as well as I can. You're always safe with me." Yeah, he had already shown me how safe I was.

As I sat in that van, holding my children, my mortal fear for them rushed to the surface. Since Joey had nowhere to sit, Joseph put a folding chair between the two seats and ordered him to sit on that. Even a three-year-old knew that that wasn't safe, and Joey didn't want stay in the chair.

He had every reason to be afraid. His father drove like a madman. He went too fast on bumpy roads, up hills, down hills, and then he braked too roughly. We were bouncing up and down in our seats, and Joey's chair was sliding back and forth. Needless to say, he was terrified. The only way I could help him was to grip his hand, while I held Alex in my right arm.

When Joseph noticed that I was holding Joey's hand, he roughly pushed mine away. But Joey kept begging me, "Mommy, hold my hand!" To avoid Joseph's rage I whispered to Joey that I would support the chair with my leg instead, so that his father wouldn't see.

But Joey didn't feel any safer and his father just kept driving like a stunt driver. My leg wasn't enough to prevent the chair from moving so I instinctively grabbed Joey's hand. Joseph of course noticed it at once. "You are not allowed to touch him!" he yelled at me. "I know what I'm doing and I'll protect him." So he deliberately terrified us. I didn't answer, just prayed to God to protect us, or even to have the police catch us.

Then suddenly the chair folded under Joey and he ended up on the dashboard. The worry for my children drove me to the edge. Joey was trembling with fear while his father was laughing. In his opinion everything was all right but it was not for me or Joey, who wanted to sit beside me.

So now the three of us were crowded into one seat as I held Joey very close to make him feel as safe as possible. I also propped up my legs to keep us stable and continued searching for a patrol car.

After some time Joey calmed down in my arms but Joseph of course didn't let us remain sitting together. He violently pulled Joey back onto the chair and started to flail around, trying to hit me. I wasn't in control of my fear anymore. The way he drove and the way he acted was too much for my nerves, and I couldn't hold back my shock. "You are insane! You ARE insane!" I kept repeating this over and over like a mantra.

It was very hard to comprehend that something like this would happen to us. Who does such things? "Don't talk to me like this in front of the children!" he snapped at me. But he could tell me anything at that point. My head was buzzing and I just kept repeating that he was insane.

Although I was the one searching for the police, Joseph noticed them first. He knew better what to look for; every time he saw a patrol car he ordered me to hide the children until we passed them. So being caught by the police was hopeless. Such a shame, as I was sure they would have been fascinated by our sitting arrangement...

Chapter 42

In Hungary he never went fishing but here in Canada he took us out in a small motor boat, ordered both children into my care, and got busy with his fishing equipment. Joey didn't stay put for one second and Alex was just as restless. I was so afraid that Joey would fall out of the boat, which was rocking a little too much. Joseph, of course, had no patience for the children's liveliness. "Keep the children in line!" he yelled at me. "How?" I asked him. "Joey is only three and a half and Alex is seven months old. You can't expect them to sit tight while you're waiting for the fish to bite. Take us to the playground instead." And he granted my wish, for ten minutes anyway, after I spent a few very exhausting hours on that motor boat.

Business was always more important though, and here he used the apartment as his office so when he worked, we had to stay in the bedroom, be quiet, and not leave it until he was done. It was a rather annoying arrangement, and we couldn't take it for very long, so I asked his permission to leave the house while he was working. "Where would you go?" was his first question. "I saw a playground nearby. I thought I could take them there and you would be able to work peacefully." And he agreed.

Now that was rather interesting. In Hungary we were never allowed to go out alone, only with him. In Canada, though, we were quite free. And why was that? Probably because he knew I wasn't able to communicate and had nobody to run to.

But the situation was completely different when he wanted to go somewhere. He stood up and was ready to leave. He never helped me and never gave me time to prepare but was always very impatient while I dressed the children. He just stood at the door, barking out orders. My only hope was for some peace when he went back to Hungary.

Before the trip, Joseph had taken our passports, and now he locked them away. I had no idea where he hid our one and only identification documents, and when I asked him to give them back he said, "I'm not going to give them back to you. Since all three of you are my property, everything that is yours is mine, even your personal papers."

"And what will happen if I have to identify myself?" I asked, but he just laughed.

"Don't worry! That won't happen because nobody is interested in you." Thanks.

So when he went back to Hungary without us, I swept through the whole apartment but was unable to find our documents. Instead, I found a bunch of porn magazines.

And the well-deserved peace never arrived. While he was away, I got sick. Then bugs, worms, and moths infested the kitchen. Wherever I reached, something crawled out. He never cleaned when he was here and now I had to spend our grocery allowance on insecticides. I was sick to my stomach just being here. And when Joseph came back, for some reason he was madder than ever. He kept provoking and pushing me, picking on me about everything. He even criticized the way I completed the household chores, which he hadn't done before.

One day I was cleaning the dining table, trying to make the black lacquer surface evenly shiny. I was fully absorbed in my work when out of the blue he started to yell. At first, I didn't even know who he was yelling at or what he was talking about. There were no signs of any problems. We had had a rather peaceful lunchtime, so I didn't understand what had happened to drive him to the edge. I looked at him with questioning eyes. "Don't smudge the table with that sponge! Use the washcloth instead!" "I like to use the sponge," I said to him but he was already all worked up. "Do what I said!" he shouted.

That was just ridiculous and more than enough. I smashed the sponge on the table and said to him, "I do it as I do it. The point is to get the table clean." I didn't see it coming. He hit me hard right across my face. I was stunned by the sudden attack. I wasn't sure yet whether there would be a continuation but I wasn't about to just stand there and let him beat me until my last breath. I was ready to fight back to protect myself and my children.

Then he hit me again and we began to grapple. He grabbed me suddenly and roughly pushed me backward. Luckily, I fell onto a loveseat. At the same time out of the corner of my eye I could see my children. Joey sat on the other couch, frozen, while Alex was crawling toward me. Joseph gave me no chance to say or do anything for them, because the next instant he grabbed my legs and pulled me off the couch onto the ceramic floor. I bumped onto my protruding spine and an excruciating pain racked my whole being.

I remained on the floor, waiting for the pain to subside. Before I could get up Joseph started to hit my head but I wasn't able to protect myself because Alex was at my side, trying to slip into my arms. Then he was on me but his father just kept striking my head, shouting endlessly. Once again, I was screaming only in my mind, just as I had a few weeks earlier, *My children! My children!* They were there, witnessing the whole terror. They weren't safe. *I had to protect them.*

I made some weak attempts to stand up because Alex was in my arms, but Joseph didn't let me. I could do nothing for Joey. To shield Alex, I turned to my right side, hoping that that was enough to keep him safe from his father's incessant strikes.

Because I had shifted my position, I now had my back toward him, which gave him free access to my neck. He just kept beating me. He knew I had Alex in my arms or more likely under me, but that didn't bother him at all.

In the middle of the blows, I could hear Joey crying. The fact that the father of my children was terrorizing them again sent me into my own fury. Using my legs, I changed position on the floor and kicked him with all my might. He fell against the terrace door. Although I surprised him, I had no time to stand up or even to crawl away. He came back at me in a flash, beating my head again with more force than before. I fought desperately, but then I lost track of time.

The next thing I knew, he was pressing my head to the floor with both of his hands. I couldn't move my head an inch. I was still holding Alex as I struggled under Joseph's weight. I felt that my head was about to be crushed. Then I heard Joey's horrified scream, "Mommy! Mommy!" I couldn't even look at him because I couldn't turn my head, but I could see Joseph's face. He was now beaming above me with the expansive satisfaction of a man who had just achieved a total victory. Yes, he had won again.

I stopped struggling under the pressure he put on my head, realizing that all my efforts were totally useless and if I tried to defend myself he would just hurt me even more. All I could do was yell into his face,

"Let me go! Let me go! Alex is in my arms. Don't you see that you stupid maniac?"

When he finally released me and I could take a look at my children, I felt beaten all over again. Alex was gasping for air, while Joey was still sitting where he had been at the very beginning. He was crying hard and his small body was shaking uncontrollably. He didn't move; either he couldn't or he was afraid to.

It took an enormous effort to gather myself. My whole body was trembling and my face was soaked with tears. I tried to stand up but couldn't, so I just crawled toward Joey, clutching my little baby to me. When Joseph looked at me, he burst into laughter. I must have been a miserable sight because I felt like a wounded animal.

In that moment, I was flooded with hatred. The feeling was so powerful that it took my breath away. I didn't know that I was capable of feeling such an intense animosity. I could have killed him with my bare hands. Every time he looked at me he chuckled, "Poor Mommy." His tone was full of pity as always, but now reached to my deepest core. I felt utterly devastated.

Before I could reach Joey, his father sat beside him, put his arm around his shoulder, and began to explain the situation to him. "You know, Joey, sometimes Mommy is stupid and bad. She just doesn't listen to Daddy. That's why Daddy must punish Mommy." Joey remained totally motionless as his father continued, "You must know, Joey, that Daddy is the boss. Everybody must listen to Daddy and obey; you, Alex, and Mommy. If you don't obey, Daddy has to punish you. So be a good boy! Do you understand?" I was still sitting on the floor, listening to Joseph's insanity pouring out of him. I didn't think that Joey really heard what his father was saying; he seemed to be paralysed with fear.

As before, Joseph took the privilege of soothing Joey but was unsuccessful. In the instant when Joey could escape he slipped into my arms. When I could finally manage to stand up, I took my children to the bedroom.

Strangely, Alex wasn't crying but he was still gasping for air. I couldn't calm him down. I was getting rather desperate because I didn't know what to do. Then I realized that I could nurse him, and that helped to stabilize his breathing.

In the room, peaceful silence surrounded us, but my mind was racing. *How can anybody live like this?* My newly discovered feeling, the

intense hatred, was still seething in me, and I was also very angry—
angry with him and angry with myself for not being able to protect my
children from their father's near-fatal rages. *Why is he doing this to us?*
What am I doing wrong? Why can't we live normally? What does he want
to achieve? Questions, so many questions, but I had no answers. Besides,
we were in a foreign country. He was home here, but we weren't. Where
could I possibly run from him?

Chapter 43

THERE WAS NO TIME TO philosophize; I had to look after my children. Not just in the everyday sense, but for the future. Somehow, I had to protect them. My children certainly didn't deserve to live in this madness. And I was literally afraid for our lives because I saw him as capable of hurting the boys, just as he hurt me.

I cuddled my babies. We were very quiet for a while and when I finally talked to them I just whispered. Joey automatically whispered back to me. We had an almost silent conversation. He had already calmed down and Alex was somewhat more settled. But my mind wasn't quiet. I had to find a way to get out but until then we had to survive his brutality; somehow, we just had to.

In the following days Joey was very defiant toward his father and I entirely withdrew. My body was aching all over. I couldn't bend my right knee, so I was limping. I didn't even know how or when my knee got hurt. My back and head were throbbing for days, and I suffered several bruises. The children started to have nightmares and became clingier to me than ever.

I had been beaten like a bad dog, but life went on. Nothing in our situation had changed, except for the three of us. I knew that my children were deeply affected, if not damaged by the events, and Joseph just kept barking his orders at us. But whatever he said, without a second thought, Joey refused to do. His father didn't ask him again but took a wooden spoon and threatened to hit him if he kept disobeying. By now, Joey was already running away in fear when he saw his father pull out the drawer.

Joey had been through enough terror already, so I asked Joseph not to hurt him; after all, he was only three and a half. But I couldn't utter one word without his being angry at me. My words, my voice, or simply I drove him to the edge in an instant. "Don't interfere or you'll get some too." I risked getting beaten again but I didn't care: I didn't want him to even touch my son.

Before I finished my thought, Joey was already on his father's knees and Joseph started to hit him with the wooden spoon. I was helpless, so miserably helpless. If he wanted to hurt us there was nothing and nobody that would prevent him.

As I stood there watching them I couldn't miss the smug expression on Joseph's face. He seemed to be enjoying what he was doing, that he could hurt us, see our fear, our pain, and our tears. To me that was unbelievable. No man with a heart and a sound mind would enjoy anything like what he did to us.

When he was finished punishing Joey, he said to him, "Joey, you have to promise me that you'll be a good and obedient little boy at all times. Mommy and Alex have to be obedient as well. If you obey me, I will love you. If you won't, I will hit you." Joey had to promise everything his father wanted to hear before he let him go.

His other punishment for Joey was to stand him in a corner, facing the wall. Joey was always so terrified that he wasn't able to stay there for one second. He was clearly suffering, trembling in his whole little body, but his father forced him back in the corner anyway.

I wasn't able to bear this. I asked Joseph, then begged him, to let Joey go. "Be quiet!" he snapped at me. "If I say that he stands in the corner, then he stands there. He must learn who the boss here is." That was always the point, wasn't it? And he taught us through terror. Because of his unpredictable mood swings we lived in permanent fear now, never knowing what he would do next.

My knee didn't work for two weeks and my bruises reminded me of the beating for even longer. I was desperate to go back to Hungary. I knew that our situation wouldn't be easier, but at least we would be home. When I was calm enough, I asked Joseph to take us home, and since he refused my request, I started to beg, again. I tried to make him understand, but he brushed me aside. When I reached the verge of tears, he threatened to put me into a mental hospital.

My tears always gave him an extra opportunity to hurt me and by now I cried every day. But I desperately fought for my dignity and self-worth, and for so many more things that he deprived me of: I fought for my life, my mere existence, for our lives. And I became more rebellious than I'd ever been.

When I cried out in pain, he always reacted the same way. "You are an insane person. You need a doctor. It would be very easy to put you into a mental institution. Obviously, you're not normal. And believe me, I could arrange to have you locked away forever." And I did not doubt him.

Actually, every threat of his was believable, but still I felt safer at home, so I tried again, approaching the issue from a different angle. I even told him that another shot was soon due for Alex. He didn't care.

Of course, the fewer people knew us, the better it was for him. He even made some promises, such as that he would give me $2,000 a month, would buy a new car and a beautiful home, to make me want to stay. But I wasn't up for sale. There was nothing he could offer me that would have kept me here. Yet I also knew that without him I wasn't able to do much because everything was in his hands, absolutely everything, including us.

Days went by, then weeks, and still we were in Canada. I felt so lost and hopeless; I was totally dependent on a man who despised me more than anybody else in my life ever had.

I knew it was quite useless, but I tried to keep my distance from him in that tiny apartment. It made me sick just to breathe the same air with him. Since we had two bedrooms, I drew away from him into the children's room, while Joseph slept in the other one.

I spent my nights listening to his every movement. I was afraid to fall asleep but most of the time exhaustion overtook me. All I wanted was to have some peace, at least at night, but even that was too much to expect.

Whenever he woke up and didn't find me beside him, he knew immediately where to find me. He came to my bedside and pulled me out of bed to satisfy his needs. And of course, I wasn't allowed to reject him. There couldn't be any reason for my not wanting to be with him. If I dared to object, he started to yell at me, waking up the children even though they were in the other room. Whenever I said no to him, he threatened that he would beat me again if I didn't obey. And that was hard, because I could never enjoy him, although he expected me to—even his touch gave me the creeps. But I had no way out. That was just part of my obligation.

The whole event took only a few minutes—extremely long

minutes—and it always happened the same way. If I hadn't felt deeply violated I could have just fallen asleep. However, in his belief he was the master of a woman's body and beyond excellent in bed. I was the one who needed serious education in this field as well, because I was frigid. Well, he certainly wasn't able to warm me up.

So, since I was the one who needed to take sex lessons, he gave me some books in English to learn how to be a satisfying lover to him. He never considered that he might be the one who needed some education. No, he was pure perfection. Every woman was dreaming about him, but I was the lucky one, wasn't I?

Whatever he believed, he couldn't force me to love him. He actually disgusted me. His presence turned me off, not just as a woman but as a human being. And there was no book that could have helped me with that.

In the past, I had wanted and tried to confide in him but that was all history. Still, I remembered very well when about six years earlier, I had shared something about my childhood experiences with him, and he had reported everything back to my parents. I could still sense their reproach. That was my first and last attempt to trust.

I couldn't even sit down to talk with him because he turned my own words against me. And he constantly repeated: "You are a defective person who needs help and I am the only one who can help and fix you. Unfortunately, you're ninety-nine percent defective, but lucky for you, I'm willing to help."

How fortunate I was, because even the beatings were for my own benefit. That was a part of his help. "I will break you in," he said. "I will hit you as many times and as much as is needed, until you become an appropriate person." And of course he was the judge of that too. The criticisms, insults and put-downs that he hurled at me were for my own good as well. Unfortunately, he was very diligently fixing me on a daily basis. And for all of this I was supposed to be grateful.

Ever since the children had been born, Joseph had kept me in fear that he would replace me as a mother. I was desperate not to be separated from my children, not even for one minute, because I only felt alive when I was with them, and I wanted to be alive. But he always had somebody in his mind that could be better for my children than I. My godmother was one of them.

About four years previously she had ended up in California, thanks to a guy who she only knew through correspondence. She gave up everything before she left; but now, since their so-called relationship hadn't worked, she wanted to go back to Hungary. But even there she had nowhere to go. She had no job, no home, nothing. To me, it was rather unsettling that my former heroine had believed in the prince and his white horse...

I never found out how it happened, but she contacted Joseph while we were in Canada and asked for his help. His suggestion was that she would come to us and be my children's nanny, so I could work with him. The idea drove me into total desperation.

I loved my godmother but I didn't want her anywhere near us. Besides her depressive mood and pessimistic attitude, I didn't want to lose the privilege of looking after my children. Being with them always gave me some distance from him, and I needed that because it was my only escape.

I, for once, defended my own needs. "Even if she comes here, I am the one who looks after the children. I am their mother. She has no experience at all. Moreover, she smokes like a chimney. I'm sorry, but I don't want her to look after them."

After that, I know they spoke to each other several times, but I never really knew what happened. In the end she didn't show up. Joseph told me that she was moving back to Hungary but couldn't afford to ship her belongings. She asked for his help to pay for the shipment, which cost over $2,000. The deal was that once she was home she would work for him to pay off her debt. So, Joseph paid her expenses, then gave her a job as my parents' assistant, and accommodation in the office building as well.

CHAPTER 44

AFTER FIVE LONG MONTHS, HE finally took us back to Hungary. I was exhilarated to be home again. Even the children were more relaxed in the familiar surroundings. Because of what he had put us through in Canada, I wished, hoped, and prayed that I would never be back. I had given him that one last chance that my father requested...

Sadly, Joseph didn't go back to Canada as often as he had before. First he had gone back almost every month, then every two months, but now he went back every three months or even more—excruciatingly long months.

The bliss of being at home didn't last because he started to push me again to work with him in the office. He asked Monica and me to work together and order thermometers. With that, Monica was done with the work and she left me to deal with the owner of the company. Fine.

I ordered several types of thermometers which the supplier could deliver at once. The payment methods were out of my hands though. That was it; I just stayed upstairs again. I dreaded being with him in his office, or anywhere else for that matter. And when he brought up some catalogues, I simply refused to work on them. Of course, he didn't like that, but I really had had enough of them. Still, I wasn't "bored" at all, because he could turn the most ordinary events into nightmares.

One day when he came up, I was in the bathroom with the children. I grabbed the opportunity of his being there, gave Alex to him, and asked him to take the children out. But Joseph didn't move, just stared at me, then said, "Do it peacefully. I'm not shy. You're mine anyway. Just do it!" I had no intention of participating in his game. It made me feel uneasy and uncomfortable, so I just gently drove them out and locked the door.

I wasn't in there for ten seconds when he kicked the door with enormous power. When I went out and took Alex from him, as soon as his hands became free he struck me across the face with such force that my head slammed into Alex's; he started to cry immediately. I was so surprised that I didn't even recognize the pain. "If I say something to you, you do it without grumbling," he thundered. I couldn't believe this. I wasn't even allowed to pee independently. His violation of my privacy left me with very few options: either I wet my pants or I did it in front of an audience.

Although I was still his "sweetheart", the beatings became regular. His voice was all sugar and honey when he called me but I could sense the venom in it. Most of the time, I didn't even know what elicited the attack.

Just a few days after the bathroom incident, we were in the living room. I was holding Alex while Joey was peacefully playing around. Joseph kept pestering me and in the next flash, bang—my head crashed into Alex's again. Then he started to shake me and push me with Alex in my arms. When his rage subsided Alex was again hyperventilating. Joey was paralysed with fear and crying silently. All three of us were trembling like leaves and this time Joey didn't dare come to me.

The whole event was painfully familiar, a repeating pattern: the terror, the yelling, our fear, the three of us crying, his blaming me, lecturing and explaining his acts, even his smugness. When he left and I pulled myself together, I said to Joey, "The next time, if your father hurts me, go and hide in your little house. Don't watch what he does to me!" It was more than enough that he heard everything. But Alex was a different story. He was always clinging to me. So the plan was set for the next incident, which came shortly. When Joseph started to toss me around, I saw Joey hide in his little house.

This time Joseph had been bullying my parents, which offended me even more than when he insulted me. My own pain and desperation gave me the power to slap him. I believed it was time for him to get a taste of his own cooking. But I had no time to enjoy my satisfaction. He hit me so hard that I fell against the wall and my glasses landed on the floor. "You know," he hissed at me, "I could knock you out with one strike, then you would be silenced for hours." I needed some time to regain my balance and clear my head, but I had no doubt that he meant what he said. One slap was enough to break my eagerness to fight him. I was no match for him, whether I liked it or not.

When he left, Joey came out of his house, trembling. The noises alone had flooded him with total fear. But he tried to be very brave. "I hid, Mommy, I hid. Am I clever?" My heart sank. *Oh my God. Are we destined to live like this?* I held both of my children as close as I could, and said to Joey, "Of course, you're clever. You did very well!"

I couldn't find the right way out of that chaos. Joseph was obviously much stronger than I was in every aspect, and he always vented his rages on me. For over six years I was a human punching bag to him, either verbally or physically. And the circus was always on. If he didn't hurt me directly, he destroyed other things. One time he smashed the vacuum cleaner on the floor; another time he threw a bowl full of soup onto the kitchen floor because I was busy with the children and couldn't serve him. He also started to criticize my cooking and refused to eat certain foods now, because to him they were only dog food. But that was rare, because I was his favourite target.

Every fight with him was very exhausting. He literally sucked the energy out of me. But after each clash I simply refused to serve him. There were occasions when we didn't exchange one word for up to seven days. And that was good. When he didn't speak to me, he didn't hurt me. And since he never beat me without yelling, that also meant that I was safe physically as well, at least for those few days.

I was well aware that we were the main subject of gossip because our life was on wide-screen display. Everybody knew everything, or at least thought they knew, and sometimes they knew more than I did.

Uncle Mike, my father's cousin, was now there to work in the warehouses too and he also lived in the office building. He had always liked to gossip and wasn't any different now. One day, I met him in the second-floor corridor. We took a few minutes to discuss the past few years and the time when Joseph had shown up in our hometown. "So much for the great future," I said to him. "I wish I'd never come here in the first place." His response was more than unexpected. "You were supposed to find a place to rent and move out of his apartment in three months." I froze. It was as if everything around me had gone still. I just stared at him in total disbelief. "WHAT?!" That was all I could say at that moment. "Yeah," he said. "You could have left in three months." I had never felt so utterly devastated. "How come I didn't know about this?" I asked him, but he just shrugged: "I thought you knew."

Well, I hadn't. Nobody had ever told me anything like that. Nobody told me that I had an option. That was too much to bear. My head was swirling. *I was set up. I was used and betrayed. Was there a conspiracy behind my back? Someone was very responsible for all my suffering, and I believed that there was someone besides Joseph...*

I was thinking about my parents and Uncle Mike's family. Why didn't anybody tell that to me? When I was taken to Budapest, I stayed at Joseph's place so that I could learn directly from him. "It's easier this way," he said. That was the first and last thing I knew about the living arrangement. There hadn't been a word about my living independently. Nobody ever told me that I was free to leave. But did it matter after so many years of suffering? He had only paid me for three months altogether, and he had clearly marked me as his when he forced himself into me. Had there really been any chance for me to get out?

I had to stop dwelling on this because it was far too late to do anything. I also had to stop analyzing my life, as doing so put me dangerously close to a nervous breakdown. It was better for my own sake not to think about all the opportunities I'd been brutally denied.

I felt so tired after that conversation. Tired of Joseph and tired of my whole life. I had already given up on a better future and now I began to pray for the end. I lived day by day, hour by hour, and when I survived one day that was like a miracle to me.

During quiet moments I fantasized about another life, where I was respected and loved, appreciated and admired, where we were safe and free. And in my prayers I asked God to set us free from Joseph. I even offered a deal to God: I was willing to give up twenty years of my life if He would just end our fear and suffering. But since there were no positive changes in our life, I took this as a sign that God didn't want to make such a deal with me.

CHAPTER 45

IT WAS EXASPERATING THAT MY life just got more and more difficult. Whenever Joseph assaulted me I confronted him; nobody stood up for me, but *I* stood up for myself, and for my children. Unfortunately, that was always a dead end, just a waste of my breath and energy, and it was also quite risky. But what choice did I have?

He was never man enough to admit that he might have done something wrong. And whenever I tried to expound my view of the events that had gone on between us, he always interrupted me, saying, "You're nothing but hot air. You have a bad attitude toward me and toward everything else. You must look for the good in me and not the bad." Well, I tried to, tried very hard, but for some reason I couldn't find that hidden good in him. I even told him so. "How do I find good things where there are none? I can't find them." But his answer was the same: "You can't find them because you have a bad attitude."

At this point some disturbing gossip raised its head and eventually reached my ear. As I heard it, Joseph would have kicked me out if Alex had turned out to be a girl, and of course he would have kept Joey. That information came rather unexpectedly and had nothing to do with my attitude.

I had two children to look after now, but Joseph still demanded to be the priority and insisted that his dinner be ready by 6:00 p.m. To me the children came first, regardless of what he wanted. I told him that I could be ready by 7:00 p.m., so we could all sit down to dine. And he agreed, on one condition: I had to call him every single day with love and devotion, saying, "Dinner is ready."

I worked very hard to keep the almost-never-existing harmony in the family, but that was like swimming against the stream—very exhausting, if not impossible. Joseph destroyed all my efforts with a single wave of his hand.

Before bedtime I read stories and sang to the children. They enjoyed this routine of ours very much, since Joseph was in his office most of the time; thus it was peaceful. But when he came up, everything was ruined. While I read the story, he kept whispering to Joey and poking him. There were times when he simply took Joey away, then threw himself on his hands and knees and began to neigh. When Joey didn't jump on his back, he blamed me. "Why don't you let the children play with me?" I could only answer him with my own question: "Why don't you join us instead of being destructive?" But that he could never do. In the end he just stormed out of the apartment. After he left, sadness settled in. The mood was so depressing that I was never able to restore the peace and harmony we had had before he came up.

During these years, I saw my whole world collapsing in front of my eyes many, many times, and just as often I thought it was the last time and I wouldn't be able to stand up again. I was certain that he wanted to destroy me, even annihilate me. It could have been much easier if he had just killed me. That would have lasted for a few minutes only, and then it would have been over. Instead, he kept torturing me year after year. And I had no idea how many years were ahead of me, living like that; every time he hurt me a small part of me died.

I wanted to get away so badly from the constant madness, but where or how? My way to the outer world was blocked, so I had to find something inside. I gathered all my stuff in our bedroom, everything that was important or significant to me: my books, my clothes, my personal items. I valued the smallest things a great deal and was attached to them even more. Literally my whole life was in this room. It contained all of my memories from earlier years and all of my hopes for the future. In this way at least I had a faint sense of being home.

I wasn't allowed to read my books but at least I could take a look at them. I couldn't wear my beautiful clothes but at least I could admire them. I had stopped wearing make-up a long time ago because I just cried it off. And I loved my high heels but those just generated more problems because Joseph was shorter than I was, and in my heels I literally towered over him. He of course couldn't tolerate that and forbade me to wear those shoes. So instead of using my wardrobe, I started to live a life through my dreams.

For him, though, it didn't take much to look good. Close to sixty, he was a rather handsome man and it was my job to keep him that way.

But doing his laundry was just another challenge for me. If I washed his shirt, that was a problem; if I didn't wash it, then that was. When he asked me to prepare his outfit each day, I did my best to put his clothes together tastefully and variedly. I even enjoyed doing that and I thought he would at least appreciate my efforts. But instead, he told me not to prepare a clean shirt every day because he could use the same shirt for days; yet when I didn't change his shirt, that caused a problem: "People might think that you're neglecting me."

He drove me crazy by frequently changing the rules. He also berated me if I didn't do the dishes before I went to bed, but then if I did them, he told me not to because Joanne could do them in the morning. I never knew which rule was in force.

Pleasing him was simply impossible. There was no way I could do anything right. He made sure of that. At the end of the week his shirt was so dirty that it could stand by itself. It was impossible to clean it properly, and once again that was my fault.

He made me responsible for all his stuff, which meant that if he put something away and wasn't able to find it, he came to me. That happened just one day before he was due back in Canada—he couldn't find his passport. He checked all his suits, he turned his office upside down, but the passport was nowhere to be found. When he had no more patience, he turned to me. "Find my passport, because I'm leaving tomorrow." It was useless to say anything. I hadn't seen his passport for a long time and had no idea where he had put it, but I had to find it.

The situation seemed quite hopeless. Still, I had to find that stupid document, no matter what, because otherwise he would be stuck there with me and I didn't want that. He had to leave!

Then an idea struck me; whenever we went to the weekend house, he always carried a sports bag with him. I couldn't think of anything else, just that sports bag. And now all my hopes and a couple of weeks of freedom were locked in it.

I asked my father to take me to the house. There, we found the bag and inside was Joseph's passport. Oh, I was so happy and took it to him proudly. He was noticeably relieved as he said to me, "From now on, you will find those things that get lost." That was very promising for the future, but for now I was relieved too, because he was leaving the next day without us!

More and more often I longed just to cuddle up to someone who didn't hurt me. I also wanted to know how it felt to be truly and honestly loved, because I had reached the point again where the suppressed desire for love surfaced in me. It was like survival equipment. I wanted to be caressed and not beaten. I wanted to hear loving words instead of insults. And because of the invisible leash he kept me on, I wanted to get away even more—to be me and live my life, not his.

While I was dreaming of the unreachable, he arrived back again. His sexual aggressiveness just got worse. He took me regularly now against my will. I could either let it happen or he would hurt me, either way… He said, "You're obligated to have sex with me. It's very important that you understand that sex is essential to a happy family life. It's your responsibility to keep the family harmony. So don't ruin it! And if you decide that you don't want me anymore, you must leave the house, but without the children."

He had also initiated quickies a short time ago. He would just run up from the office, take me, then go back to work. I felt used and violated every time he touched me. His quickies were sickening and utterly humiliating. I didn't feel any more valuable than a trash can. But for my own sake I had to cooperate.

Ever since he had begun to beat me, I wasn't able to even pretend that I wanted him. "How could I be intimate with someone who beats me?" I asked him. His answer was very quick: "Then don't make me hit you." And he laughed as if the fact that he beat me was nothing but a good joke.

More often, though, he completely denied his acts or simply rewrote history. "What are you talking about?" he would ask innocently. "I've never hit you. That's only your illusion. You always make things up. You have a very vivid imagination." He could be so convincing that I almost doubted the facts.

Interestingly, he accused me of being a witch who had put some kind of spell on him. There were times when I felt that he was actually afraid of me, and I had to admit to myself that that truly amused me. If I'd really had any magic power, I would have changed him into a frog—or something worse—a very long time ago.

∽

Even after six years, the company wasn't stable, so much so that in the fall a group of liquidators showed up at the office building, and in December, right after Joseph left the country, they moved in. Monica kept me updated about the situation. The problem was more than serious; the company was in great danger of being swept off the earth.

Mysteriously, Joseph didn't arrive when he was due to be back. As I heard, he was advised by his confidants—whoever they were—to stay in Canada until the problems were smoothed away. Supposedly, he was at great risk of being arrested. Thus, he was away for six weeks and we had a never-before-experienced peaceful Christmas. Even though his faxes were rather demanding and could easily drive me to the edge, this was the first holiday in years when I didn't cry.

1997
Enough!

Chapter 46

THIS YEAR WAS VERY HECTIC. Events sped up and I felt that he and the circumstances he created were really pushing me to extremes.

I had already told Joseph several times that Joey needed to be among children, that it would be very good for him to attend preschool. His father, though, simply forbade me to carry out my plan. But while Joseph was away, I registered Joey. And what a good thing I did.

Joey loved being at preschool. He loved the children, the teachers, and even the food. More importantly, he was well liked too. I was so very happy for him. Finally, there was something normal in his life, and I was determined to keep it for him.

When Joseph was able to come back, I told him straightforwardly what I had done while he was away. I also told him how happy Joey was there. I was beyond astonishment when he told me that I had done the right thing.

His reaction was so unexpected that I didn't know how to respond. It was just too good to be true. But my experience with him didn't let me rest. Something was wrong with this new picture; something was hiding under the surface. I knew that it was only a matter of time before he would show his true face and that kept me in constant agony, because I didn't know when or how he would blow up. I just knew that sooner or later I would have to pay the price for my action.

After six years and two children, I was sure that my life was supposed to be as it had been. While I tried very hard not to react to his provocations and mocking, he also tried very hard to take advantage of my weaknesses. My passive behaviour fired him up and he didn't leave me alone until I just couldn't take it anymore and broke into pieces. And when that happened, my anger and pain gave him an extra reason to hurt me even more. "You're a mould and a rot. It's your fault that our relationship has deteriorated. And your relatives! You're ruining me and my children! You don't deserve any good, only beatings. And you'll get that from everybody, even from your own children. Nobody will tolerate you, ever."

As frightening as it was, after all those years of constant verbal attacks it was easy to believe what he said. And no matter how strongly I pretended not to be affected, the truth was that his words always hurt me.

Attacking my personality was one thing, but attacking me as a mother was more than I could take. Being a mother meant much more to me than I had ever expected. It became my most important job in the whole world, my mission, and I took it very seriously. I was determined to do my best, to be a good mother to my children, to protect them with all my strength and support their best interests in all matters. I felt important and needed in their lives. But his slandering words always made me feel worthless. "You're a bad mother! You're simply not able to offer any good to the children. Moreover, with your disobedience you're a bad role model for them. They'd be better off without you."

Years of insecurity started to catch up with me again and at these times I always wondered whether he was right. But I didn't want him to be right, so I worked even harder to become an even better mother. And learning from my own experience, I could never let my children down, no matter what kind of situation we were stuck in.

Still, the so-called "intimate" times were the most difficult ones. I couldn't help it. I was physically sick of him. But I could never escape my obligations unless, maybe, when I had my period. But one time he didn't even believe that. "You're just saying that," he said, "to make me suffer. Okay, enough of that! Let's go!" I was shocked by the way he spoke.

"I can't!" I said, but there was nothing that would have convinced him. "That's a lie! You must come at this instant!" It really hurt that he didn't believe me. Regardless of the circumstances in which he kept me, I was quite honest with him, which was probably a big mistake. To prove my truthfulness I said to him, "If you don't believe me, check the garbage can." Now that stopped him cold. He looked at me with clear contempt. "You must let me know when you've finished it!" he said and started to walk away, but then he turned back to me and asked: "You want me to die, don't you?" His question was more than unexpected, but I said to him, "You can't hide from God. He sees everything you do."

"Oh, don't worry about that. I will haunt you anyway," he said, and my skin broke into chills. I was relieved to get away from him that time, although it never occurred to me that he might count the days…

I was always looking for some reason not to be near him, but to go out somewhere when he was around remained out of the question. Even if I had a doctor's appointment I had to ask Joseph's permission to leave. If I got lucky and he let me go, that meant that I had a couple of hours of freedom. Therefore, I wanted "to go to my doctor" diligently. Unfortunately, that didn't always work because he usually had excuses why I shouldn't go. He even told me, "You don't have to go to your doctor. He won't do any good. I'm the only one who can go down there anyway. If there's anything wrong, I can fix you." It didn't seem that he cared much about my well-being, did it? And he wasn't joking. He did forbid me to go to my appointment.

But at least I could still take Joey to preschool. Even though it was only a tiny part of the outer world, to me it meant the whole universe. Joseph represented my prison, with the chains tightly around my neck, but he wasn't there. My brother took us! That gave me an extra opportunity to catch up with him, because otherwise I hardly ever saw him. I enjoyed his company and our well-earned freedom enormously. And it showed.

I was sure that Joseph could see my happiness because I was glowing. Therefore I wasn't surprised when he broke my joy into tiny pieces. "You sent the child among plebs? That place is for low-class people." So that's what was wrong with the too-perfect picture. It was only my opinion, though, that he behaved in a lower manner than any low-class people ever could. "I think that place is great and the people are wonderful," I told him. "Joey likes it and so do I." He was quick to reply: "Of course it's good because you don't know any better. You came from a pigsty. You're just like them. And now you want me to sink to your level?" I couldn't answer him. I didn't think that there was any correct answer to his question. Despite his reaction, though, he didn't take Joey out of the school.

During these years I had heard Joseph over and over again slander his mother-in-law, his wife, his previous wife, then of course me, and more and more often my mother. I took his insults daily. "You are more stupid and primitive than anybody else," he said. "Nobody will ever love and appreciate you, only me. And you won't be able to find a better, smarter, and more loveable person than me, not even if you live for a thousand years, so don't even try. You must love and appreciate me; otherwise you'll lose me and the children. And then you can cry your eyes out." Or he would say: "If you lose me you will never succeed, ever. You are nobody without me, just a pig. So be careful what you wish for." Oh, I wished so many times to lose him, but he had already eaten himself into me like rust into metal, corroding me.

All of this, though, didn't mean that he could descend upon my mother. He was so full of hatred when he spoke about her that I really didn't know what to think about his intentions. I experienced a sudden clarification when I realized what the problem was: he obsessively hated mothers in general.

It aggrieved me deeply that he always spoke about my mom in such a condemnatory manner. He didn't respect her at all, and was now blaming everything on her. Even though we resided in the same building, we could have lived on two different planets because we hardly ever spoke. Still, every single detail that went wrong between the two of us (and there were many!) was my mother's fault. "Your mother is filling your head with ideas against me. She is the one who alienates you from me. It's her fault that you don't love me anymore."

Poor Ma! She did just the opposite. She was always more on his side than mine. Between us she usually called him "our father". I knew that she was greatly hurt by those lies. And despite the differences between my mother and me, I felt for her. I even tried to help her deal with all Joseph's accusations. My mother took everything to heart to such an extent that one day my father came to me saying that their marriage was on the brink of divorce. The unjust accusations were driving them apart.

And as if this situation wasn't serious enough, those thermometers from the previous year came back to haunt me. When I had ordered them, I truly hoped that the whole business deal would be problem-free. It seemed so simple. I never expected that the man wouldn't receive his payment for months, not even after the products were sold. Since his rightful request was constantly ignored, he turned to me for help.

He called me several times and literally begged me to ask Joseph to pay the bills. I always passed on the message and apologized to him profusely for something that wasn't my fault. I felt so ashamed, because nothing seemed to happen. Then one day another phone call came. "Thank you so much for your help. I finally got my money."

CHAPTER 47

THE IDEA OF MY PARENTS divorcing was the most shocking news I had ever heard. It never even occurred to me that they would consider such a thing. My father was devastated but I had mixed feelings. The possibility of breaking up their unity scared me a lot, but I felt angry too, angry at the whole situation that had brought us to such an extreme level. And I was angry with my father. "If you think that I would take my children separately to their grandfather, then to their grandmother, you're wrong!" I couldn't handle the simple thought of not having my parents together.

Although I showed my anger to my father, I blamed Joseph. He was the one who brought the constant curse on our heads. At this time, though, he kept the pressure on my mother. She was his new scapegoat. "Your mother is evil. It's her fault that our relationship is ruined. She's brainwashing you." If he only knew: she was so devoted to him, even humble, so why her?

Joseph manipulated everything. He drained my strength, killing off my self-confidence and my joy in life. He even robbed me of my identity, because I was nothing else but a stupid slave called "sweetheart". He was so malicious and so powerful that it was beyond my understanding. So when he ordered me again to stop communicating with my mother once and for all, I didn't even try. His demand was so offensive and ridiculous that I didn't take it seriously.

And just as our daily lives didn't get any better, our nights got worse as well. In the last couple of years, Joseph's snoring had become unbearable. Since all four of us slept in the same room, I was worried about the children because they were tossing and turning, while I wasn't able to sleep, night after night. But of course, neither problem was Joseph's concern. I knew that if I dared to bring the issue to his attention, he would just hurt me. But the lack of sleep quickly caught up with me. I had difficulties functioning because I was like a sleepwalker all day long. I had to speak with him and I obviously needed his cooperation so I could get some rest.

I asked him to use the other bedroom, so we all could have a good sleep. There was absolutely no reason for us to be sleeping together. He went to the other room for a couple of nights, then refused to do it. I knew that was it, so I started asking and then begging him to turn on his side. I hoped that would do the trick but unfortunately it didn't work too well, if at all. So while he slept his sweet dreams, I stared at the ceiling, crying quietly. I didn't dare to complain anymore because he would just yell and wake up the children, as he had many, many times before.

One night, though, I had to ask him again to either go to the other room or change position. His reaction had never been better: "You're obligated to let me sleep. Be a good common-law and get used to it. You must learn to enjoy my snoring. And don't wake me up again." I was suffering from severe headaches and I started to lose weight again, which I could never afford. All the sleepless nights, the stress, not to mention the enormous noise he made—it was too much for me to bear.

"But I can't sleep," I said to him. "I have a constant headache, and I'm worried about the children. They're tossing and turning in their dreams."

"They sleep very well," he said. "They're enjoying my snoring. You should do the same thing. And if you don't, then it's your fault because you have a bad attitude toward me." Of course, what else?

I had to figure out something, so I changed my tactic. Instead of begging him throughout the night, I waited until he fell asleep, then I took the children one by one to the other room. I held my breath as I tiptoed out of the room with them and only dared to breathe again when I was far enough from Joseph. Finally, I could have a few hours of peaceful, very much needed sleep. But that didn't last either.

When I was awake all night beside him, he never woke up, and didn't even stir. But as soon as we weren't in the room, he was wide awake. When he discovered that I had snuck out, and had taken the children with me to the next room, all hell broke loose. "How could you leave me? And how dare you take the children? Your place is at my side. I don't want to sleep alone," he whined.

He was complaining as if I had taken the children to another planet, and the arguments went on night after night. Then one night he told me: "Okay, I'll sleep in the other room, but I'll take Joey with me." Then he just picked him up and took him to the other room. From then on, besides Joseph's having tantrums, Joey cried. Since Joseph didn't let me comfort him, I couldn't do anything but listen to my little boy crying himself to sleep.

The whole circus was unbearable enough, but as always Joseph was the mastermind of making bad situations even worse. Several times I heard him threaten Joey that he would get one if he didn't behave. I knew that Joey would struggle to get free and when that happened, his father held him down or put his leg across Joey's tiny body. It didn't take much effort for him to defeat a four-year-old child. I couldn't bear to see my little boy suffer, so I told Joseph that it was possibly better if we slept all together again, even though the problem remained.

As with many times in the past, I felt again that I couldn't live like this and I didn't want to. And to worsen the situation, he came up with Canada again. I had to remind him about what had happened the previous time. "Last year I was there with you and you beat me so badly that I could hardly walk. So why would I go anywhere ever again with you?"

"Oh," he chuckled, "you did that to yourself. If you love me, you obey me. You have to do what I say." I could very well have answered him back, but I had to be careful what I said because he was always ready to hit me now. And I also had to keep in mind that I still wasn't allowed to say no to him. In the early years he only lectured me when I said no, but now I was risking my physical well-being when I dared to go against his demands.

In April both boys came down with chickenpox. Joey was the first one, then a week later it was Alex's turn. Joey was very, very sick, covered with spots from head to toe. He had a high fever and was so weak he couldn't walk without my support. But I had to keep the spots clean. When I gave him a quick bath, he was clearly suffering; he shivered uncontrollably and didn't feel well enough to be up even for those few minutes.

I was carefully drying Joey off when his father showed up. He watched us for a few seconds then told me to wait till he got his camera. "No way!" I said to him. "I can't wait. Joey is way too sick. I have to look after him as quickly as possible." But he was already there, ordering me how to pose my sick child. I got so mad at him. "Forget it! Don't you see how sick he is? He's shivering so badly he can't stand." By then Joey was crying and Joseph was yelling, "Don't be smart with me. You're the one who prolongs the time."

When I covered Joey with a large towel to keep him at least a bit warm, Joseph bawled at me, "Get that thing off him!" With that he pushed me aside and took some pictures of the child. I had never before seen anybody suffering and trembling as much as Joey. "There," said Joseph. "This will be a very nice memory one day."

He made me sick. I could almost feel the spots of frustration coming out on my skin, and now I was the one who pushed him aside so I could tend to my sick child.

Alex was luckier in every aspect. He had a high fever but just a few spots, and Joseph wasn't interested enough to take photographs of him.

Then my birthday came, my twenty-seventh. I never celebrated my birthday, but I always noted its significance. After all, it meant that I was still alive. I never really got any presents from him, but this time he gave me a beating. Just as always he went straight for my head: always and only for my head and the nape of my neck. Maybe he wanted to beat me until I really lost my sanity. In that case he could have locked me away in that so-often mentioned mental hospital for the rest of my life, and I wouldn't even have been able to object.

Again, I didn't know why I was being punished; perhaps I had breathed the wrong way. I couldn't escape his striking hand. I tried to protect myself but he gave me no chance. That was the most memorable birthday present I ever received. It also made me feel that it was probably a huge mistake that I had been born.

CHAPTER 48

EVEN THOUGH I FELT LIKE giving up and said so, I wasn't able to. Something in me was pushing me toward a better existence. I was still hoping for a miracle, any kind of miracle that would end our nightmare. I prayed that one day an authority figure would recognize the wrongness of our situation and help us to get out of it. I wanted to be safe and I wanted to keep my children safe. So when our paediatrician recommended a psychiatrist, which was a new source of hope, on May tenth, I went to see her.

At first I was timid about talking to her, because I didn't know how she would react. I was also ashamed of my situation. Fortunately, she was very friendly and understanding. Although I couldn't pay her for every session, she told me that I could see her regularly, or as often as I could get away.

Through my meetings I was able to open up and told her everything that went on. One of her common-sense questions was, "Is he drunk when he hits you?" I had never even thought about this before. And I had to admit that I had never seen him drunk, only tipsy. At those times he was never violent, just playful, although he was as strong as when he was driven by rage. Whenever he attacked me he was sober, so I couldn't blame his violence on alcohol. He'd beat me up without a single sip of booze...

Ever since the food discount store had begun operating, I was drawn to the place and to the people there, although I knew I couldn't really trust anyone except very few of them. Of course, we weren't allowed to spend time there except to buy our groceries, but I took the risk and chatted with the employees. Even the boys befriended some of them. It was a great pleasure to see my children having some good times. Their joy was worth every possible consequence that I knew was waiting for me.

Since Joseph still loved to sneak up on me, I always kept an eye out for his unexpected appearance. None of us needed his insults and threats, and I also didn't want those good people to get into trouble just because they socialized with me. He was the boss, he was the owner, and everything was under his control, including people's paycheques.

Of course, there were times when he caught me speaking to somebody or Joey playing with someone. At these times, ignoring all the people around us, he bellowed at me, grabbed my arm, and pulled me away from the person I was talking to. If he saw Joey interacting with other people, he ordered me to go and take Joey away. Then he ushered us back to the apartment and came at me with full force: "You must follow my orders! Don't show the children how to disobey me! Don't break my rules anymore if you want to live here! I am the head of the family and in my house everybody does what I command!" We were grounded. He took my keys away and locked the door on us, or he took Joey to his office while Alex and I had to stay in the apartment.

He just didn't get it; the more he isolated us, the more I wanted to get out and be with people. The more he forced himself on me, the more I wanted to get free from him. The more he hated me, the more I wanted love. And I tried to get whatever I could.

I liked the doormen very much and so did the boys. They always had a few good words for us. Being with them was rejuvenating. Even though Joseph ordered me to walk by them without a word, I never did that and I also didn't want to; we always chatted for a short time, laughing and joking. It was so nice to have a carefree conversation with them and I treasured every second of those times.

Yet while we had to steal a little fun time for ourselves, Joseph didn't waste any time when it came to having some fun on his own. Actually, he had all the fun he desired. He was continuously flirting. To him, age had never mattered. Young girls or women in their sixties or whoever dropped by were sure to experience his charm. To them he was irresistible; to me he was intolerable.

No wonder I was always more comfortable with men, as women were too responsive to Joseph's appeal. He wasn't wasting his kindness on me anymore but he was a real charmer when he wanted somebody on his side. I knew that already.

He also impressed people by taking the stairs with triple steps. Whenever my parents saw him they always marvelled about Joseph's physical condition. "This is just unbelievable," they said. "He's close to sixty but stronger and fitter than many forty-year-olds." While Joseph's physical endurance kept my parents and others in awe, I felt rather uneasy about it. His irresistible vigour didn't ensure my physical safety.

He even courted one of the young women, who also could easily have been his daughter. She had a small girl, but instead of looking after her, she was at the office from early morning to late evening, and often stayed into the night working closely with Joseph. I barely knew what they were working on, and didn't even care. I was kind of grateful to her that she took some of Joseph's attention off me. The only problem was that he used her, too, to put me down.

He wanted me to befriend her so I could learn her qualities, like how to behave, how to smile, and whatever made her smart and irresistible in Joseph's eyes. She could have been a goddess when it came to Joseph. To him she was even a better mother than I was, although she clearly neglected her only child.

Then one weekend Joseph came to me saying, "I'm going to Lake Balaton with Emily and her daughter. We thought that we would invite you as well. So you can come along if you wish." That was unbelievable. I was actually invited! But I was neither honoured nor happy. I felt really offended so I refused his invitation as politely as I could, although I was steaming: "No, thank you."

That was the only thing I could say. I didn't care where he took his girlfriend, but inviting me along was a little too much for me. I was hoping to have a few hours of peace, just the three of us, when Joseph dropped the bomb. "I'm taking Joey with us. You know, we've been thinking about combining our families. So it would be her, her daughter, Joey and me." The hatred was seething in me. I could only spit the words out: "In your dreams."

That situation clearly reminded me of what Monica had told me. I also remembered my mother's reaction as she viciously turned against Monica, accusing her of making trouble between her father and me. Sadly, we didn't need somebody else's assistance to have problems, because the troublemaker was right there. He had just proved that Monica was speaking the truth, again. He was doing the same thing to us: he had brought a "new mother" into the family. And he took Joey with them. I stayed at home with Alex and couldn't get what he had said to me out of my head.

Monica and I still spent some time together whenever we could manage it. It felt so good to be with someone who knew and understood what I was dealing with. Once, she had an interesting comment: "You're not the last one. He's been doing this ever since I can remember." Now that was quite reassuring. So there was hope after all.

I carried so much pain inside of me that I didn't know anymore how I could put up with him. My daily goal became to stay away from him, to escape every connection and every communication. I loathed every moment of being with him, and just as much, I hated my life.

I was desperately looking for the slightest chance to get out of the terror, but I also knew I had no chance against him. I had already seen how he smoothed over problems when he was trapped. I was quite sure that he could wipe me off the earth if he wanted to. I was very close to giving up. But my soul remained restless. It was driving me to get what I longed for.

Of course, there were no secrets from him. I always assumed that he knew more than he told me about my "social life". Whatever percentage I was punished for, though, it was enough. And he didn't have to hit me to hurt me. His words were like sharp weapons and he stabbed me with them mercilessly. "Wherever you go, nobody loves you. People tell me that. The only reason they tolerate you is because they know that you belong to the boss." Among the many cruelties he showered me with, that was something I heard repeatedly. And because of that, my way to escape was cut off before I could even attempt my first step to leave him. Who would ever have helped me?

This had been the seventh year with him and I was very tired. It was extremely exhausting to live with him. His continuous demands, as to smile 24/7, drove me up the wall. Nobody grinned like a pumpkin, with or without reason, at all times. After such a long time I forgot to smile. I just couldn't pretend to be happy when it came to dealing with him; I couldn't smile at him anymore. But even when I did smile, my eyes were mirroring the pain. Maybe I could have fooled him, but I certainly couldn't fool myself. Yet it's also true that my smile was available to everybody else who didn't hurt me.

I wanted more out of my life, more than being a live target. I was tired of my fake happiness. And he always noticed my reticence immediately. His favourite question was, "Are you happy?" No, I wasn't happy. But I couldn't tell him that, although he knew, otherwise I don't think he would have asked. I could not tell him that I was beyond miserable and unhappy. My children were my only happiness, but he clouded even that.

So if I said yes to him, then he demanded that I show it, although I didn't know how. And then if I said no, he said, "You have no reason to be sad. You have everything. You have me!" Bingo! That was exactly the main reason for my unhappiness.

The other question he so frequently asked—although the answer was obvious—was, "Do you love me?" That was the toughest question of all. No, I didn't love him. I only got hatred and contempt from him, and I still didn't know how or why to love someone who detested me so much. But of course, that question had to be answered. Being truthful caused me a lot of trouble. "How come you don't love me? You have every reason to love me. You won't be able to find another man anyway, because nobody will ever tolerate you. You're luckier than you realize for having me. If I hadn't made children for you, you wouldn't have any, ever. Nobody wants you, don't even dream about it!" Only a few sentences and I was destroyed. He didn't hit me, didn't even touch me, but I still felt beaten and ugly and undesirable. Was I really that useless and unlovable?

Yet if I lied and said yes to him, he would eagerly urge, "Then run and hug me." At these times giving him a hug was pretty easy. If a hug was enough to prove my non-existent love, then so be it.

He also wanted to initiate a new game. Just to reassure himself that I really loved him, he wanted me to tell him ten times a day, "I love you." But when I tried to say those words, I felt like I would choke on them. And at these times even hugging him took such a physical effort that I was literally in pain.

CHAPTER 49

JOSEPH WAS ALWAYS VERY BRAVE and "manly" when he beat me, but when life challenged him he remained hidden. One night we were woken up by some noises. We could hear people talking, coming and going around the factory ground. It seemed that there was a break-in at the back of the food discount store. The guard had discovered the burglary and a few people were already at the scene. But the owner remained out of sight, only peeking out of the window. I couldn't resist telling him, "Don't you think you should go down? Everybody is there but you." It was surprising that he didn't snort at me. "You think I should go down?" he asked. "Well, yes. After all, this is your company. It looks weird that the owner himself has no interest in what happens to his property." It was interesting that he didn't start to yell at me because I was being "smart" with him, but instead put on his clothes and went to the scene. To me his behaviour was very strange. I had never seen him act like that.

His cowardliness didn't last long, though, and then he was back to his original self: the power, the all-familiar domination over us, everything. He arranged an outing for us to go to Lake Balaton, which could have been a wonderful excursion, but I was rather nervous about the day ahead of us. Whenever we had gone out before, he had used the time for lecturing, criticizing, and bullying me. If he was finished doing that I had to entertain him, only I had nothing to say. My mind was empty and even my vocal cords stopped functioning. Besides, I was literally afraid to speak so as not to say anything wrong.

For some reason, there was no mention of his girlfriend this time; it would be just the four of us. I wasn't sure anymore which version was better: us being with him or me staying behind in total humiliation, worrying about Joey. But if we went out, I at least wanted to enjoy the time.

It was hard to understand why I wasn't allowed to experience such a simple joy, though. Once again, we weren't even permitted to listen to the radio because we had to listen to him. To make sure he had our attention, from time to time he expected us to answer him, which mainly consisted of mumbling. I played with the children instead, to show him how "busy" I was. And if they slept I buried myself in silence and just watched the clouds. Observing the sky was far more fascinating than listening to him.

On that particular day it was very hot and being in the car for hours made everyone grumpy. I always liked to travel with the window open but because the car had an air conditioner we weren't allowed. It was such a relief when we arrived. Finally, we could open the *door* and get out.

We went for a walk first, and then Joseph took Joey into the water while I stayed on the shore, holding Alex. I'll never know why, but Joseph didn't go to the beach area where he could have easily walked into the lake; rather, he lowered himself into the water right at the sidewalk, then lifted Joey in.

Under the water I could see huge rocks, which were obviously very slippery because even Joseph had some difficulty keeping his balance. He put Joey on one of the rocks, then came back to get his camera, leaving him unattended. The water reached Joey's small chest and the alarms of my motherly instinct went off immediately.

I begged him not to leave the child alone but he didn't listen. In that instant a wave knocked Joey over and he went under water. Joseph was still busy with his camera and didn't pay attention to Joey at all. He couldn't swim and he was also out of his father's reach. I was paralysed with fear for my son, and I could only scream, "Joey is under the water! Joey is under the water! Get him!" But for some reason Joseph didn't even budge. He just stared at me. I didn't know why he wasn't acting. It swept through my mind to put my baby on the ground, jump into the water, and save my other one, but that was only my mind working; my legs were rooted to the ground.

I kept yelling to Joseph, pointing into the water. Finally, with great difficulty, he got the picture and went to get Joey. Poor child, he was absolutely terrified, but otherwise all right. I could have collapsed to the ground in my relief if I hadn't been so mad at Joseph. It shocked me even further that he was actually laughing at the situation. Or maybe he was laughing at us, as always.

That was enough water for Joey. He didn't want to stay in the lake any longer, but his father took him out into the middle of it anyway. In the end Joey had a great time, and it was only me who wasn't able to shake off the fact that my little boy had almost drowned before my eyes, just because his father had been so careless.

We had dinner a few hours later, but still I couldn't relax. Joey seemed to have forgotten the incident, but to me, it was a true miracle that my baby was actually sitting at the table with us.

I felt so out of place. I wasn't in the mood to chat, but was just quietly observing the people around us. Some of them were walking hand in hand, young couples were snuggling up to each other, and others were just talking. Everything was so peaceful. Only my soul was disturbed.

I wanted to be one of those people around us. I wanted to experience the freedom they enjoyed, the love they shared. They looked so happy and carefree in those moments. I had to admit that I envied them all.

I imagined myself walking in the park with someone special who loved me enough to care about me, but that just left me even sadder. My only option was to walk with him, but that made me want to run away. I had to realize over and over again that happiness or even simple normality just wasn't for me, that the present situation and Joseph were my destiny.

Year by year, my allowance had shrunk. Soon I was compelled to buy our groceries on credit. I was so ashamed but I had to feed my children, whether he supported our needs or not. When Joseph discovered that I had credits at his food discount he got very angry with me. "You can't do that! You're the boss's common-law. Don't humiliate me!" As always, he was worried about himself. "Then give me enough so I can buy what the boys need," I said to him. "You must behave first," he retorted. "Be an obedient and loving person; then you'll get what you need. If you don't obey, if you don't behave the way I demand, I won't give you any money for your supplies. You have to merit everything first."

Our weekly allowance was 5,000 forint, about $45 for the four of us. This didn't bother him since he could go out and eat at restaurants. And me? I had to be a real magician to stretch the amount I got so it would cover our needs. And just to make sure I didn't waste the money,

I had to give him a detailed account of every penny I spent. Also, before I could buy something I had to give him a thorough explanation of why I needed it. If he thought I was reasonable enough, I got some money; if not, I didn't get any.

For instance, buying a toothbrush wasn't reasonable to him, because in his view, "You can use a toothbrush for years. You don't have to change it every three months. That's just your stupidity." And he did use his toothbrush for years—at least, it looked like that—for his dentures, and he expected me to do the same thing. After this I started to collect toothbrushes.

Joey was four years old now and he had to go to the business meetings regularly. He had hardly ever seen a playground in his life but was forced to sit among over one hundred strangers. "Dress him up nice. He's coming with me. He has to learn the business." And if that wasn't enough, from time to time I had to sit in with little Alex as well. Let him learn the business too.

I opposed all of his demands now, and fought for Joey's best interests. "Joey needs some air, to go out and play. He doesn't need to sit among strangers and listen to their mumblings for six to eight hours." Of course, Joseph didn't like what I said. "I'm the boss," he said. "So you do what I say. Make him ready for the meeting. It's good for him. He can at least learn something. On the playground he can't learn anything. That's just a waste of time."

I was so tired of fighting him to make him understand basic concepts. Joey wasn't even five years old, yet he wasn't allowed to be a child and have fun. Joseph combed his hair the same way he did his own, and Joey looked like a tiny old man instead of a carefree little boy. My heart always sank when Joseph dragged him out.

I went to the psychiatrist as often as I could. My sessions were something I refused to share with Joseph. It was better that way because his treatment got harsher and harsher, if at all possible, and I continued to lose weight. Besides the constant stress, I was still lacking sleep. I also became sick more and more often. Without any warning I would run high a fever or vomit uncontrollably.

I didn't even get proper help from him when I wasn't feeling well. It happened a few times that I was so sick I could only drag myself to the toilet and just sit in front of it. While I was getting everything out of my system, little Alex crawled into my lap and Joey was also right beside me, while Joseph just stood in the living room, watching me suffer.

When I didn't throw up the way he thought was right, he started to bawl at me about how I was supposed to do it. He ordered me to stand up, but he missed the point that I was too weak to stand. Besides, Alex was lying on me and Joseph wouldn't even help to get the children away from me. I was totally on my own in this miserable condition too.

When I was all done and my stomach was pretty calm again, I dragged myself back to bed, taking my children with me. I began to feel better and even a little stronger. Only now Joseph finally dared to come closer, bringing me a cup of milk. MILK!

He tossed it at me and literally demanded that I drink it. I was quite frightened by the offer. "Milk is the worst thing you can have when your stomach is sick. I'm not willing to drink that!" But he kept pushing the cup at me. I refused to take it from him, even though I could see that he was losing patience. "I'm smarter than you are," he said. "If I say the milk is good for you, then you drink it without question." He was standing there, holding the cup of milk, staring at me with full expectation. I knew he wouldn't leave me alone until I did what he said and I had no energy to fight. Thus, I took the cup and in one breath I drank the milk. Wait for it…In a few seconds, everything came back.

When I was once again done, I just looked at him, assuming that he would get the point. He was so smart that he had made me even sicker, and a nagging question took form in my mind: *Had he done that on purpose?*

But when he got sick I was right there at his bedside looking after him. Although I knew he didn't deserve my attention, I loved to help even him when it was needed. I made one mug of tea after another, and I would have looked after him with more compassion; I would have soothed him, made him more comfortable; I would have done anything to help him get better if only he'd let me. But my caring wasn't good enough for him. He was more overbearing and hurtful than usual. My devotion was totally in vain and it hurt me very much that he didn't appreciate my efforts. Therefore, after some time I simply refused to look after him. But then he just whined endlessly, "How come you don't look after me? Don't you love me?"

Then one morning he was strong enough to go to his office and, as a token of his gratitude, he left me a half mug of phlegm, which he spat into the remainder of his tea but which I had to clean up after him. That was more than my stomach could take. I was retching out of control while I cleaned his mug. And that was only the beginning of a nasty series.

After that he left the bathroom sink filthy. Cutting his moustache in it was one thing but leaving his snot stuck to the side of it was a little too much. But then he regularly didn't flush the toilet in the morning, leaving everything behind. That was his way of greeting me at the beginning of each day.

After waking up, my first thought was of what I would find in the bathroom. There were mornings when his stool was smudged on the toilet seat. Several times there were pieces of his stool in the bidet. Swallowing my tears of humiliation, piece by piece I cleaned up his waste.

I had never felt so low in my life. The only way I could interpret his acts was that he despised me so much that he didn't even bother to clean up his own waste. He couldn't have mortified me more. When I asked him to flush the toilet, he found my request rather amusing. "You can do that. You have plenty of time." He wasn't ashamed at all. To him that was just another joke.

My mind was full of those bathroom scenes. I couldn't control myself. "But it's your shit!" I broke down. He of course had to answer. "If you love me, you love my shit too." And he was gone, leaving me feeling dumbstruck. I stood there for a while, trying to comprehend what had happened, but it was beyond my understanding. And that was the man I was obligated to be intimate with. The bare thought of him touching me made my stomach jerk.

Chapter 50

At twenty-seven, I was still desperately seeking my parents' understanding and love. I thought that if they loved me enough, they would at least show me some compassion. So far, my hopes or dreams of being rescued by my father were in vain; therefore, I at least wanted to be listened to.

I tried to tell him what I was dealing with—like he didn't know—and I also tried to tell him what I missed and longed for. I went back to my childhood and told him how much it hurt me that they ignored me every time I needed them. I also told him that I missed my mother's being like a mother to me. But my father was very defensive. "I don't believe that we were such bad parents. After all, you were never cold or hungry." That was all true but I wasn't talking about that. I never complained about being hungry. My soul was starving, and that he never understood.

And Joseph? I wanted to be free of him and I acted upon it. In spite of his prohibition, we went to the food discount daily. Not shopping, but to have some company. There my children befriended one of the security guards. He was unfamiliarly kind and humane, and very quickly became the boys' favourite. He always knew how to treat them and it was obvious how much he loved being with my little ones. I was very worried about leaving them with him, because I was always afraid of the consequences, but the children were drawn to him and seeing them as happy as they were with that man made it worth any scolding or even beating that might await me. So I wasn't able to stand between them.

Adrian just took their hands and walked around with them between the aisles. They chatted, played, and laughed together. The whole scene was so touching to me that I had a hard time concealing my tears. That was what my children deserved—being cared for, having some true good times instead of the constant terror we were destined to live in. They deserved to be children, real children, instead of victims.

They had never experienced such warmth and kindness from any other man before, and I knew that this guy had won my children's hearts. I wanted to join them so badly but I didn't dare. Instead, I let them be while I guarded those precious moments for them.

Then at the beginning of June Joseph went back to Canada again, and I had a rare chance to look after myself. On the eighth of June I had laser eye surgery. After sixteen years I was finally free of glasses and contact lenses. It was exhilarating.

My father took me there, waited for me, and took me home. Right after the surgery I had to wear sunglasses, and was advised to avoid every kind of light. Thus, I was wearing my sunglasses day and night. I went for a walk around the factory ground in the evening, sometimes late at night. Joseph wasn't there so I was free to do anything I pleased or needed. Whenever the children's buddy was on duty, he accompanied me, which gave me a chance to know him a bit better. He offered me a glimpse of normality, like having fun, a good talk, laughing and simply being ourselves. I was never afraid of being myself around him, and it felt so good to be with him that I started fantasizing about certain things...

Although my freedom evaporated when Joseph came back, I didn't even mind that because my head was filled with Adrian and the fun we had had together. I couldn't even remember when I had had such a great time.

I never really thought about what Joseph would say about my eye surgery; after all, it happened without his knowledge. He was only curious about where I had gotten the money. I told him that my parents had helped me out. Hearing this he just couldn't resist commenting, "I didn't know they were doing that well." Whatever that meant.

Throughout my recovery, Joseph threatened to hit me several times. I was so afraid for my healing eyes that I debased myself and literally begged him not to hurt me. I was horrified that the powerful blows he always inflicted on my head could damage my eyes.

Meanwhile, he came up with another idea: he wanted penthouse on the top of the office building. The work was underway when he asked me to choose the carpet and the kitchen cabinets. I was interested in interior decorating, but in that case I was unable to think straight. It felt so ironic that he was asking me to decorate my own prison where I would be regularly beaten, raped, and slandered. There were beautiful textile patterns but nothing fit into our living circumstances. If I had had a happy family life and a real home, I could have done wonderful things there, but I had no desire to beautify that place.

Nevertheless, I chose some carpets, and despite the obstacles I was satisfied with my selections, but he wasn't. "You don't even have any taste." Now that hurt me. It hurt me more than being called stupid all the time or a stinky skunk. I knew I had good taste, but the way he spoke to me always diminished the tiniest remainder of my confidence.

I really didn't want to move up there. I loathed every additional change in our lives because that just reminded me that months and years were passing by and I was still chained to him. And the fact that I had absolutely nothing to say to him just made everything even more difficult. I answered him when he had a question but that was it. I either pretended that he wasn't there or I wasn't. I couldn't look at him, couldn't speak to him, not to mention the obligatory smiling, which I wasn't able to do either. When it came to him, I was utterly burned out.

My eyes healed. I couldn't feign that I was still recovering because I wasn't. So when he had another reason to beat me, he did. The scene was the same as always. The children were stuck in the middle of his physical attack again…

When he stopped striking me and I could look into his face, I was so shocked at what I saw that I almost forgot the beating. I didn't even recognize him. His face was enraged and twisted, his pupils were dilated, his glance deranged. All he lacked was a foaming mouth. He looked like a lunatic. I was more afraid of the way he looked than of his actual attack. His contorted face haunted me for a very long time.

We were at war; there was no doubt about it. It felt as if our lives got worse every minute. I was wired 24/7 and the fear for my children's safety kept me on the edge. I didn't have to wait for the next attack; it was already happening. After being beaten again I tried to shield the children from him but I failed; he got Joey and wouldn't let go of him. He pulled the child into the bedroom and bolted the door.

Alex was in my arms but all I could think of was my little Joey stuck in the room with his raging father. I knew he was terrified and I wanted him out of that room, out of Joseph's claws. I lost my sense of reality; the only thing I wanted was to free Joey. It didn't matter that he had already beaten me up and my body was throbbing with pain—I tried to break down the door so I could rescue my child.

The scuffle went on for a long time and was clearly audible on the third floor, because my father appeared in the doorway. I didn't even know that the door was open. "Oh my God!" he exclaimed and stopped abruptly. "Help me!" I screamed. "Help me to save my son! He wouldn't let him go and Joey is terrified. I have to save him! Help me!" I felt my sanity slip away in my desperation, but I didn't care. I had to save my little boy.

My father tried to get into the bedroom but he couldn't so he asked me several times to go to their place, but I wouldn't leave Joey behind. "We can't do anything," he said. "Just leave Joseph alone and you can come back later. Both of you have to calm down first."

I dragged myself out, clutching my baby. In my parents' apartment I sat on the couch, trembling all over. My father sat in front of me, and my mother was pacing around. For a while we just sat there in silence as I tried to regain my composure.

Then I waited and hoped that something miraculous would happen, but neither of them offered any help or support. I was actually waiting for some affection from them, either toward me or toward my trembling little baby. But nothing came. Neither of them seemed to worry about me, their only daughter. Neither of them made any fuss about me; neither of them comforted Alex or me. Neither of them showed a spark of love toward us.

They said nothing and I became very uncomfortable in that silence, so I started to explain what had happened and I showed the bruises, which were already noticeable on my arms. My father didn't say anything, just kept on sighing. But for some reason my mother was angry. "If you two don't get along, what will happen to us?"

I wasn't able to utter a single word, although my mind was racing. I wasn't actually sure that I had heard my mother correctly but they were looking at me, waiting for an answer I couldn't come up with. But I had some questions of my own. *Am I responsible for them? Is it my duty to provide for their happiness and sense of security? Is our living situation my fault? Do they blame me? Are they angry with me? Well, my mother obviously is. But I am their child, am I not? How can they let me down in such a crisis? Do they expect me to sacrifice myself for them? Would that make everybody happy? Why is it that everybody is more important than me?*

I couldn't breathe; I had to get out, so I walked to the door without saying a word to them. Neither of them walked me out or offered anything. My father remained in his seat while my mother called after me, "Make things right!" So after all, I was the one to blame again. I was responsible, as always. She had already told me that I wasn't kind enough to Joseph, that that was the major problem.

My head was buzzing, and my only answer to her was, "Try to live my life!" But I only answered in my head. I couldn't believe that they hadn't even asked me how I was.

CHAPTER 51

THE NEXT TIME I WENT to see the psychiatrist I told her about Adrian, although I felt guilty about him. I knew, though, that I deserved such a positive experience, finally. His kindness felt extremely good but also very strange. I wasn't accustomed to such humane treatment, but in this case, I didn't doubt its honesty. It also helped me to realize that I was still somehow capable of managing a healthy relationship and that meant I wasn't entirely destroyed. Not yet, anyway, which was good to know. The doctor fully supported my friendship with him.

Visiting my therapist gave me an extra opportunity to meet Adrian outside of the factory ground, far away from Joseph and his spies. From time to time I took the children with me to my appointments. While I was in, Adrian played with them in the hospital's beautiful park; then when I was finished all four of us had some good times before we headed back to our prison. Those free moments were mesmerizing and I felt myself falling under their spell.

Whenever I could, I still visited my friend at her boutique. Only now I had no money at all, so I just admired her beautiful collection while trying to ignore the nagging pain in my soul. Whenever I was there, we chatted for a long time.

I told her and her employee about Adrian. I was very excited and felt very adventurous to have him in my life. At least one of the locked opportunities was opening up for me. My friends shared my delight and said that I deserved to have some happiness.

We stood at the front door, chatting endlessly, when an older man came in. His presence made me weirdly uncomfortable as we stood at the lingerie rack. First, I thought he was a homeless person, but his clothes were neat and clean, although rather old-fashioned. He looked so out of place.

My friends were giggling, but I couldn't even crack a smile. I felt so strange, like I was in a different dimension. There was something unnerving about that man but his face was so loving, so caring and peaceful, almost angelic. And he was smiling so beautifully, so gently. I kept staring into his face, feeling weirder and weirder, and I couldn't have explained the feeling that engulfed me. Obviously, he hadn't come in to buy anything. He said a few words to my friends, and then he turned to me, still smiling. "Why do you lack self-confidence? You have such a beautiful forehead and you are very intelligent. You shouldn't feel bad about yourself." Then he was gone—he just disappeared.

I couldn't say anything, just stared into the air. My friends were giggling encouragingly but I couldn't laugh with them. That man had a huge effect on me. I felt strangely calm. Although I didn't necessarily understand why he would say such things to me, his words and his ethereal face remained with me for a long time.

In the fall, Joseph fired my parents again, along with my brother. This time they also had to move out, so they went back to our home town. Sadly, my parents' presence never really provided much support for us, but now that they weren't there, I missed them. I felt very alone and even more isolated from the world. It was even harder when at Joseph's suggestion Adrian was transferred to some other place.

He had become an important part of our lives and it was painful not to see him at the food discount. I actually felt the emptiness. Fortunately, we could still keep in contact. I called him from different phone booths when I was out taking Joey to school. I also knew Adrian's schedule.

After my brother left, Joseph assigned one guy from the warehouse to drive us to the school and he became a good pal. That went on for a while, but then he started to blame me for keeping his employee away from work. Therefore, Joseph himself volunteered to take us—except he didn't even have the patience to wait while I dropped Joey off.

He was sitting in the car and when I went back to him, he was already fuming. "Where have you been? What have you been doing in there? What took you so long?" I told him, but he didn't like my answer, so the next morning he came in with us.

While I changed Joey's clothing and said goodbye to him, Joseph was standing over our heads, watching like a predator. The following day, he refused to come in, but called after me, "Just throw him in! You don't need to fuss about him that much."

Well, that was his idea of love, but I wasn't able to do it. His insensitivity constantly shocked me. I told him that I needed to see that Joey was all right before I left. How could I just throw in a five-year-old child? It was very depressing to start every day listening to Joseph's whining. I couldn't take it very long, so—in spite of his disapproval—I switched to the bus.

That was a rather new experience for me. I had never taken the bus with my children before. People were always so nice and helpful to us and they always gave up their seats. I put my children on the free seat but remained standing. Then one day an old man spoke to me. "You should sit down!" He took me by surprise and I felt rather dumb. It had never occurred to me that I should take the seat.

After I took Joey to school I didn't even go back to the office building. I needed some time to sort out my life. Even though I was totally alone in my misery and could only count on myself, I had reached the point where I wasn't only thinking or dreaming of getting away from him, I was actually planning it.

There were days when Adrian waited for us and if he was off duty, we spent half the day together. I shared my life and my plans with him. I was determined to carry out my escape, but I was also afraid of being alone with my children. I wished I had someone I could rely on at least a bit.

I was toying with the idea that I would "invite" Adrian to come with us. We had gotten pretty close by then and that gave me the extra push to take the risk and ask him, despite truly believing that I had no right to request such a huge favour. But the safety of my children was my priority before everything else and I felt I needed Adrian around us. He was a good and decent man, and I knew I could trust him. I could hardly believe it when he said yes. I was and remain immeasurably grateful to him. God bless him.

Somehow, I managed to save some money although I almost didn't even realize that I had something to reach toward. It wasn't enough to start a new life, but at least it would give us a head start. Adrian took the responsibility of locating a place, and when he found one, we went to check it out together. He did a great job. On his second try, he found an apartment that was suitable for our needs and was available from the first of December, which was approximately a month away. I was looking forward to my new life and my new home, and I was sure that

I would be able to manage those few remaining weeks with Joseph. And since we were moving—either to the roof or to somewhere else—I boxed and bagged all of our stuff.

In the meantime, the penthouse was almost done. Joseph moved up there, taking Joey with him and leaving Alex and me in the nearly empty apartment on the fourth floor. For several nights, we slept totally separately. Having Joey away from me filled me with never-ending worries. I could only imagine how hard it was for him, because he was forced by his father to sleep with him night after night.

At dawn, when he went to his office, he left Joey all alone in that huge, unfamiliar apartment. When we had a chance to speak, Joey told me that he wanted to come to us in the early morning but his father wouldn't let him in. I had no idea. And that happened repeatedly. Then one morning, at about 4:00 a.m., I was awakened by my little Joey. He was cold and barefoot, but at least he was with us. When I asked him how he had gotten in, he said that finally his father had allowed him to come to me.

This was senseless torture and it was hard to understand why he would do that to a five-year-old child. He could have let him in before that. But I knew that it was just part of Joseph's sick games. So in my opinion, my plan to leave him was highly justified. During those nearly seven years, I had experienced more than enough reasons to get out of his claws. Now there was no turning back. I had to do it for my children and for myself as well. Only it wasn't time yet; there were two more weeks and I had to be strong.

Despite all we had been through, the children kept growing and they needed shoes. I couldn't reveal the little money I had saved, so I told their father that the children needed new shoes. I thought he could do at least that much for them. Well, he didn't. He simply refused to buy pairs of shoes for his sons, because as he said, "You have to be a good common-law first. Love me and appreciate me first, then you will get what you want." It didn't matter that the children, not I, needed shoes.

CHAPTER 52

SINCE JOSEPH'S COMPANY NEVER SEEMED to be very strong or stable, it came to a point where more money was needed to keep it alive so he approached me again. But this time he wanted about 60 million forint, which was about $537,000CAD, borrowed on my name. I had already helped him to carry out his dream with that 40 million in '92 and there was no way that I would give my name again, not to mention taking on the responsibility. I had learned my lesson. Besides, I had been advised by a lawyer, an acquaintance of our paediatrician, not to sign anything. So I didn't. I told him that much when he came to me with his commands. When I refused to obey, he began fuming with rage. But he didn't have too many cards in his hands because he had already fired my parents and my brother, so he could no longer use them against me.

I thought he would beat me up again because I wouldn't do what he wanted, but instead he put all the responsibilities on my shoulders. "If I don't get the money," he shouted, "the company goes bankrupt and I'll be ruined. By then I'll have nothing to live for, and because it's your fault I'll kill all three of you!"

The children were right there with us, and I didn't know whether they understood what he had just said, but I did. I looked at him and the blood stopped running in my veins. Just that one look was enough to convince me that he meant what he said. He actually threatened our lives! I felt the fear sweeping through my body and I certainly didn't want to die by his hands, although whenever he had beat me I felt that he could have killed me easily. I also feared that one of these days he really would finish what he started and I didn't want to wait for that. But even after his threat, I still didn't sign those papers.

Then his lawyer and my adviser drew up a paper in which I handed all responsibilities for the company to Joseph. Two witnesses signed it and with that my name was cleared. That was a huge relief, but Joseph wasn't happy. He gave me a last ultimatum. "You have to decide whether you want to live with the children and me or not. I want your answer by this Saturday, the twenty-second." That was nine days earlier than we could occupy our new place and I had no idea where we would stay until then because I knew I wouldn't be staying at the office building.

He left for Romania on Wednesday, so I had two or three days to answer him. I reconsidered my choices and knew it was very unlikely that I would ever have a normal or safe life with him. I felt I had played out all my cards. I had adjusted to his treatment in as many different ways as I could. I had even used methods I saw on TV, like putting my hands gently on his shoulders when he was upset about something other than me, but he just shook them off. After seven years of constant agony and desperate tries, nothing had worked. None of my methods had the result I was longing for: no harmony, no love, no respect or appreciation, only tears, pain, terror, and fear.

He also held everything against me; everything I said and nearly everything I did. I had never been an equal part in this relationship, only a worthless creature—a big nobody and a big nothing. Once again, it hurt me to realize that he had never loved me, never even liked me, that I was never important to him and never even counted as a living, breathing human being who had feelings. He never wasted his time to actually get to know me, he was never interested in me or who I really was. Just like my parents.

Ultimately, he never wanted that particular person who was me; he just wanted to have another him. But whenever he needed somebody to kick, I was very handy. And after these long years living in constant fear and uncertainty, I was beyond exhaustion. Living up to his unlimited and ever-changing standards was simply impossible. I was dying in this so-called relationship.

Besides, I was simply too worried for my children to stay, afraid for our lives. So on Friday evening I packed a few necessities and wrote a note to Joseph: "I have decided. I cannot live like this any longer. We'll spend the night somewhere else and I'll be back tomorrow, so we can discuss the situation. Do not worry, we are fine."

I was too afraid to wait for him and tell him face to face, "I can't do this any longer!" I was sure that he would kick me out but without the children. I couldn't let that happen. Saving my life but leaving them behind would have killed me—I wasn't able to betray them. So, I saved what I could, if nothing else but our lives. I put the note into an envelope and left it with the doorman, whom I didn't even recognize.

We took the first bus and headed into the darkness to find a safe place for the night, although at this point I still had no idea where that would be. But for some reason I wasn't worried about that because I knew I was doing the right thing in order to save us. I was always very afraid that one day he would treat the children just as he treated me. I already could see the first signs of that toward Joey. I didn't want my children to have to directly experience the same terror I had been put through. They had already seen and heard more than enough.

The bus was nearly empty and that gave me some sort of comfort and even a sense of safety. And by now I also had a plan. When we got off it was pitch dark. The streetlights didn't work, taking away my sense of safety. My stomach trembled as I inched along in the darkness to find the house where I wanted to leave my children for the night. Alex was half-asleep held in my left arm and clutching my neck, while on my right side I held Joey as close to me as I could manage. I was scared because I was still kind of expecting that someone would stop me and take us back to Joseph.

When I finally found the house I was overwhelmed with relief that we hadn't gotten lost. But we were just standing in front of the house for a while, because I didn't dare to ring the bell. Since I had no other choice and I had to provide a warm bed for my children, I had to gather all my strength just to ring it.

Joanne was extremely surprised when she saw us. I told her what had happened, that I was running for our lives, and asked her if she could take my babies in for the night; I would be back after I spoke to Joseph tomorrow. Thankfully, she offered her help. I felt so grateful that I almost choked on my emotions. But I had to be strong and not let my tears come because that would have opened the floodgates.

When my babies were settled, her husband called me a cab and I was on my way. Even though I had no place to sleep, I didn't even ask Joanne whether she could take me in as well. My children were the first priority and I didn't want to burden her further.

Everything was so peaceful around us as the cab smoothly glided in the dark. The driver put on some music and finally I could relax a bit.

My children were safe for the night and I wasn't really concerned about myself. I knew Adrian was on duty, and since I had nowhere else to go, I went to visit him. Unquestionably, he was very supportive.

At his post there were a few chairs and two tables. I occupied one of the tables and Adrian offered his backpack as my pillow. He took a chair and bent over the table to get some rest while his colleague did the rounds. I slept an hour or so and the next morning I went back to Joseph for the discussion.

I was so sure and confident that I would be able to talk some sense into him, and I also planned to get some warm clothes for myself because I was shivering. I had only a light coat on, and since it was almost the end of November it didn't provide enough warmth. The weather was getting colder by the day.

I went to the fourth floor and tried to get into the apartment but my key wouldn't open the door. First, I didn't understand why it wouldn't work, so I tried it again. After these unsuccessful attempts, I turned to go and look for Joseph but I almost bumped into him. He already knew that I was there. "I have to get in," I said without greeting him. I was rather surprised to hear myself because I couldn't recognize my own voice. "I'm cold. I need a few sweaters." He looked at me ever so coldly. "You'll get nothing," he said, "not even a sweater until you bring my children back." His face was locked in a stone-cold but clear expression. I could see that there was nothing that I would be able to discuss with him so I just left without saying another word or even looking at him. I wasn't about to bargain over my children's lives.

Later that day, I signed the rental agreement, paying the first month's rent and the security deposit. Now the place was surely ours. Still one week was left, though, until December first, thus I had to find another solution. Adrian's mother offered a bed for the next night, so after I picked up the children from Joanne's we went to her.

It was a surprising and huge help that she took us in. She was very kind and also grateful to me, because her son had had a drinking problem, but had totally given that up since I had come into his life.

Now we had a place to stay for the upcoming night, but we had no place to stay for the upcoming week. I had to find a motel or something in the area, so I checked out a few and luckily found a very nice, quiet place. I took one room with a bathroom attached. It was comfortable and clean, which was more than I could hope for in those circumstances. After all, we were escaping. When everything was settled, I picked up my children from Adrian's mother and went to the guesthouse, which became our home for the next week.

Adrian was always there for us. He brought fresh food to us every day because I was too afraid to go out. But I still had responsibilities. I couldn't really stay in hiding for who knows how long. I had to go out to the school and explain to them the situation, tell them that Joey wouldn't be coming for some time.

While I was engulfed in fear and worry about what would happen to us, Adrian gave me a sense of safety and much more than I could ever have asked. He stayed with us for the night whenever he could. I felt so very grateful for all his help, and deeply touched that such giving and helpful people still existed. I was very lucky to have someone like him at our side. He did more for us than anybody else, but that's how he was. No wonder he was so special to us.

Even though I had bravely carried out my plan, I was terrified of the consequences, which were constantly hovering over my head. I was very afraid of Joseph, both physically and emotionally. Still, I wanted to solve the problem with great diplomacy. So on November twenty-fifth, I wrote a statement to Joseph's lawyer, in which I explained my recent acts:

"The past circumstances weren't safe for the children or for me. In the last seven years I have suffered from my common-law's treatment. He has blackmailed, threatened, and physically hurt me, he has kept us in total financial withdrawal, and slandered and bullied me throughout the past years. I cannot take this any longer.

"My children have had no peace and no safety. In the circumstances in which Joseph kept us, I wasn't able to provide much-needed safety for them. There wasn't a bed or a corner where they could be. I feel that it is my responsibility to rescue the children from that unbearable and dangerous situation.

"For their stability and healthy development I was compelled to create totally new circumstances, in which I'll do everything to provide the best for the children. Besides, on November 19th, 1997, the father of the children threatened to kill us. On November 21st, 1997, I left the factory ground with them. I indicated that I would go back to discuss the situation, which I did. As his response Joseph had changed the lock on the door, thus I could get none of my belongings.

"We'll have a new home by December 1st."

Chapter 53

I didn't reread my statement to check whether it was clear or not. I was emotionally overloaded and I just wanted the main facts out of my system. I knew it wasn't at all professional, but in those circumstances I was quite satisfied with my efforts. What else could I have said? I tried to squeeze seven long years into a few short sentences. And I really didn't want to go into all the details of violence and brutality Joseph had put us through. I just wanted the lawyer to get the picture and I could only hope that he actually did. I dated and signed my statement, and the next day I asked Adrian to mail it as a registered letter.

On December first, we left the guesthouse and the four of us occupied our new place, a quite large apartment with two bedrooms on the eighth floor, high enough so I felt safe there. The apartment was furnished. There were two beds, one sofa bed, one coffee table, one desk, one wardrobe, a bench, four chairs and a small dining table. As far as I was concerned, it was perfect.

We had nothing else, though: no bedding, no cutlery, no plates, no pots; nothing, only the four of us. Adrian and his mother helped us to get some basic necessities, plus a small radio and a black and white TV, and we were in heaven. My children were relaxed and happy. They danced and played for hours. I had never seen them like that before. They had such a party that the neighbour below us came up. Their joy convinced me even further that I had done the right thing.

I had to call my parents, though. I didn't want to, but I felt that I must. It was always easier to speak to my father, so I was glad that he answered the phone. Without any introduction, I just blurted out, "I left Joseph. I could not take his terrors anymore." After my father was able to respond to me, his first question was, "How are you going to support the children?" "I have help," I answered him but I didn't start to explain.

It really saddened me that I had to actually convince him that the circumstances with Joseph had become unbearable, not to mention unsafe. He should have known better. We were on the phone for a while, but once again they didn't offer any kind of help or support to us, nothing. That was always one of the reasons I never considered going back to them; I knew I wasn't welcome. There were no questions such as, "What can we do to help you?" or "Is there anything you need?" Absolutely nothing, but I could hear and sense the unspoken accusations in their voices.

I knew they weren't happy about my decision. All my father kept repeating was, "I don't know, I don't know." And of course there were the very familiar deep sighs. I felt myself to be a very heavy burden because my father could never do anything but heave sighs. Anyway, I told them what I thought I had to. And since they didn't care enough to help, I really had nothing else to say.

On December second, a lawyer wrote a letter to Joseph to tell him that I had ended our relationship, and asked him to release our personal belongings. A short time ago he hadn't even allowed me to get one of my own sweaters, so it was no wonder that he didn't respond to the letter. Then my lawyer asked me to write a list of what I was claiming of the common acquisitions. That was also sent to Joseph but again, there was no answer.

Although his arrogance infuriated me, it felt so good to have some peace at our new home. Finally, I could get some real sleep. But this new situation had its own challenges. Very soon I realized that my savings wouldn't last as long as I had expected. I had absolutely no experience of what it meant to live independently—and it did cost. We needed more money for a brand new start, and we needed it urgently. I was casting about in my mind to find somebody who could help, and found one option that wasn't really one, but I had to take the risk anyway.

One of my parents' acquaintances had his own business and he was quite successful. My mother always praised him exuberantly, so I thought I would ask him for help. Humbling myself to that level was the hardest thing I had ever had to do, but the circumstances demanded it. I was very nervous and even more ashamed, but I had to swallow my pride and dignity.

Alex was with me and now it was my turn to cling to him. When we arrived at the man's office, I had to gather all my strength not to turn and leave. *I am doing this for my children*, I reminded myself over and over again. I had to convince myself, otherwise I wouldn't have been able to do what I had come to accomplish.

In the office I felt very uncomfortable, and was certain that I had made a huge mistake. But I was already there, just unable to say anything. The man's unfriendly manner didn't help me at all. The minutes were ticking by and I knew I was wasting his time.

He offered me a seat but remained standing. His polite but reserved voice gave me the much needed opening to tell him why I was there. I told him in a few words what had happened and that now I wished to start a new life and keep my children safe, but I was short of money. He didn't have to think twice to refuse my request. I didn't really know why, but I felt deeply hurt by his cold rejection, despite knowing he had every right to say no. And with that all my hope was crushed into tiny pieces. What hurt me the most was that he knew who I was. He respected and liked my parents (mostly my mother), yet he didn't even have a single encouraging word for me.

I was terrified as the uncertainty of our future swept through me all over again with more intensity than before. But I gathered myself enough to apologize and left the office as calmly as I could.

I was so ashamed that I wasn't able to look in his eyes when I said good-bye. On the way back I scolded myself for being so stupid as to put myself into such a self-destructive situation. What was I thinking?

We had to be very careful how we spent our little money. When we had left the office building, I had taken only a small bag with us. I couldn't have carried more anyway, and because of that now we had no clothes to change into, plus we had no washing machine. In our situation even the most basic things were a luxury. We were back in time; I had to wash our clothes by hand, but I didn't dare to wash the children's winter coats.

Although we had peace within those new walls, life went on. The lawyer who wrote the letters to Joseph seemed to take my case, even though he knew I was unable to pay him. Lack of money was only one side of the problem; the other difficulty was that to see him, I had to leave the apartment. So, I only ventured out when it was dark. It was pure luck that this lawyer only saw clients in the evening. Still, I was always watching my back.

The lawyer was within walking distance, and when I went to him I always remained in the protection of the houses and tried to avoid the streetlights. But one day I ran into someone I knew and in that instant I was certain that I'd been found. I wanted to turn back and run to the protection of the apartment because I was sure that my safety had just blown away. On the other hand it was vital that I see my lawyer so instead of cowardly running, although I was trembling in my whole being, I walked quickly to his office. All the while, the realization of my failure to remain safe was weighing on me heavily.

The lawyer was very nice and sympathetic. I trusted him, maybe because there wasn't any other authority figure I could rely on. I gave our passports to him for safekeeping. And after a few words were exchanged, I couldn't hold my tears back anymore. Even though I was sitting with my lawyer, I felt desperately helpless. He already had a picture of the situation we were in, and now he looked at me and said, "You are just as alone as a plucked grape." Unfortunately, that was a very fitting remark.

I had so many details to cover, and I just didn't know how to provide proper protection for my babies and myself. I also felt responsible for Adrian, even though it had been his decision to accompany me. Still, *I* had brought him into this circus.

I had always sensed that I wasn't "alone" in the dark because Joseph had hired people to search for us, but now I wasn't sure whether he knew where we lived or not. That was the most disturbing question of all. Up to this point we had always kept the shades down, and now we closed them. From time to time we peeked out to see whether we were safe enough to go out and get our groceries. Total devastation settled in when we realized that one of Joseph's henchmen was hanging around the main door of our building.

He was there for thirty minutes or so, then disappeared. Although we were on the eighth floor, I could only whisper, "He was waiting for us. They know where we live." I could barely keep the terrorizing fear at bay. I was thinking about my children, what would happen to them. I had done my best to save them, to protect them, and I had failed— failed them and failed myself as well. Everything was crumbling down on me. The whole situation was slipping out of my hands and I knew there was much more to come.

For the next few days I was too afraid even to go to the window. I just didn't know who I would see. My fragile freedom and security were lost, as if they had never even existed. It had been a beautiful mirage but now it was completely gone.

CHAPTER 54

JOSEPH LEARNED THE PHONE NUMBER of Adrian's mother and harassed her daily. What was going on between my parents and Joseph was a complete mystery, but I was sure that they were deeply involved. Since obviously they weren't on my side, I was certain that they would hook up with Joseph just to make me jump out of my hiding.

Then the message came. I was expected to attend a meeting at the bank where I had had to sign the loan in 1992. The time was set for December sixteenth, 10:00 a.m. The appointment was quite a surprise, but I didn't question its purpose. I believed that it was necessary for me to go there. I didn't want any extra burden on my shoulders, so as a woman of integrity (or stupidity) I wanted to solve this puzzle and do what was right.

The date of the appointment was rather convenient because on the same day I was due to take Joey to his psychologist, so I took him with me. I planned to take him to the hospital right after the meeting.

I was so nervous about being outside with my son that I was literally trembling. At the bus station I checked all the people and noticed a young guy using a cell phone. For some reason I had to look at him several times. His skin was covered with acne scars and he was rather skinny. I didn't know him, but I had an uncomfortable feeling about him. (Such things only happen in the movies, right?)

When we had to switch buses, he was there again using his cell phone. By now, I was openly staring at him and when he caught my eyes, he turned his back on me. Then he was gone.

On the way to the bank I couldn't stop thinking about that young man. I was so suspicious of him that it hardly seemed real, and the fear numbed my mind so much that it was difficult for me to think logically anymore. Still, something about him was really bothering me. Even around the bank I kept searching for the guy, but he was nowhere to be seen.

At the bank we met Joseph's lawyer and my adviser, who I was surprised to see there, so my attention was diverted. These two people had helped me to grant all financial responsibilities to Joseph the previous month. I didn't know what was going on, or why they had to be there, but I didn't question them. After all, who was I to doubt two lawyers' intentions?

We went in and waited for five minutes or so. When we were motioned in, the bank worker was very relieved to see me, saying, "We were very worried that you had disappeared. But now that we know you are here and well, everything is all right."

They needed my new address. That was it—the meeting was over and I still didn't know why I had to be there. (I guess my inner alarm didn't work.) We were out within ten minutes, including the waiting time.

After the so-called meeting Joseph's lawyer invited all of us for a cup of hot chocolate. We talked about the recent situation. I told them what we had been through with Joseph, and they seemed to understand my point of view. Then we went our separate ways and I never saw them again.

I had thought that the bank appointment would be longer and now it was too early to go to Joey's appointment, so we headed back to the apartment.

We were just a few metres from the door when Joseph approached us, grinning widely. I stopped the instant I saw him, not because I wanted to but because I was rooted to the spot; I couldn't move or speak.

He happily greeted us, squatted down in front of Joey, lifted him up, and started to run. That shook me up. "Hey, what are you doing?" I yelled after him, still unable to make a movement. But he just kept running. I heard him laughing while Joey was desperately screaming and kicking. Then finally I was able to make a step forward, was ready to run after them, when a voice stopped me. "You have no right to touch that child!"

When I turned, I faced the man who had been lurking around the building a few days ago, Joseph's head henchman, who had originally been just another security guard. I noticed his gun and baton, which were far too obvious. And then I spotted the scar-faced guy. "He was the one who followed us," I whispered. "That's right," the henchman said, and with that all my strength left my body. I felt like a rag doll that would drop to the sidewalk at any moment. I had to hold on to the man as I begged him, "Please, help me. My baby, help me to get my baby back." I could have felt so pitiful, but I felt nothing. I was numb emotionally and physically. "I can't," he said. "I'm sorry!" Then he advised me to get married, or get a job, or do something else, because till then I had no right to my own child.

I didn't thank him for his advice, just slowly dragged myself to the door. Joey was gone and I felt weak, so very weak and lifeless. I didn't understand how I was able to stay standing on my own two feet. My keys felt so heavy that I had to use both my hands just to put one in the lock and turn it. Then, with my whole body weight, I pushed the door open just enough for me to squeeze in. Somehow, I could manage the elevator, which was like an old wardrobe, but I wasn't able to open the security gate to our apartment. I gathered all my strength to turn the key, but I couldn't.

Adrian heard me and came to my aid. "I can't open it. I can't open the gate. I cannot," I whimpered. "I'll do it," Adrian said and finally I was in the apartment. But as I stepped in I could go no further. I just collapsed onto the small bench we had in the foyer. "Where is Alex?" I asked my friend, but didn't hear what he said, if he said anything at all. "Alex? Where is he? Is he here? Is Alex here?" I kept asking the same question over and over again. "They took him already," Adrian said quietly. "What? Where is Alex? How?" But I didn't wait for his answer. I continued my mindless chant. "But now at least they are together, right? My children, they are together and that is good, right?" I was reassuring myself more than I was talking to him. I didn't cry because I couldn't cry yet. But as the events slowly sank in I started to sob.

It felt as if I had lost everything. No—everything had been taken away from me. With Joseph, I had lived imprisoned. My whole life was overshadowed; all opportunities were cut off. Once, I had been full of dreams like every other young woman. And now even my precious babies had been taken away by the one person from whom I was so desperately trying to protect them.

Joseph had never let me enjoy my motherhood; he made sure that my happiness was non-existent, and this was the cherry on top. I couldn't take the thought that my children were back with that maniac, who had never cared about them, only terrorized and used them ever since they were born. They were back with that sick freak, who had threatened to kill them and from whom I wanted to save them. But I lost. I had never even imagined that my luck would run out so quickly, not to mention those two lawyers' betrayal. Their behaviour made me wonder about the validity of the papers I had signed six weeks ago. Did I really transfer the responsibility for the 40 million forint to Joseph?

I lost all hope. That was it. That was the end. I sat on that bench for a long time. The thoughts were coming and going in my mind, but I had no answers, no solution for the problems I was facing. On top of everything, I was so weak that I couldn't even untie my shoes. It took me a couple of hours before I could listen to Adrian, who told me what had happened with Alex. "While you were out with Joey I took Alex for a walk around the building. Then Joseph appeared with two men and simply took Alex from me. When I objected, Joseph told me that he was the father, and I couldn't argue with that. Besides, they outnumbered me. There was nothing I could do."

I was still nursing Alex. The simple thought of that made me want to scream my head off. *Poor baby, what will happen to him?* I had to do something, I just didn't know what. I had seven years' experience of living in terror but I had no experience with how to solve the never-ending problems of my life. I felt totally hopeless about the future. Although Adrian was a rock-solid support, I was completely alone when it came to dealing with Joseph.

Later, in the afternoon, Adrian convinced me to call my lawyer, who advised me to call the police. He told me what to say, so I did as I was advised. Involving the police gave me a slight hope that they might help me to save my children. I called and told them what had happened. I also told them that I was still nursing my little one, and that the children were in serious danger because their father was very unpredictable.

The officer asked me, "Was there any blood on the scene?" I wasn't expecting such a question and answered him rather hesitantly but truthfully, "No."

"Then we cannot help," he said. Now that made me lose my composure. Before he could hang up on me I thundered into the receiver, "Then what should I do?"

"Abduct them back the same way he did," said the officer. "How can I do that? I can't do that." But his answer was the same. "We cannot help unless there was blood on the scene."

I slammed the receiver down. My own blood was boiling as I turned to Adrian and told him what the man had said. Then I started to yell again. "What do they want; someone to die? Then they would do something? They actually wait until someone dies, or at least bleeds. I can't believe this. They are the police! They're supposed to help, serve and protect, and they don't do any of that." I had no idea what to do next.

I called my lawyer back. He wasn't surprised about the police's attitude. I wasn't really surprised either, but I was utterly disappointed. I was a good citizen who needed their help and got none. The lawyer's next advice was to contact the district family/child protection service, then go to the court to give my statement about the past and recent events.

I contacted the family protection service in the children's district, but a woman just rudely interrupted me before I could explain why I was calling, telling me to call the office in my residential area. Her unfriendly and snappy tone shook me but I called the other place anyway. There, I was pleasantly surprised that they actually listened to me and considered my case serious enough to open a file and set up an appointment. The woman said, "The father has no right to lock the children away from their mother. I will contact him." Once again, that sounded very hopeful and promising.

I was very happy that finally I had an authority figure who promised to act on our behalf. I truly believed that something positive would happen, and that finally I had the help I was seeking to protect my babies. At least, that was what I thought, what I hoped, what I expected.

CHAPTER 55

EVEN THOUGH ALEX WAS TWO years old, I was still nursing him and that made me look like an abnormal person in everybody's eyes. People around me, like the police operator, the family protection worker (the helpful one), Joseph of course, and even my parents were against it. They all said that Alex was way too old to be nursed.

Maybe so, but they all missed the point or simply didn't care that it was a pure miracle that after all the beatings, all the rapes, all the intimidations, all the terror I had been put through, I was still able to comfort him. Moreover, that was the only way I could calm him down after his father's attacks. And I was the insane one? I just did what I could to survive and save us. In my eyes, it was a superhuman act. And yes, it was also very important to me because I had only been able to nurse Joey for ten weeks. I didn't want that to happen with Alex.

But who understood that or even tried to? People ignored the fact that Alex might need that special connection with me, and claimed the right to judge me, even condemn me. But they could've said anything. I was proud. Not surprisingly, though, nobody judged Joseph's actions.

After the abduction, I got sick from the accumulated milk, and had to drain my breasts so I wouldn't run a fever. I cried every day as I washed my precious milk down the sink along with my tears. Alex would have needed it.

On December nineteenth, I went to the courthouse with Adrian, who remained my one and only support during the whole crisis. There, I was asked to write a statement, which would be handed to a judge.

For a while I was just standing there, toying with my pen, because I had no idea where to start. The clerk gave me some basic idea of what to include in my statement and that helped me start writing.

When I was finished, I had a three-page, handwritten affidavit; still, I felt that I had missed a lot of important details. I wasn't satisfied but was very exhausted and the clerk said that it was good enough. So, I trusted his judgment. At least that was done; now I had to work on getting used to a life that didn't include my children.

Without them my life was dull and purposeless. I wanted to see them, to be with them or at least to know something about them. To support my case it was essential to go and visit them, but my fear of Joseph, his henchmen, and the experience I had been put through stopped me.

I imagined going there and asking the doorman's permission to see my children, then leaving them; but the simple thought of facing Joseph again petrified me. I wasn't strong enough to deal with that humiliating task. I was their mother, but that obviously didn't matter to anybody.

On the twenty-third, I received a telegram. I opened it reluctantly and as I started to read it, my stomach turned. It was an invitation from Joseph for a Christmas dinner at 3:00 p.m. He invited me to have a Christmas dinner with my children! Just like any other guest. To me this was filthy insolence and I was deeply offended.

I didn't even answer him and I didn't go either. Even though I was desperately longing after my babies, for their own protection I kept myself away. I didn't want to hurt them with my being there then leaving them, as I was certain that Joseph would kick me out after the dinner was over. I didn't dare to imagine what that would do to the boys. We had grown far too close to each other in those horrifying periods of Joseph's insane rages. We were like one soul in three bodies—too bonded. I knew every vibration of them. Thus, I just stayed away. Still, I needed a back-up, someone who would understand my decision and tell me that I was right. So I spoke to the paediatrician and Joey's psychologist. Both of them agreed with me that it was best for the boys if they didn't see me so as not to cause them more emotional turbulence.

Christmas…and I thought that the previous Christmases were sad. This one was simply unbearable. Still, Adrian and I went out to do Christmas shopping. People were in high spirits, and children, oh God, children were everywhere. I was constantly swallowing my tears as I looked at them but thought of my two little boys.

I wanted a small tree for my children. Or maybe I needed that tree. We even bought a few presents for them. Although they weren't with us, I had to do that. I decorated the tree with colourful ribbons, and put the presents beside it. We didn't have Christmas lights, but the silky ribbons sparkled on their own. The tree looked beautiful but also very lonely. And I wasn't celebrating there; I was grieving at the tree, which stood like a tombstone in the darkness.

On Christmas Eve I just sat in the dark room, silently singing the Christmas carols I knew. I looked out of the window and could only pray that my babies were all right. And since I wasn't with them, I asked God to look after them for me.

Close to the end of this horrible year, I got lucky when, with Adrian's help, I was able to contact one of the doormen who my children and I liked so much. Surprisingly, he still worked there and I hoped that he would be able to tell me something about the boys. "I haven't seen them ever since they were brought back," he said solemnly. "But their father is telling everyone that the children are very happy without their mother. They don't miss her at all and have already forgotten her. He also hired some woman to look after them."

I knew my children. There wasn't one living person on earth who knew them as much as I did. Therefore, I also knew that whatever Joseph was telling other people couldn't be true. Still, it hurt me tremendously that I was so easily disposable, and Joseph's bald-faced lies made me very angry.

He had taken the children from me just to pass them off on a stranger, and to keep them like hostages. Shocking. My worry for my children escalated minute by minute, and my anxiety and depression reached their peak. I could feel that they weren't all right. And gossip spread like wildfire. The news reached us as well that the doorman who had told me about my children was fired.

I paced aimlessly from room to room, or just sat hugging and rocking myself, which scared Adrian a bit. "What are you doing?" he asked, looking at me rather strangely. "Rocking myself," I said and although I noticed his discomfort, I continued. I needed that solace.

I felt so empty—more than empty, I felt dead. I dragged my body from one day to the next, but my spirit was gone. I couldn't function without my children. Adrian breathed for me and made life go on. He pampered me and kept an eye on me. Every morning he brought me fresh baked goods, and cooked for me daily. He was always there when I needed him, and he left me alone when I needed to be alone.

But even in my misery, I couldn't deny the ironic side of the situation. From our apartment I could clearly see the office building. I tried to force myself not to look out of the window, but I did it anyway. I just stared at the building and imagined my children in that prison where Joseph kept them locked away from the whole world.

I dreaded starting another year, which was already on our doorstep. Somehow each year had gotten worse and worse. And now there was a new one to face. I wasn't sure I could do it.

1998
The sacrificial lamb

CHAPTER 56

IT HAD BEEN OVER THREE weeks now without my children. I had suffered enough throughout the last seven years, but these three weeks had been the most unbearable times of all. I was a mother, a good mother, but my motherly privilege—my pure rights—were brutally taken away. To me, my life was over and I couldn't find any reason why I should continue to fight.

Adrian regularly took me to my psychiatrist. Because of the severe crisis I had suffered she gave me a prescription to help me regain myself a bit. She also spoke to my friend and told him that the best way to shake me out of my despair was by taking me out of the apartment. That I didn't want to do because whenever I went out I saw too many children and that made me even more miserable. There were no pills on earth that would have made me not miss my babies.

But just to show that I was cooperative and wanted to get better I took the pills for awhile. Whatever their purpose was, they didn't make any difference for me. I still jumped out of my skin when the doorbell rang, and I hid when I heard people talking in the stairway. My nerves were always at their breaking point. I simply wasn't able to control my fear.

Then one day I thought I would take the whole box. I was sure that would do the trick. With this decision I started popping the pills out, one after the other. There was no use in my living and I didn't want to suffer any longer. Anything was better than living like this, not to mention facing Joseph again, which I dreaded the most. I had been pushed over the edge.

When I had about five pills in my hand, Adrian came to me and gently took the medication away. I had no strength to object but I still hadn't given up ending my miserable life. If I couldn't take the pills, there were other options, like Adrian's gun or a jump from the balcony.

Although I didn't find the eight floors high enough, I was drawn to the possibility. Maybe if I flew out instead of jumping...

But Adrian was always there. He wasn't only my friend; he was my guardian angel. And he was also one step ahead of me. After he took the pills, he locked away his gun and made sure that I wouldn't go near the balcony.

There were days when Adrian was simply too afraid to leave me alone for even one minute. And when it was inevitable that he had to go out, he left his guard dog with me and made me promise that I would be a good girl and not do anything foolish. Sometimes I was hesitant about promising him anything, but then he wouldn't leave until I agreed to stay alive while he was away. I gave my word and I kept it. Day after day, when he arrived home and found me unharmed, he let out a sigh of relief.

In the middle of my emotional turmoil my inner voice was getting louder and louder. Every time I was tempted to do something or even just thought about it, that voice was there, saying, "Your children need you! They *need* you!" And I had to realize that if I threw away my life, I also would throw away my children's lives. And that I wasn't able to do. That inner pleading convinced me that even though my children weren't with me at that point, they needed me.

My flirtation with death ended right there, and instead I sat down to write. I poured out all the pain, disappointment and frustration. For hours I did nothing but write. It was a new feeling and a very rejuvenating one, since it helped me to feel better.

I also started to focus on myself a little bit. It was still very hard to go on without the children, but at least I made some effort to gather myself together. I started to do things that I hadn't been allowed to do for seven long years: I read, whenever *I* wanted to; I watched TV, if *I* wanted to; I could even take a bubble bath, when *I* wanted, and I could sleep. With Adrian I was a free individual and that felt wonderful.

He also dragged me with him whenever he had to go out. I still didn't want to leave the apartment but he didn't let me stay in. He promised my doctor that he would get me out of there and he did.

I was so grateful to him, which I was sure he didn't know, and it would have been unfair to make his life more difficult, because everything he did was in my best interests. I knew I had caused enough headaches for him already and he deserved much better. So I tried to be cooperative. I followed him like a puppy, although I couldn't enjoy the outings very much. I felt branded and out of place, as though my shackles were clearly visible. I knew that my face reflected the pain I carried and even Adrian's face showed exhaustion. The whole ordeal was affecting him a great deal.

We went for long walks and took buses to get around. On one service, we sat clinging to each other, when a woman's voice attracted my attention. She sat in the row beside us with her friends. She was laughing so hard that she was almost choking. As she tried to say something to her friends she kept looking at us. When she finally could get the words out, I caught what she said: "Such a pretty picture. It seems love can be found in the bottle. It's very romantic." Then she laughed even harder.

Her words hit me with full force. *She thinks I am a drunk. I look like a drunkard?! How dare she?* I felt the anger welling up in me. I wanted to shake her off her seat or simply slap her around. But before it was too late my common sense took over: *She's just too dumb for her own good. She isn't worth any attention.*

But she wouldn't shut up. I listened to her cruel remarks for some time but after a while I had to get off the bus. I thought that some fresh air would help me clear my head, but her laughter and words haunted me for days. Whenever I was among people I wondered whether they thought of me as a drunkard.

Adrian was continuously a strong support. Good days or bad, he was there for me, with me. He was the only one who held my hand when I needed encouragement. He never blamed me for anything, never called me names, didn't manipulate or blackmail me, didn't force me, never held anything against me, and never yelled or hit me, whether I was annoying or not. He never had a bad or angry word for me. It seemed I was tolerable, even at the lowest point of my life. He made me feel important and likeable. Nobody had ever cared about me with as much devotion as he did.

He always tried to create a pleasant atmosphere, making me laugh and trying to please me no matter what time of the day. To keep my mind busy, we played *Words Up*, dominoes, and card games. We put together several jigsaw puzzles, watched TV, and cooked together. He made me feel like a queen and treated me accordingly. I was more grateful to him than I could ever express.

One day a very unusual event happened: we went to the movies along with my brother and his girlfriend! I hadn't been to the movies for eight years at least. I was so nervous that I was literally shaking. I just wasn't used to such occasions, such freedom. Once I overcame my uneasiness, I felt pretty joyful, only the movie itself, *The Devil's Advocate*, was too much for my nerves. I kept hiding behind Adrian's back throughout the film, which he found very amusing.

But without the children, time seemed to stop. Every day was painfully long and empty; only Adrian remained as he had been, always caring and helpful. Even when the children had been with us he would sit down to play with Joey. They played for hours, and I knew that that made Joey feel well loved and happy. He had never experienced anything like that before. I also knew that he grew very close to Adrian and loved him more than he loved his own father. The affection between them spoke volumes.

Since Adrian was there for me whenever I needed him, he deserved to see that his efforts yielded some results. I tried to relax and breathe, and enjoy our time together. But one time his playfulness caught me off guard. He unexpectedly reached toward me, which made me shield myself in an instant. I knew he didn't want to hit me but the abrupt movement made me tremble with fear. I felt very foolish and I could see that he was offended by my instinctive reaction, for which I apologized. He never again played with me like that.

And I had to regain my strength because the court notifications started to arrive. After my handwritten affidavit I was the plaintiff in the case and the first court appearance was set for March 10, this year.

Still, in mid-February I received a letter from Joseph's lawyer. He wrote to me on behalf of Joseph saying that he was in Canada at the time but after the seventeenth, he wished to see me in order that I visit the children and discuss the current situation with him.

The only thing that stuck in my mind was that he wasn't around. This was my chance, now or never, to try to get in and see my babies on my own without being supervised by Joseph.

I went to the office building, shaking like a leaf, and told the doorman, who I didn't know, why I was there. I fought the sense of deep humiliation—after all, I was asking a total stranger whether I could see my own children. He was well trained because he didn't let me in but called Monica, who called her father in Canada. Within minutes I spoke to Joseph. "I'm sorry, I cannot let you see the children," he said. "But when I'm there, you can come any time."

There weren't physical walls around me but I felt like walls were closing in as I tried to maintain my dignity. I thanked the doorman and slowly trudged away, feeling like a wounded dog. Joseph did what he had always said he would do: he took away the children from me. In this case, though, he didn't just take them away—he literally locked them away from me and from the entire world as well.

A month after the first court notice, an order arrived saying that Joseph had already taken action against me on November 28, 1997; therefore my case must be closed and the hearing that was set for March 10 had been cancelled. Very quickly, I went from plaintiff to defendant. But the most disturbing fact was that even my lawyer had no clue that Joseph was one step ahead of us.

The fact that he had just left the children with a stranger he had hired filled me with apprehension and anger. He never bothered with them. Moreover, within a couple of weeks I heard that he was out of country, again. Why had such a person ever wanted children?

Of my family, I only remained close to my brother, so I asked him to go and see the children for me. Who knows why, I was hoping that at least my brother could visit the boys, but he was also sent away.

My family was another enormous heartache I had to face. I was aware that they only wanted to brainwash me, so I didn't want to speak to them at all. I had already said what was necessary to say. Then one day, totally unexpectedly, my parents, my brother, my grandmother, and my godmother somehow got into the building and lined up in front of our apartment. I knew that they hadn't come to help me…

I didn't let anybody in. I wasn't able to face all of them at once, and I had no strength to protect myself from the enormous pressure and the flood of accusations. They were only my enemy's messengers and I was afraid of them.

CHAPTER 57

I WANTED TO BE LEFT alone, but they settled down on the stairs and refused to leave. Hours went by and they didn't move. Their presence irritated me tremendously and after a while they got on Adrian's nerves as well, so he made an attempt to convince them to leave.

He spoke to my father while I tried to vanish. I felt like a trapped animal. I knew that I was expected to listen to them and take their advice, but to be honest, I wasn't interested. They were always ready to lecture and blame me, and I didn't need that at all. Just because I was the youngest woman in the family, I was continuously disregarded.

After a lengthy negotiation between my family and Adrian, he came to me and asked whether I wanted to see my godmother—then they would leave. My childhood memories came to the surface. When I was a little girl, I loved her so much and looked up to her. And now, I was hoping that she would also remember those times. Still, I was reluctant to let her in, but since I wanted them to leave, I agreed.

My godmother came in and Adrian left us alone. As she sat down, she said, "What are you doing here? You have two beautiful children waiting for you. They need you and you deserted them for a fling?" The moment she opened her mouth I knew it had been a big mistake to let her in. I was shocked by what she said. "What fling?" I asked her. "I did everything to protect them but I am all alone. Joseph doesn't want me there. In his opinion I'm a bad mother. Besides, he regularly beat me up. I cannot live like that."

But she was very angry with me. "Get off your high horse! You're so spoiled. If I was your mother, I would've raised you differently. You think the whole world is about you? Everybody makes mistakes, but he is a good man and a good provider. Remember how happy you were when you could buy two pairs of shoes at once. Have you forgotten that you can thank him for that?" *Him?!*

After seven years my godmother threw those shoes at me, shoes for which *I* had worked very hard. How long and how many times had I had to pay for them? "Yeah, that was seven years ago. But last November he refused to buy shoes for the children. He only terrorizes us. Don't you get it? I don't want to be beaten and live in fear. How can I or anyone live like that?" By now I had great difficulty controlling my tears and frustration. "He is the father of your children," she said. "You should appreciate him. Don't forget that I couldn't have a baby. You must be grateful to him. He has only given you good."

She also brought up 1996, when she was in California and wanted to come over to us in Canada, but because of *my jealousy*, she couldn't. I didn't even know what she was talking about, and I wasn't able to listen to her any longer. I buried my face in my palms and screamed, "I can't live like that! I can't live in fear! I can't!" And my godmother kept yelling at me, "You'll regret this. You'll cry your eyes out. You must get off your high horse and learn to show some gratitude. He will take the children away from you, you know, and you don't have the slightest chance to win here. NONE!!!" With that she stormed out.

I was so tormented that I was shaking in my seat. I felt beaten all over again. She robbed me of my painfully gathered strength. That was my loving and supportive family. I didn't understand why they detested me so much, why they punished me.

That was exactly why I hadn't wanted to speak to any of them. They treated me like I was nothing but a slut, rather than a mother, a daughter, a goddaughter, a grandchild who was in great need of help and support, not to mention love, which I hadn't gotten for a very long time. Maybe their love for me never had been honest. And those nagging questions rushed back to me: *Was I really that intolerable and unlovable? Why do they hate me so much?*

It felt as if they had ripped my heart out and stamped on it. I was longing for my family's support and understanding, but instead I was accused, blamed, and threatened. All my pleas were in vain. And it hurt me so much that my godmother had violated my trust. I let her in and she just continued what Joseph had started. She and everyone else believed him but not me. WHY?

Again, only Adrian was there for me. He held me tightly while I cried my pain out on his shoulder. "It's not my fault that she couldn't have children, is it?" I sobbed. "Am I supposed to pay for that too? They just don't get it. Why is that?"

⌒

On March thirteenth, my brother came to us with an invitation from Joseph. He invited my parents and me for dinner on the upcoming Sunday. My first reaction was that he could eat his dinner alone. "I'm not going!" I said to my brother. The slightest thought of seeing Joseph again, not to mention eating with him at the same table, flooded me with terror.

It didn't surprise me that our parents had already accepted the invitation. I called them to say not to expect me. But of course, as always, my refusal wasn't acceptable to them. And now, instead of forcing and pushing me, my mother tried to buy me: "Joseph has changed. He admits that he also sinned and that he has to change too. He regrets everything that happened. He wants to buy a house outside of the factory ground. You can go back to school and get your further education to make your dreams come true. You can do whatever you like and are interested in. He also wants to take you to Canada, just for a few weeks, so the two of you can get closer again. Give him another chance." Hadn't I heard that before?

These promises were more than a honey-string could bear. But my mother went on and on, promising the starry sky and everything I was longing for. It made me dizzy. My mother was so enthusiastic and convincing that after a while I couldn't think clearly. Even though I wanted to have all that was said, I didn't believe one word of it. I knew him too well and I knew what he was capable of.

Then the promises turned into threats. Now that was more familiar to me. My mother continued, "But if you don't come along, he will take the children. You'll lose them. Take his offer! You'll have a wonderful life!" Wasn't this what they had said when they pushed me to take his job offer? How wonderful my life had turned out to be.

I was so tired of being manipulated and pushed around, and I was also terrified to go back to the terror and be a prisoner again. But then, I wanted to be with my children so badly. I hadn't seen them for three months now!

And my mother wouldn't stop. As if I had already accepted the invitation, she started telling me how to look. "Put on some makeup and dress pretty. Look irresistible. Wear a miniskirt, so he won't be able to resist you." So far, I had been treated like a slut, but now I actually felt like one. Listening to all this nonsense made my head spin. Then I heard myself interrupting her. "Okay, okay! I'll go. I'll go. Just stop it!" And they were happy.

On the fifteenth, around 1:30 p.m., my parents came to pick me up. I followed my mother's advice to dress nicely and also applied some makeup. Adrian was certainly very impressed, although I felt like a cheap whore. And when my parents saw me, they couldn't have been more pleased with me.

I was trembling in the car all the way to the office building and when I got out I had to gather my composure because I was sure that my shaking was clearly visible, and this wasn't the place to show my weaknesses.

Joseph greeted us without the slightest trace of a smile, holding a small child who I didn't recognize. When I passed by them and looked the child in the eyes, the recognition hit me hard. It was my little Alex. *Oh my God! I didn't recognize my own son!*

He was so pale, filthy, and ragged. He sucked his thumb, which he had never done before, while his index finger was in his nose. The snot was smeared all over his face. He didn't make any sound. I almost choked on my tears, but I didn't dare to touch him.

As we entered the penthouse, my godmother was there. She was also very pleased to see me but remained very cold when she said, "I'm glad that you came to your senses. That was a very adult decision. Look at your children. They need you. Don't ever dare to desert them again!" I didn't reply to her. There was nothing to say.

I was in deep shock at the appearance of my children. Joey looked the same as Alex. Their eyes were so empty, looked so sad, and they were deathly quiet. They looked like two frightened animals or ghosts. I wasn't expecting my boys to jump onto my neck, but I was hoping to at least hear some noises from them. Instead, they looked so lifeless. *What had their father done to them?*

I wanted to scream. I turned to my parents, ready to blow up. "Do you see this? Look at the children!" I fumed. "Hush!" my parents silenced me. "Joseph might hear you."

"I don't care!" I snapped. "My children look dead!" They hushed me again. "Put on your poker face and smile!" my mom said. Then it was my father's turn: "Oh, by the way, that list you sent to Joseph about those items was really stupid." That cold remark hurt so much that with the same effort he could have just hit me instead. They even knew about my visit to their acquaintance, for which they felt ashamed. How could I have done that, right? But nothing was as important as walking to the dinner table with a wide smile on their faces.

I felt myself facing a guillotine instead of that table. My stomach was upside down. I'd never seen my children so dirty and neglected, and I couldn't care less whether my parents liked my list or not. The fact that they were able to ignore their grandchildren's condition was simply unbelievable to me.

CHAPTER 58

ABOUT FIFTEEN MINUTES AFTER WE arrived, Joseph called me for a private meeting. My father nodded reassuringly as I was led into another room. Joseph shut the door on us and we sat down facing each other.

He looked stone cold and I could feel the nausea forcing its way up in me. He got to the point at once. "This is your last chance to learn to respect, appreciate, and love me. I have done only good things for you; therefore, you're obligated to follow my instructions and must obey me. I know what is best for you. And just to show you how good I am, I forgive you and am willing to take you back if you promise me that you will behave; otherwise you won't see the children ever again and you can cry your eyes out. I don't need you to raise them. I can do a perfectly good job without you."

I sat there dumbstruck. What was I actually expecting? Since I wasn't able to say a word, he continued, "The family protection worker called me and I invited her here. I showed her around and she was in awe of everything I have accomplished here. She told me that a normal person wouldn't have left me or my milieu." Family protection worker! It seemed that the woman had forgotten what her job was. I couldn't believe my ears. My only hope had been that worker, but she betrayed me as well. No one would have helped me because Joseph twisted them all around his finger. Just because I wanted to stay alive, protect my children, and live under normal circumstances, I was considered insane. In his opinion I'd always been an unfit mother, so he did everything to prove that.

I was completely alone; the police, the lawyers, that worker, my own family, Joseph—everyone who could have done something good and positive was against me. All the help I needed was denied, one time after another. I honestly believed that not one of these people actually cared about my innocent children. I no longer thought that I had any chance there. I was trapped forever. Plus, everything was my fault. I was the bad guy here, the guilty one, because he had all the support that *I* needed. And of course he used everything he had access to so he could stomp me into the ground, deeper and deeper. He said not a word about those promises with which my mother had filled my head. No house, no school, no dreams, and no normal life for me whatsoever, just the last ultimatum.

For the time we were in the room, hatred, condemnation, and blame were pouring out of him. When he was finished with all his insults, he expected me to be grateful. He also mentioned the list of belongings my lawyer had sent him. "Such a pathetic list," he said. "You have no right to any of it. You came here with nothing; you will leave with nothing." Then he asked me, "Do you promise that you will never leave me and will never lie to me again? That you will love me and respect me?" I promised him what he wanted to hear, although I knew I wouldn't be able to keep my word, because he would do anything to make sure that I failed. But that was the only way I would be allowed to come back to my children.

Then he started to laugh and gave me a detailed list of one of our grocery bills. Whoever had watched Adrian and me was much closer to us than we had ever considered. And obviously that person gave a very precise report of us to Joseph. With that, our private meeting was over. Before we left the room, he told me, "You can come back, but you must move back immediately."

The dinner was very painful. My appetite had vanished long before and now I was completely drained. Those beautiful promises that had come only from my parents, Joseph's terrible words, and my children's catastrophic appearance were all beyond what I could take.

Throughout the dinner Joey sat across the table from me, but he was so scared he didn't even dare to look at me. He was also quite hostile toward me, which hurt me a lot, but I had to understand.

And who understood me? Instead of being helped to rescue my children, I was blackmailed, threatened, and manipulated all over again so I would come back to the terror and fear. I had no idea how I was going to manage the same life I had been trying to escape from. He always pushed me until my defence or reluctance cracked.

After dinner I went back to Adrian and I told him what had

happened. "It's no use, Adrian. He's going to take my children away from me if I won't go back. And believe me, he has all the help he wants. I can't lose them. They're my life, you know that. And the way they look, they need me desperately."

I believed in myself, and I also believed that I was the only one who was able to restore all the damage that had been done to them. Adrian couldn't keep his tears at bay and I cried with him, but I had to be strong for the four of us. I got my very few items, thanked him profusely for everything he had done for us, and then I was on my way back to the prison from which I had desperately tried to break free.

The next day, on the sixteenth, Joseph came forward with an agreement typed by his lawyer. Reading the paper, I couldn't believe my eyes. I would never have thought that a sane person could put something like that on paper. That so-called agreement was my death sentence. It was simply impossible for me to comply with. He demanded that I give up my basic human rights, my dignity, my freedom, my children—my whole existence.

"Agreement,[1] which happened today between
J.S. and E.P. with these conditions:

Considering that Erika left Joseph, she took Joseph's children, she lied, she stole from Joseph, and now she has made a statement that she would like to come back and continue the common-law relationship.

Talking and thinking over the facts, sizing up the emotional conditions, considering the common and the family interests, we present the following decisions:
1. / Joseph takes Erika back. He will love her as his common-law, as his children's mother, according to what she deserves he will appreciate, help, guide her with good intention and he will do everything for Erika and the children, so they can live in the best, happiest mental and financial circumstances.
2. / Erika promises that as a good mother and common-law, she cares about Joseph and also about the children in the same way. She makes every effort with love, helpfully and in self-denial, for the family's harmony and

---

1   The Agreement was written in Hungarian, originally. I've translated it as closely as possible to give a sense of Joseph's writing style, including the grammatical errors as well.

happiness.

3. / Erika promises that she will always be faithful, honest and decent, she will always share her thoughts, feelings, dreams, worries, sadness and happiness with Joseph. Joseph as a good common-law and good father will consider those with good intentions and ask for Erika's opinion before he makes a decision, which decision Erika is obliged to follow—as her own—without any arguments.

4. / Erika promises to help Joseph six hours a day in his business efforts to be more successful. Her efforts and helpful work help to increase the family's financial well-being in the morning 8:00 a.m.-10:00 a.m., then in the apartment.

5. / Erika irrevocably agrees that Joseph is the sole guardian of the two male children, Joey and Alex, and she will never argue against it.

6. / In the case that Erika doesn't follow any of the paragraphs above, after a warning she must leave Joseph's house and she cannot have any kind of compensation.

7. / The parties sign this Agreement in free will in the presence of two witnesses.

Budapest, March 16, 1998.

To complete the above, today Erika promises and places herself under an obligation that she will obey Joseph's advice, directions and commands 100% without any argument."

I think it is unnecessary to say that nothing was discussed, ever. And even if it had been, it would have been totally pointless. He said to me that this paper secured every right for him, and every judge would be on his side after they read it, so "Don't even hope for anything."

To me that was proof of pure insanity, but I had to choose my words very carefully before I spoke to him. "Why do we have to involve a lawyer, who is a total stranger, after all. Let's do it just between us." Whether it made any difference or not, I didn't want a lawyer to be involved. By the same token, it was hard to believe that an attorney would help to destroy someone's life, although nothing surprised me anymore.

Luckily, Joseph agreed. He went to his office to get the original, handwritten version, and then gave it to me. (After all these years he couldn't even spell my name correctly.) "Study the Agreement and think it over. If you have any suggestions, feel free to share them with me."

I had already read the typed version once and it was clear enough. I interpreted the writing to mean that my life was over and that I had no right to *my own existence*. I was stamped to be a slave, or who knows what. I didn't even know what to call someone in my position, because I felt beyond victimized. I also didn't know whether to cry or laugh about this situation. It was so pitiful, so ironic and lame, like a really bad joke. That was why I couldn't resist telling him to include me in the fifth point too. It didn't make any difference because he had already taken over my life completely, so why not let him be my guardian as well? He had done that already without any agreement, and he was certainly old enough for that role. And that was the paper I had to sign…

But to take that much control over me wasn't enough for him. The same day he started to demand our passports. "I don't have them," I said. "If you don't give them to me at once, leave my house!" he snapped at me. I feared that from now on if I didn't meet his commands, he would just kick me out. "I don't have them," I repeated. "I left them with a friend."

"Then go and get them. You must give them to me; otherwise I'll throw you out with the guards."

That I didn't doubt. I had already learned that his men were very supportive in his attempts, and I was afraid. "Okay," I said to him. "I'll go and get them on Thursday." But that wasn't good enough. "Why not now?" he asked me. "Because they are with my lawyer, and I can see him on Thursdays only."

Despite Joseph's threats, I was more than happy to be with my babies again. Poor children, they were so neglected. Joseph and the nanny weren't even able to keep them clean.

Alex relaxed very quickly with me but Joey remained distant. He told me several times that he didn't love me and wanted me to leave. His words burned my heart but I knew it wasn't him talking. I had to be extremely patient with him to gain back his love and confidence. It was so painful to see that my little boy was very confused and possibly hurt. I had to help him.

The nanny told me that Alex had run a very high fever after he was brought back, and they were unable to reduce it for days. But he wasn't taken to a doctor. My children's condition already frightened me enough but that was just too much. So on Tuesday the seventeenth, I took them to the paediatrician.

He had seen the boys about three months ago and now he was shocked. "In my practice, which is over thirty years, I have never seen such devastating damage to children after only three months. Look at this," he pointed at Joey's lips. "He redeveloped the sucking reflex and he is almost five and a half years old. Show him to the psychologist. He needs help urgently."

At first sight, I had known that they were damaged but now that the doctor confirmed my observation, I couldn't say a word. I asked the doctor to write down what he diagnosed but he refused my request. "I can't do that because I'm not their doctor officially." Well, that was true. He had been recommended by Dr. Lane as someone who took house calls but he wasn't our district doctor. It never occurred to me that one day that could be a problem. I felt utterly disappointed. I almost broke into tears. The last straw I had been clinging to was pulled out of my hands.

CHAPTER 59

AFTER ONLY THREE DAYS ALEX and I were inseparable again but Joey needed more time. Still, I trusted that my love and patience would eventually bring me some result, that slowly but surely Joey would find his way back to me.

Alex refused to sleep without me and since Joseph slept with the children in the same bed I was stuck between them. But my being there angered him. "Let the child sleep. Why are you bothering him? Get out of here!" He was shouting like a madman and made the children cry. But I didn't let him frighten me. Alex was snuggled up, holding me tightly. "He wants me here," I said to Joseph.

Alex's affection was so obvious that after a while Joseph settled down and didn't try to kick me out of the room. I could stay there holding my babies and now all four of us slept in the same bed. Joey was at the wall, next to him Alex, me, and then Joseph. I tried to occupy the smallest space I could to avoid the slightest body contact with him, but if my children wanted me there, having body contact with Joseph was the least thing I was worried about.

And the shocking surprises just kept coming. "Joey told me that Adrian beat him with a wooden spoon on the sole of his foot."

"What?" I asked him in total shock, "What are you talking about?" He kept telling me that that was the truth, and that Adrian belonged in jail. "Do you know that once that was the harshest punishment, beating someone's sole? The prisoners were tortured that way." No, I didn't know that, but obviously he did. "That never happened! He never touched them. He loved them dearly." I couldn't believe this impudence. I was getting angry. "Are you accusing the child of lying?" he asked me. "He even told me that you just stood there watching the whole scene, but did nothing. He said that all of you were very afraid and were crying." Oh my God. Now that sounded very familiar, but

269

it happened with Joseph and not with Adrian. I could only shake my head in disbelief.

Joseph was the one who had used a wooden spoon on Joey. And I just couldn't believe that a five-year-old child could have come up with a story like that by himself. That was just too adult for a small boy. I truly believed it was Joseph's fabrication. "It never happened, never!" I said to him.

I was offended for Adrian, who didn't deserve such accusations. I couldn't let go of the thought that Joseph was responsible for that ugly lie, and used Joey as a scapegoat. I had to know the truth. I had to ask Joey, when he was ready to talk to me about it. He still needed time to be more comfortable with me, but the time was coming.

Joseph also told my parents about this make believe incident, and I told them the same thing as well, that it had never happened. But they didn't believe me, just looked at me accusingly. I didn't tell Joseph, but I told them that we didn't even have a wooden spoon when the children were there. No use. I could see that they weren't convinced at all.

On Thursday afternoon, the nineteenth, around 3:00 p.m., I went to my lawyer to pick up the passports. He was reluctant to give them to me because he feared that I wouldn't be able to keep them safe. First he made me promise not to give the documents to Joseph, and only then would he give them to me.

I also showed him the Agreement, which was yet unsigned. He just shook his head but told me, "Do not worry about this paper. No judge will ever take it seriously. You can sign it."

The lawyer's opinion calmed me a little but didn't take away the sharp edge of my fear. It wasn't about my signature, but about my whole life. I had to sign it over to Joseph as if I didn't even exist individually. And that horrified me.

After seeing the lawyer, I went back to the rented apartment to get some papers I had forgotten to take and to leave my keys there. Adrian was home. Poor man; he looked very sad, as if he had been crying for the last four days at least. I spent some time with him trying to reassure him that everything was going to be all right, even though I didn't feel that way at all. I owed him that much after what he had done for me.

It was about 8:30 p.m. when I got back to the office building. Unsuspectingly, I headed toward the gate and was more than surprised when the doorman didn't let me in. He called Joseph instead, who came down immediately.

He came right to me, demanding the passports and an explanation of my whereabouts all afternoon. Then he said: "I know where you were. I know everything. You were followed all afternoon." I didn't even know anymore what to feel about being violated all the time. I wondered whether anybody else had to live like this. "So, then why are you asking me?" I asked him. "You know things better than I do." He said nothing to that, but switched back to the passports. "Where are the passports?"

"I have them," I said, "but I cannot give them to you." He didn't like that. "I won't let you in unless you give them to me right away."

He was serious, I could see that, but I didn't dare to give him our documents. I was thinking about my lawyer, who had been very firm about not giving the passports to Joseph. I tried to live up to my words. "I told you that I have them. Why isn't that enough?" To him the most important thing was to break me so that I would obey his every word. "Because I said so. You must give them to me right now!" He yelled at me then grabbed my arm and shook me.

His head henchman and another guard were pacing nearby. The next moment he dragged me into the boiler room. My first thought was that he wanted to hit me. The second was that he would ask his men to hold me down so he could search me. I was truly astonished when neither happened. After almost two hours of argument and struggle he still didn't have our passports. "You cannot come in to the children. You can go back to your friend," he said and left me on the sidewalk.

It was about 10:30 p.m., dark and very cold, although it was already March. My light coat didn't protect me at all from the chilly night and the way Joseph had treated me. I was shaking uncontrollably, and I wasn't able to take a step forward. I sat down on the roadside and tried to take control of my trembling. After just four nights I was without my children once again because I had tried to do the right thing.

I couldn't stop thinking of them. I was certain that they were waiting for me, and I couldn't go to them. I did what I was advised to do by my lawyer and I ended up on the street. The pain and the helplessness I felt was core deep, but I couldn't even cry anymore, although I had every reason to.

I had been sitting in the icy darkness for a long time when Joseph's head henchman came to me. "You must go to a warm place," he said softly. "You'll freeze here. Go back to Adrian." And he was right. I couldn't do anything else, because I had nowhere else to go.

It took all my effort to stand up. I was already turning purple and I knew I had to move. Once again, I was defeated. I just kept turning the incident over in my mind again and again. It was maddening how much right Joseph claimed over something that absolutely wasn't his.

At that point I really had no idea how I could possibly protect us. There was no way; *I* had no way to keep the three of us safe from Joseph's lunacy. I also knew that he was filling the children's heads with lies that covered up his acts and put all the blame on me. He had the ability to make everybody believe that I was a bad person and that every problem which occurred was my fault.

Adrian was very happy to see me but I couldn't share his joy. "I knew you would come back," he said. That was a rather surprising statement, although I didn't ask what he meant. I didn't want to be back. I wanted to be with my children. My place was with them.

Then on Saturday evening my parents and my brother showed up at the apartment again. I was anything but happy to see them there. I didn't try to hide from them but went out to face the inevitable. "You must come back," my father said. "You are the mother of those children; they need you."

I was losing my patience very quickly. "I know I am their mother," I thundered, "that's why Joseph didn't let m…" Before I could finish my sentence my father lifted his hands defensively. At the same time, Joseph stepped out from behind my father. He was shorter than my dad so he could easily hide behind his back. I didn't even know he was there. "Come back," he pleaded, "the children are waiting for you." Well, that was it for me. I couldn't do anything else but stare at them. Joseph would have deserved an Oscar for his performance. And I was sure that my parents knew nothing about what had happened on Thursday, at least not the way it had really happened and why I was at Adrian's again. They probably didn't even want to know. It was always easier to treat me like an awkward child. So, I said my last good-bye to Adrian and then they took me back as if I was a prisoner. I never saw Adrian again.

That night was different. In the first days after my return, Joseph had wanted to kick me out of the children's bedroom but now he expected me to be with him, willing and devoted. And I had to be, no matter what or how I felt.

I was fighting off nausea while I pretended to enjoy him. I felt nothing, only the violation of my body. And after he was done, he didn't even look at me.

On Sunday, March twenty-second, it was time to sign that deadly Agreement. He had his two witnesses: my parents. For the last couple of years Joseph had blamed my mother for the problems between us, yet now there she was helping and reassuring *him* that she was indeed on his side, which meant that she had never poisoned me against him. This was the perfect opportunity for her to prove that she was clean.

The threat was in the air again: if I refused to cooperate, he would throw me out, and he guaranteed that I would never in my life see my children again. The last three months had been enough proof for me to believe him. I just didn't know how I could sign over my life and my children's lives to someone who had already threatened to kill us. My situation was painfully ridiculous and horribly frightening. My whole life depended on that piece of paper, and on Joseph's mood.

And the more I thought about it, the more I felt that I wasn't able to comply. "I can't do this," I said to my parents. "How can I sign something so insane? Who could ever carry such things out?" I felt like my whole being was denied. My father only whispered to me, "You can do this."

"How?" I panicked. "Have you read it?" And my parents nodded. So they knew what was awaiting me, but did nothing. They just let it happen. Moreover, they were the chosen ones, the witnesses! "This is simply impossible to carry out, impossible!" I was losing my nerve. "You can do this. You must! You have to sacrifice yourself for your children," my father said.

The word "sacrifice" hit me hard. *So I don't count,* I thought. "If I sacrifice myself that won't help my children. Do I have to stop living? Would *that* be enough sacrifice for everyone?" For this my mother snapped at me, "I thought you were more intelligent."

But I was scared out of my mind. When we headed to the office, I grabbed my father's arm. "Please don't leave me alone! Please!" I pleaded to him, but I also was begging for my life. And my father promised, "We won't."

CHAPTER 60

IN THE OFFICE, MY MOTHER sat on my left, my father on my right, and Joseph sat facing us. "You must sign this agreement and carry out every single paragraph otherwise we can't make this relationship work. It is in everybody's best interests that you sign this paper," he explained. If I had any way out, I couldn't find it. I felt as if I was sitting in an electric chair and was about to be executed with the help of my parents.

My father said nothing on my behalf, and I didn't see, hear, or feel any sign that he would keep his promise of not leaving me alone. They were there physically, but not morally. Both of them pushed me to sign the paper, with no objection to those dreadful things that were written in black and white. I knew that if I walked out of the office without signing that nonsense, I was sure to be kicked out of my children's lives forever. That was made clear enough.

I just sat there for a long time, staring at the paper. Joseph and my parents were staring at me with great expectation in their eyes. The question was whether I was stupid enough not to sign it. "I can't do this," I whispered. And my mother chimed in again, "I thought you were more intelligent." I had heard that enough, but what did it mean?

Her words tore at my heart, though. I felt so humiliated by her remark. She actually put me down right in front of Joseph, again. When I scratched my name on the paper my parents let out a burst of nervous laughter. Their relief was unmistakable. But then they asked me to sign it again. "You can write much more beautifully than this," they said. Joseph said nothing. I was sure he enjoyed my torment very much. "I've already signed it. Haven't I?" But they kept mocking and pressuring me as if the situation was funny.

They seemed very eager to do a good job for Joseph. All I wanted to do was scream into my parents' faces: *How many more times will you leave me in the lurch? How many more times will you betray me?* But I said nothing. I was thinking of my children. *I* couldn't betray them.

I was pestered until I scribbled my name once again on that piece of dirt. Both of my signatures clearly showed the disappointment, the anger, the pain, and the humiliation I was repressing. But my second signature wasn't nice enough for them either. "No, no, that's not it!" my parents teased me. "Beautifully, sign it beautifully!" But I had had enough of their games, "NO!!!" I hissed and that settled them down at last.

Then the two devoted witnesses, my parents, signed my death sentence as well. And now everyone was satisfied with the result they had achieved through my blood. He and my family had made me pay an enormous price for something so natural and right as being the mother of my own children.

But that wasn't the end of it. Joseph had a new idea, which he added to the agreement, although it was already double signed.

"Erika agrees that Joseph will take the two children and her to Canada on April 2ⁿᵈ, 1998."

And with that, my fate was sealed. Unambiguously, they made it clear that I had no choice, that my life wasn't mine after all. The decision was made for me once again, but *I* had to deal with everything. Nobody did anything for me.

While the three of them were casually chatting, my head was spinning. I was scared, angry, disappointed, and hurt. Besides, I didn't believe at all that my place as a mother was safe, despite all the written rules I was supposed to live by. And I dreaded going to Canada with him again.

It was quite incredible how much nobody cared about *me* as a person, and that also showed me how much they didn't care about the children. Maybe they forgot that I was their daughter and the boys were their only grandchildren, who they stated they loved very much.

We had ten days before our departure. He said that we would go for a three-week visit, so I packed for three weeks only.

In these days, Joey had opened up toward me completely. Now he let me kiss and hug him without asking his permission first. Thankfully, both of them were very much attached to me once again. Joseph saw this as well and he wasn't able to control his jealousy. He yelled at me, threatened and humiliated me daily in front of the children and the once-to-be nanny, who was the housekeeper now. He also began to force me to have sex with him regularly as a good common-law was supposed to do. And I had to kiss him every time he came up from the office. I had no stomach to do any of those things, but that just angered him. One time he grabbed my chin and turned my head so abruptly that I felt as if my jaw had been torn off. But there couldn't be any excuse; I had to kiss him. He even dropped me a note:

"*Erika,*
Please, think hard about your behaviour. I expect and demand that I and also you comply with all the paragraphs we agreed upon. Read it through again and express an opinion on what I didn't keep and what you didn't."

And another one:

"*Erika,*
For our happy and successful future, we have to make every effort to keep every paragraph of the Agreement.
Love, Joseph"

Well, I didn't know how. And his "love" hurt me so much I really didn't want to be the privileged one. But still, I tried. I tried everything to be good enough by keeping those annihilating rules.

Prior to our departure, I also used the time to look around in the apartment because I knew, I just knew that Joseph had gone through all of my packed stuff. So, while he was in his office I went through the whole place and sure enough, found some of my personal belongings hidden behind his...

I didn't even let my children out of my sight. We worked together to build each other up again When Joey started to talk with me and asked me to stay with him, I knew that was the right time had come to ask him about Adrian and the wooden spoon. "Tell me, Joey, what happened. When did Adrian hurt you?" I asked him. "I don't know," he said. "Did you cry?"

"No."

"Did it hurt?"

"No."

The whole story didn't make any sense to me and I still didn't believe that a five-year-old could come up with such a far-fetched story. I couldn't rest; I had to ask him the most important question: "Why would you say something that isn't true?" His answer was very mature and I knew it was the pure truth: "Because I was afraid of my father, that he would be angry if he knew I love Adrian more than I love him."

Poor child! I knew how he felt, but he had never actually put his feelings into words before. However, I still wasn't convinced of Joseph's innocence in that matter, although I didn't pressure Joey any further. Whatever the truth was, I understood my son.

The time I dreaded so much had arrived. We were leaving our country. I was worried in advance about every moment I was to spend with Joseph. And the problems didn't end there.

When lunch was served on the plane and I wanted to take my first bite I was shocked to realize that I wasn't able to open my mouth, not even for a small bite. I felt myself sink in my seat. The shooting pain in my jaw and the right side of my head made me cry.

The incident when Joseph had grabbed my chin came back vividly. He was eating with relish, and I wasn't able to have one morsel without the excruciating pain. I said nothing to him, but forced the food into my nearly closed mouth. After a few tiny bites I was soaked in perspiration. I was in such pain that I had to give up trying to eat. Needless to say, the trip was again a total misery from the beginning to the end.

When we arrived I felt better but the memory of the extreme pain still haunted me. Pulling my strength together, I put on my poker face and tried to force a positive attitude for the next few weeks, which I could only hope that I would survive. I said to him, "Three weeks, right? That's okay, I can do it, and after that we'll be home again." My positive attitude was roughly interrupted by Joseph's laughing: "Ha-ha-ha; we will never go back again. Never!"

Chapter 61

My optimism disappeared at once as fear gripped me from every angle. I had done what I was expected to do, hadn't I? I was looking for the positive. Although I wasn't able to find any good in the situation I was given, at least I put on an attitude of optimism and enthusiasm. Still, I was on the losing end all the time.

I was beyond exhausted again after the plane trip. And being here in Canada didn't solve any of the existing problems. Everything started again, or rather continued. Joseph was more aggressive, more violent than ever. He took me repeatedly against my will. Without a doubt, he was punishing me for what I had done—leaving him and everything.

At home, in Hungary, he couldn't avenge himself on me anymore because I'd put us into the spotlight. But here there was no one; only Myrna, who was after all still *his* employee. Nobody else knew us, nobody cared. The verbal and physical attacks were more vicious, more brutal, and more frequent. And now he even used against me the fact that I wasn't at home anymore but he was, and threatened repeatedly to kick me out of the *country* (without the children, of course).

We arrived on the second of April and on the fourth, we had already had a huge argument, because once again, he was forceful with me in order to have sex. The pure thought of it made me physically sick and it was the very last thing I desired, in fact it wasn't even on my list. But it was inevitable. I knew I could only stall so long without risking my well-being. On this point, though, I was wrong. The moment I refused the idea, refused him, he became violent. He dragged me out of the children's room (where I accommodated myself) and pushed me roughly onto his bed. He sat on me. With one of his hands he bunched together my wrists above my head, then started to threaten me, saying: "I will hit you if you don't obey. Sex is very important for a happy family life. And don't show a bad example to the children. You have to do what I say."

I tried to get out from beneath him but he kept my wrists in an iron grip, holding me down while he was tearing at my clothes. I became frantic. Then suddenly, he pulled me up in a sitting position and "hugged" me so hard that I thought he was about to crush my ribs. I couldn't breathe and soon I ran out of air. My lungs began to burn and I was gasping for air quite desperately. I felt that if I didn't get some air very soon, I would suffocate. I started to hit his back, because I wasn't able to utter a single word, but instead of releasing me, he just laughed.

Because of the struggle, *my* struggle, Alex cried out. After a seemingly very long time Joseph finally let me go, blaming me of course, saying it was entirely my fault that the children were alarmed. I shouldn't refuse to have sex with him.

I went to the children's room, where little Joey was crying as well, trembling in his whole body. He just whispered to me, "Mommy."

On April twenty-ninth, Joseph went back to Hungary. At this time Myrna took me to a Hungarian lady, who then introduced me to another lady who worked at Family Support Services. And there they told me: "You don't have to tolerate and suffer the battering. If you call the police, they will help you here." Finally, I had something to hold onto, a tiny ray of hope to save my children and along with them, myself. Still, I had some difficulty believing what I heard. *Why would anyone want to help me?*

On May twenty-third, Saturday, Joseph came back. The same evening, I put the children to bed, talking and singing to them as I always had for years now, only that when Joseph was around he never let us be in peace. At this time also, he was more important than anybody else, so he came to me saying that I had to go to bed with him and just leave the children alone, they would fall asleep on their own. "Why are you bothering them anyway?" he asked me. "They don't need what you do. Your obligation is to be with me."

Neither the children nor I wanted to end our time together so I tried to reason with him calmly and kindly. I thought that the nice words would work but I was wrong, again. Joseph was shouting now, threatening me. He ordered me to put the children into their places. Joey obeyed him, trembling fearfully, but Alex was clinging to me. I got more and more frustrated and asked Joseph again to let us be for the time being—but no!

He grabbed my arm and tried to pull me out of the bed. Since he didn't succeed he grabbed my leg and violently pulled me off the bed, then he pulled me out of the room by my leg like one would do with an animal; I was never more than that in his eyes, anyhow. At the doorway, in front of the children, while I was still on the floor, he started to pound on my head, beating me like there was no tomorrow. Alex cried out and so did I because of the extreme pain.

Then somehow, I stood up, but he grabbed my arm and continued to beat my head. I heard him saying how much he loved me and that he only wanted good things for me but I was so bad and disobedient that he had to teach me to be good. He felt sorry for me but I needed his help. My brain was buzzing, and then I could only hear my own screaming. I was quite sure that the neighbours heard me. Good. Even though nobody came to my rescue, I knew already what I was going to do. For the last couple of weeks I had done nothing but harbour the advice I had received earlier from the support worker. If only I could get away from him before it was too late.

Finally, I was free. I went back to the children, picked up Alex, who hugged my neck tightly and calmed down nicely while little Joey remained in deathly silence. When we could exchange some words, he said to me: "Mom, I didn't cry; only Alex did. I covered up my ears and refused to hear what happened." I wanted to hug him, to comfort him, but he wouldn't come to me. Instead, he said: "I don't want to snuggle up to you, because Daddy will see it."

That said it all. They once again had seen and heard everything. Joseph left us alone but I wasn't able to sleep. I was afraid to. I felt that something was on its way, that the war wasn't over yet.

Around 3:00 a.m., after the children were finally asleep, Joseph called me out to the living room for a meeting. That meant he was talking and I was listening. His lecture contained the same subject: me, the bad mother, who showed bad examples to the children. "I know, you want to go back to Adrian, so go, but don't even dream about taking the children with you. You have signed the Agreement, in which you gave me every right, and I am sure that no matter where I show this paper to a judge, they'll give me the children immediately. So use your head and see that it's better if you obey me, because if you won't, I'll put you on the first plane and I guarantee that you won't see the children ever again."

After this I barely slept. When I woke up, I could only drag myself because I was in so much pain. My body was bruised in several places and my head was throbbing. Every step, every movement hurt. But I didn't care, because my plan was set.

I was in luck when the next day Joseph left for a meeting, a Sunday afternoon meeting, taking Myrna with him. I was left behind with the children and Myrna's daughter. After they left, and I made sure that they were really gone, I was very distracted and very afraid to make the most important phone call of my life. I was circling the phone for a while, thinking about how to say what I had to say. But since my English was close to nothing, I was worried out of my mind: *What if the policeman won't understand me? I won't understand him, that is sure. How will they help us? What if they won't help? What will happen to us if Joseph finds out what I did?* On and on, my mind wouldn't shut up.

I was trembling so badly, but I had to make that phone call. I wanted to make that phone call! I felt that I didn't have much time because a Sunday afternoon meeting couldn't be that long. I had to do it. I had to pick up the receiver and press three numbers. Only three!

After a seemingly long tug-of-war with myself, I called 911 from Myrna's apartment. I was able to tell them the address and that my husband was beating me. Whatever the operator asked me, I did not understand. Then, I just wasn't able to keep it together anymore; I fell apart and broke into tears. Besides the pain, I felt so ashamed. The day before I had "forgotten" to cry, but the floodgates were open now, and the frustration of not being able to express myself in English just added to the package. But I had to pull myself together because I was there with three children to supervise.

After the phone call I remained extremely nervous. I was pacing around in the apartment and looking out of the window every five seconds. I was filled with dread at the thought that Joseph would arrive before the police came. *What would he do to me then?*

It seemed to be an excruciatingly long time, two hours or so, when I finally heard the sound of the buzzer. The police had arrived.

Of course, they wanted to know what had happened, so I did my best to explain that to them, using my hands and legs to make them understand. And the bruises spoke for themselves. They got the picture quite clearly, but what happened was that they wanted to wait for Joseph now. Just what I needed. If there were any nerves left in me, they were history. The emotional and physical beatings and the events of the last twenty-four hours were beyond my ability to handle.

We waited for an hour at least, but Joseph did not arrive. So they took the three of us to a safe house. In the van each of the boys got a teddy bear, which became the symbols of our rescue and freedom.

"Father, forgive them, for they do not know what they are doing." Luke 23:34 NIV

Or do they?

Epilogue

"GOD HELPS THOSE WHO HELP themselves." Many people just scoff at this saying, waiting for God to drop their wishes onto their laps, and if that doesn't happen when and how they want it to, they hold a grudge against Him.

Yes. We all have dreams, no matter what our backgrounds are. Dreaming is good. It puts us into a different world, a world where we actually want to be. But those dreams are powerless without a sound plan. Even if we frantically pray about them, praying without taking action does little to nothing, although sometimes it's enough. I've learned that. So keep praying, keep believing, *and* do something in order to get closer to your dreams. Show God that you mean business, that you want your wishes to be fulfilled badly enough to take the necessary steps. God will appreciate your efforts and help you to get what you truly want.

It's been almost thirteen year—thirteen long years—since the police came and took us to a safe place. I do realize that without my taking advantage of the information I got, meaning lifting up the receiver and dialling those three numbers, I probably wouldn't be here today. He would have made sure of that.

Even though we were uprooted by the abuse and betrayal inflicted on us, and our homeland and the people that were involved—either as friends or as enemies—are left behind, we are now safe and free; at least physically. I still marvel at this miracle. Even though I'm thinking of visiting Hungary, to be honest, there is not much left there for us. One day, maybe…

Our home is in Canada now, and we haven't been back to Hungary since we were brought here. We have very limited contact with my family. They are as unreachable as ever, only the reasons are different. I guess some things just never change.

If nobody listens to you,
        listen to yourself;
If nobody cares about you,
        care about yourself;
If nobody encourages you,
        encourage yourself;
If nobody shows appreciation for you,
        appreciate yourself;
If nobody praises you,
        praise yourself;
If nobody celebrates you,
        celebrate yourself;
If nobody seems to love you,
        love yourself without conditions;
and remember, always remember that you do not depend on anybody for your happiness; you are a free individual and God loves you, no matter what.

/EMP/

"The Lord is my light and my salvation-
          whom shall I fear?
The Lord is the stronghold of my life-
          of whom shall I be afraid?
When evil men advance against me,
          to devour my flesh,
when my enemies and foes attack me,
          they will stumble and fall.
Though an army besiege me,
          my heart will not fear;
though war break out against me,
          even then will I be confident.

One thing I ask of the Lord,'
          this is what I seek;
That I may dwell in the house of the Lord
          all the days of my life,
to gaze upon the beauty of the Lord
          and to seek him in his temple.
For in the day of trouble
          he will keep me safe in his dwelling;
he will hide me in the shelter of his tabernacle
          and set me high upon a rock.
Then my head will be exalted
          Above the enemies who surround me;
at his tabernacle will I sacrifice with shouts of joy;

I will sing and make music to the Lord.
Hear my voice when I call, O Lord;
      be merciful to me and answer me.
My heart says of you, "Seek his face!"
      Your face, Lord, I will seek.
Do not hide your face from me,
      do not turn your servant away in anger;
      you have been my helper.
Do not reject me or forsake me,
      O God my Saviour.
Though my father and mother forsake me,
      the Lord will receive me.
Teach me your way, O Lord;
      Lead me in a straight path
      because of my oppressors.
Do not turn me over to the desire of my foes,
      for false witnesses rise up against me,
      breathing out violence.

I am still confident of this:
      I will see the goodness of the Lord
      in the land of the living.
Wait for the Lord;
      be strong and take heart
      and wait for the Lord."

                              Psalm 27, NIV

Acknowledgements

I'd like to thank Greg Bailey, Publishing Consultant at iUniverse, for taking my call when I finally decided to make it. Thank you for giving me the necessary information and the best deal possible.

I'm grateful for the Editorial Evaluation. It was very helpful and eye-opening. All of the suggestions there have benefited my book.

I'd like to thank Gregory Eckart, Content Advisor, for giving me the "green light".

I'd also like to give a heartfelt word to Sarah Disbrow, Editorial Consultant Manager and to Alexandra Jones, my Publishing Services Associate, for their further help and patience, and I thank the whole team of iUniverse for working so conscientiously on my book—inside and out—making it marketable and high standard. In short, thank you for manifesting my dream.

I am ever so grateful to Dr. Tanya Wulff for her irreplaceable help and support. Thank you for believing in me and in my message. And thank you for finding me an editor, Dania Sheldon.

Dania, you are my English knowledge. Thank you very much for your tireless work and devotion.

I also like to thank Trudy Barton for her encouragement and for keeping my spirit up.

And my Dear Reader, thank you for reading *It Is Forgiven*. If you would like to contact me, please write to: emp.erika@hotmail.com.

I bless you all with the love of God.